Natsuki Hokami

While I was drawing, I remembered
something: I really like those jelly
drinks that you have to shake. There
was a vending machine at the high
school I went that sold a mango gelatin
in the summer, and I bought a ton of
them. I suppose those gelatins are
probably gone by now.

Natsuki Hokami's first serialized manga,
Hell Warden Higuma, was published in
Weekly Shonen Jump in 2018.

Demon Slayer: Kimetsu Academy

VOLUME 2
SHONEN JUMP EDITION

STORY AND ART BY
NATSUKI HOKAMI

Translation / John Werry
Touch-Up Art & Lettering / E.K. Weaver
Design / Yukiko Whitley
Editor / Andrew Kuhre Bartosh

KIMETSU GAKUEN! © 2021 by Koyoharu Gotouge, Natsuki Hokami
All rights reserved.
First published in Japan in 2021 by SHUEISHA Inc., Tokyo.
English translation rights arranged by SHUEISHA Inc.

The stories, characters, and incidents mentioned in
this publication are entirely fictional.

Printed in the U.S.A.

Published by VIZ Media, LLC
P.O. Box 77010
San Francisco, CA 94107

10 9 8 7 6 5 4 3 2 1
First printing, April 2024

VIZ MEDIA
viz.com

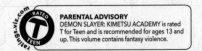

SHONEN JUMP

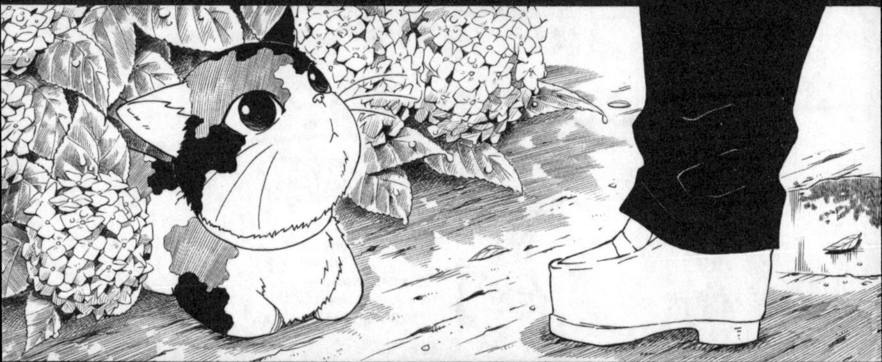

Story and Art by

Natsuki Hokami

Based on Koyoharu Gotouge's *Demon Slayer: Kimetsu no Yaiba*

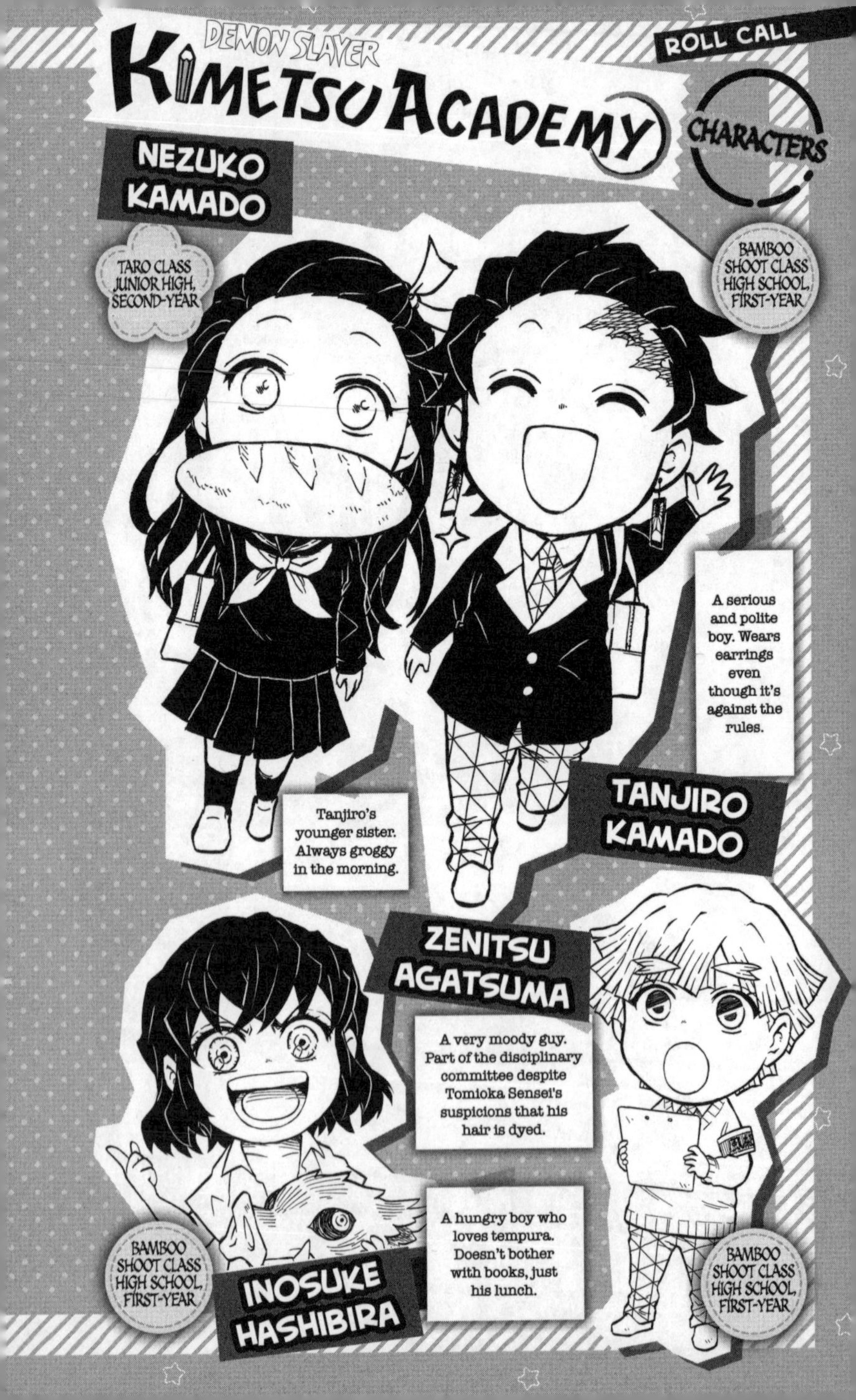
DEMON SLAYER
KIMETSU ACADEMY
ROLL CALL
CHARACTERS
NEZUKO KAMADO
TARO CLASS JUNIOR HIGH, SECOND-YEAR
Tanjiro's younger sister. Always groggy in the morning.
BAMBOO SHOOT CLASS HIGH SCHOOL, FIRST-YEAR
A serious and polite boy. Wears earrings even though it's against the rules.
TANJIRO KAMADO
ZENITSU AGATSUMA
A very moody guy. Part of the disciplinary committee despite Tomioka Sensei's suspicions that his hair is dyed.
BAMBOO SHOOT CLASS HIGH SCHOOL, FIRST-YEAR
A hungry boy who loves tempura. Doesn't bother with books, just his lunch.
BAMBOO SHOOT CLASS HIGH SCHOOL, FIRST-YEAR
INOSUKE HASHIBIRA

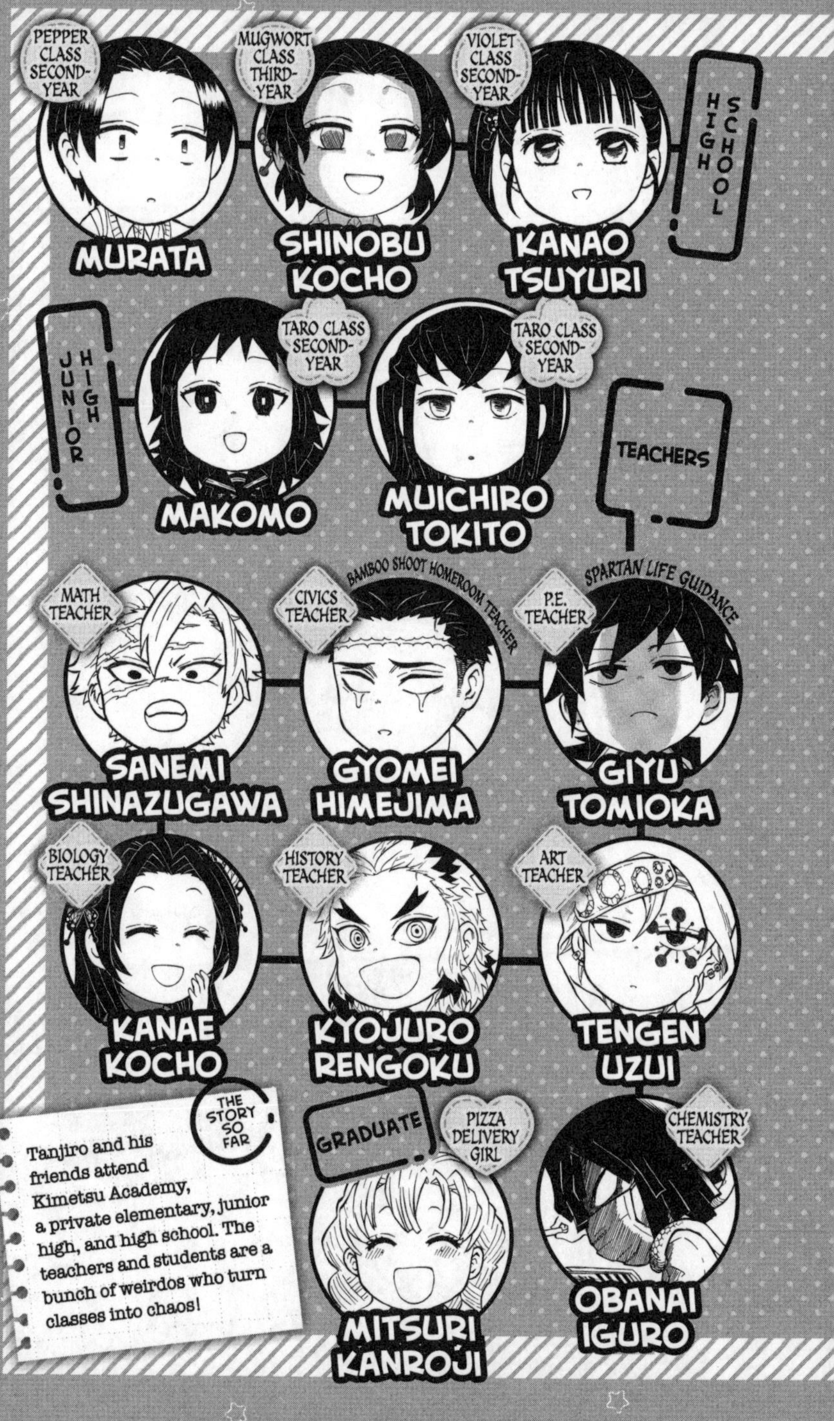
HIGH SCHOOL
PEPPER CLASS SECOND-YEAR
MURATA
MUGWORT CLASS THIRD-YEAR
SHINOBU KOCHO
VIOLET CLASS SECOND-YEAR
KANAO TSUYURI
JUNIOR HIGH
TARO CLASS SECOND-YEAR
MAKOMO
TARO CLASS SECOND-YEAR
MUICHIRO TOKITO
TEACHERS
MATH TEACHER
SANEMI SHINAZUGAWA
CIVICS TEACHER
BAMBOO SHOOT HOMEROOM TEACHER
GYOMEI HIMEJIMA
P.E. TEACHER
SPARTAN LIFE GUIDANCE
GIYU TOMIOKA
BIOLOGY TEACHER
KANAE KOCHO
HISTORY TEACHER
KYOJURO RENGOKU
ART TEACHER
TENGEN UZUI
GRADUATE
PIZZA DELIVERY GIRL
MITSURI KANROJI
CHEMISTRY TEACHER
OBANAI IGURO

THE STORY SO FAR

Tanjiro and his friends attend Kimetsu Academy, a private elementary, junior high, and high school. The teachers and students are a bunch of weirdos who turn classes into chaos!

CONTENTS

2 The Kimetsu Academy Night Tour

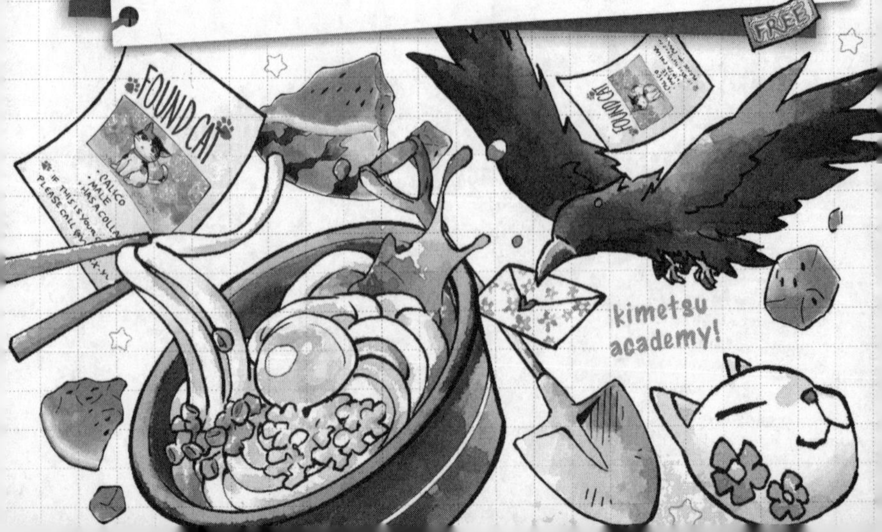

FOUND CAT
kimetsu academy!

CHAPTER 6: CATNIP FOR KITTIES, KITTIES FOR HIMEJIMA

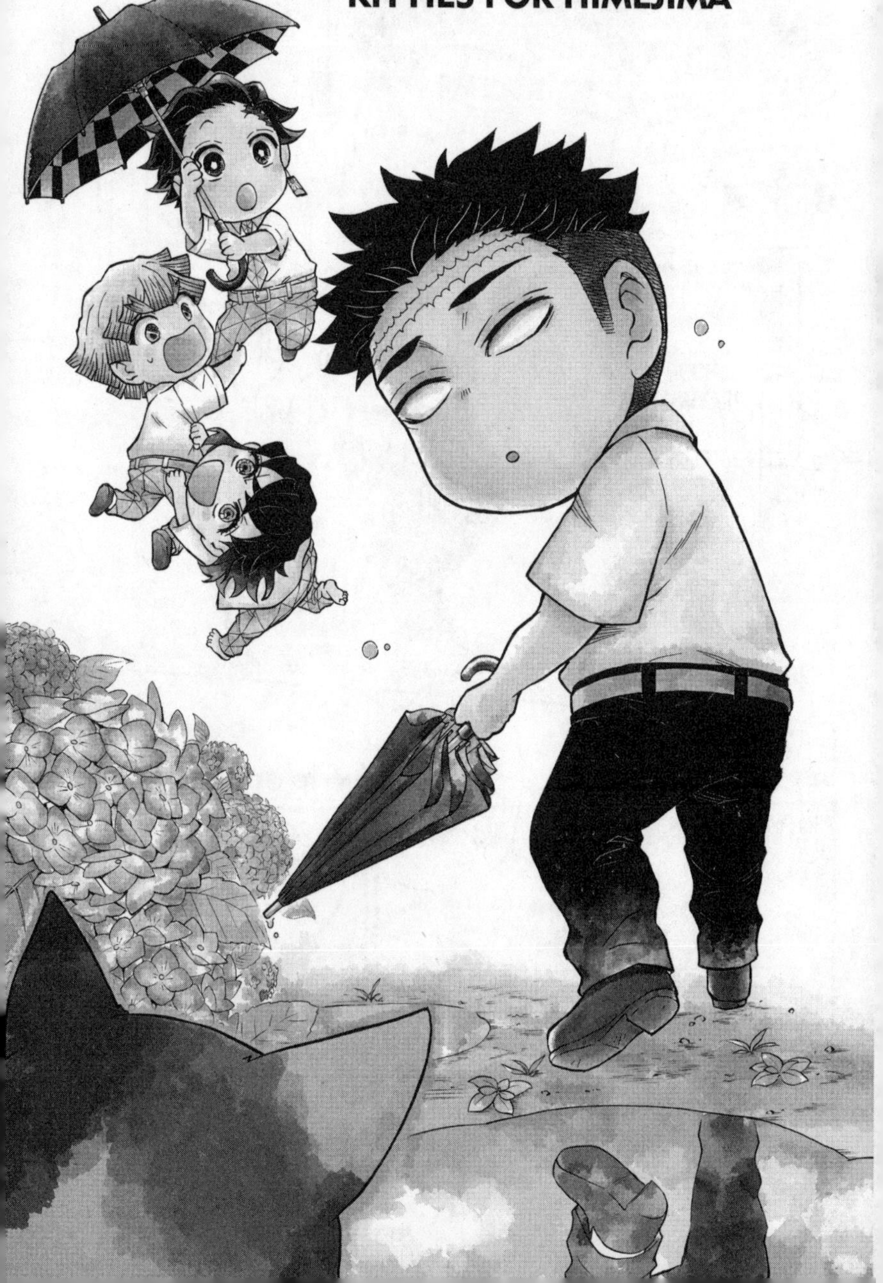

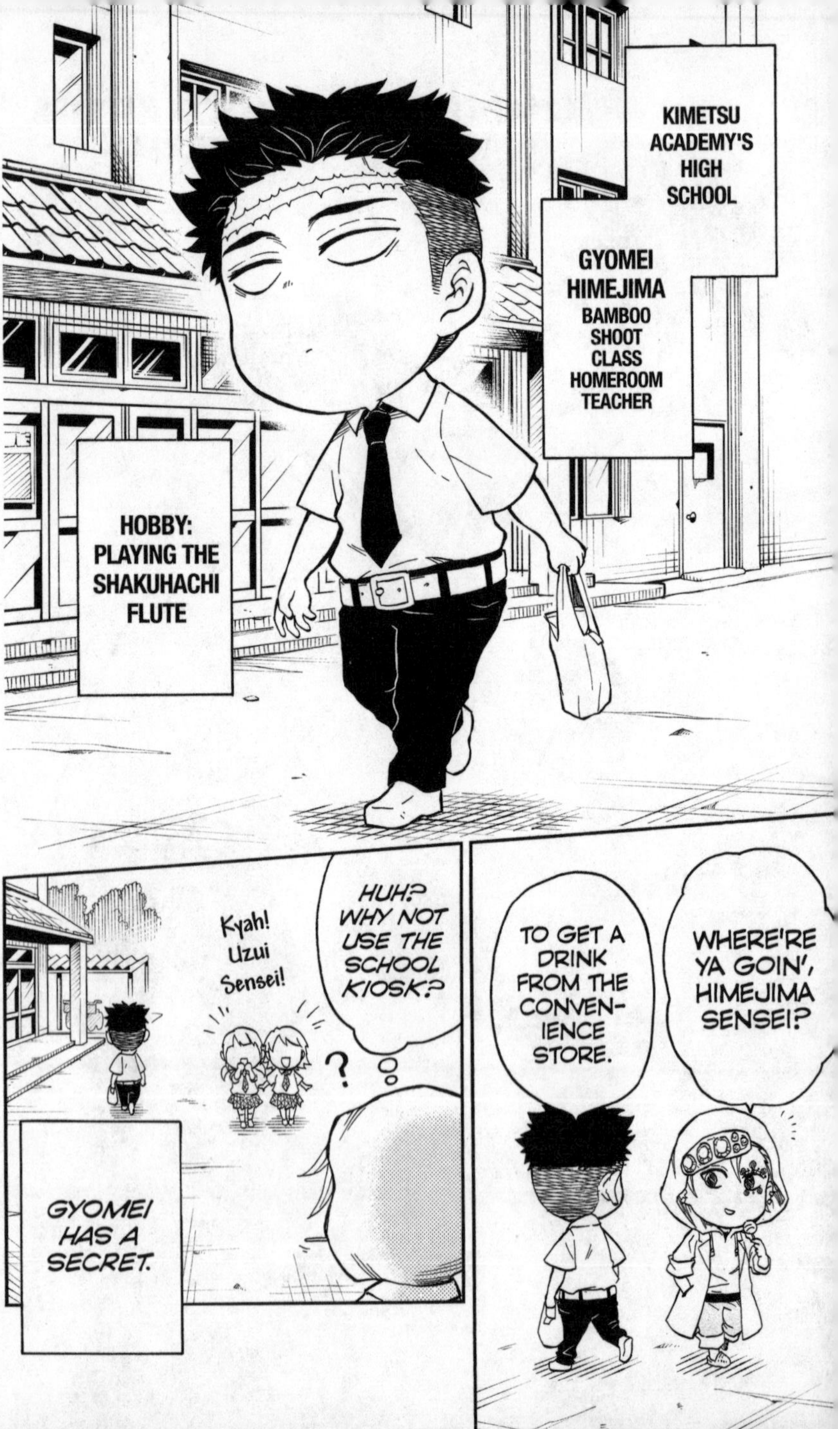
KIMETSU ACADEMY'S HIGH SCHOOL
GYOMEI HIMEJIMA
BAMBOO SHOOT CLASS HOMEROOM TEACHER
HOBBY: PLAYING THE SHAKUHACHI FLUTE
WHERE'RE YA GOIN', HIMEJIMA SENSEI?
TO GET A DRINK FROM THE CONVEN-IENCE STORE.
HUH? WHY NOT USE THE SCHOOL KIOSK?
Kyah! Uzui Sensei!
GYOMEI HAS A SECRET.

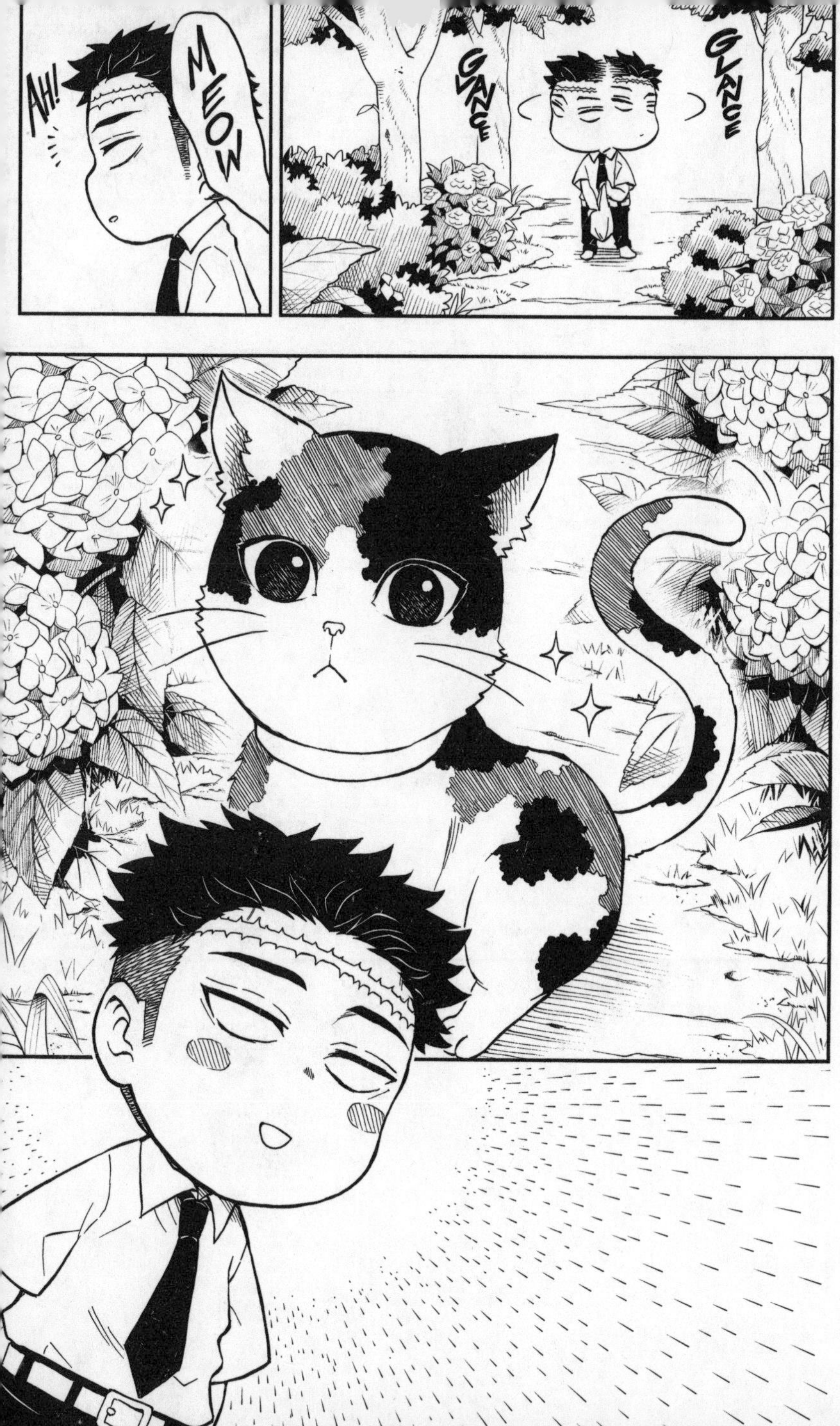
GLANCE
GLANCE
MEOW
AH!

AND IT IS SO...

...CUTE!

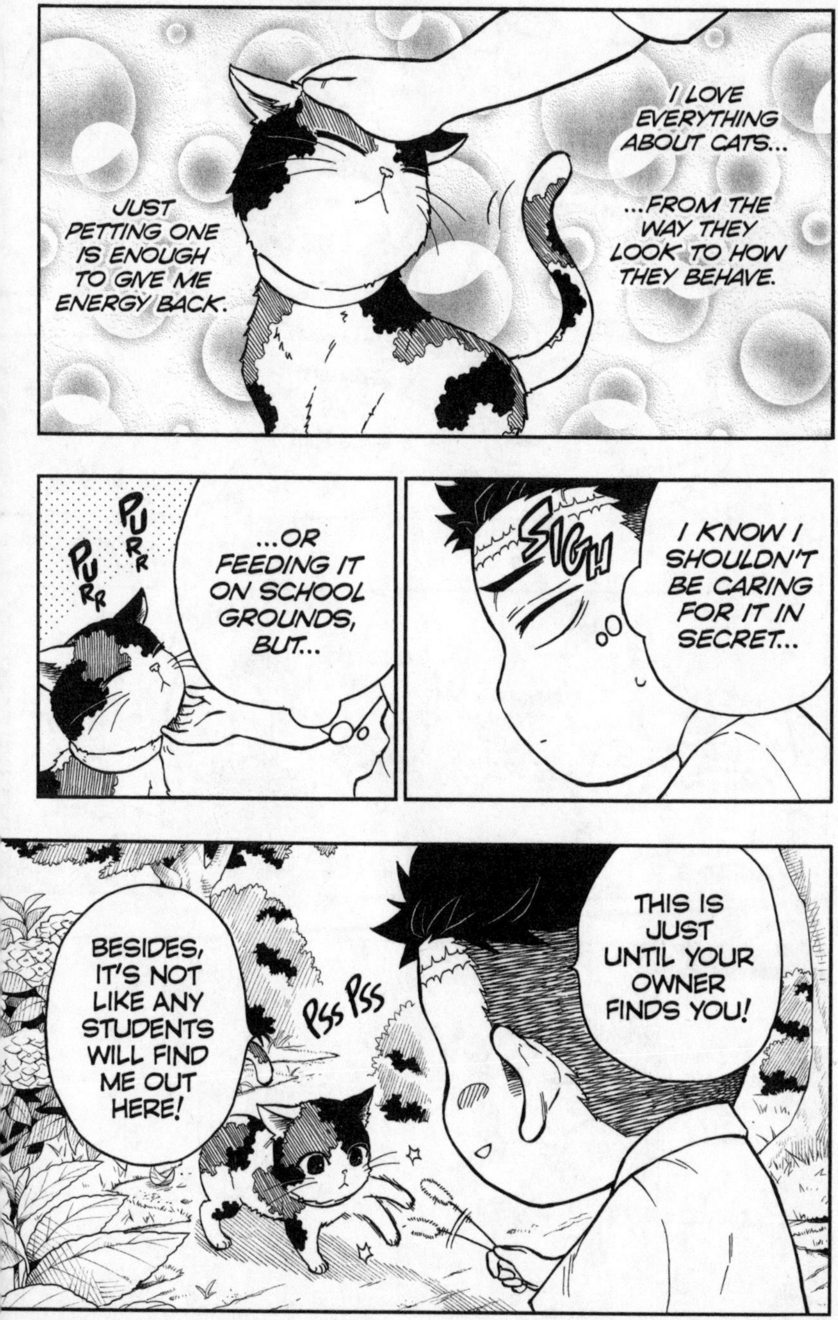
I LOVE EVERYTHING ABOUT CATS...
...FROM THE WAY THEY LOOK TO HOW THEY BEHAVE.
JUST PETTING ONE IS ENOUGH TO GIVE ME ENERGY BACK.
SIGH
I KNOW I SHOULDN'T BE CARING FOR IT IN SECRET...
...OR FEEDING IT ON SCHOOL GROUNDS, BUT...
PURR
PURR
THIS IS JUST UNTIL YOUR OWNER FINDS YOU!
PSS PSS
BESIDES, IT'S NOT LIKE ANY STUDENTS WILL FIND ME OUT HERE!

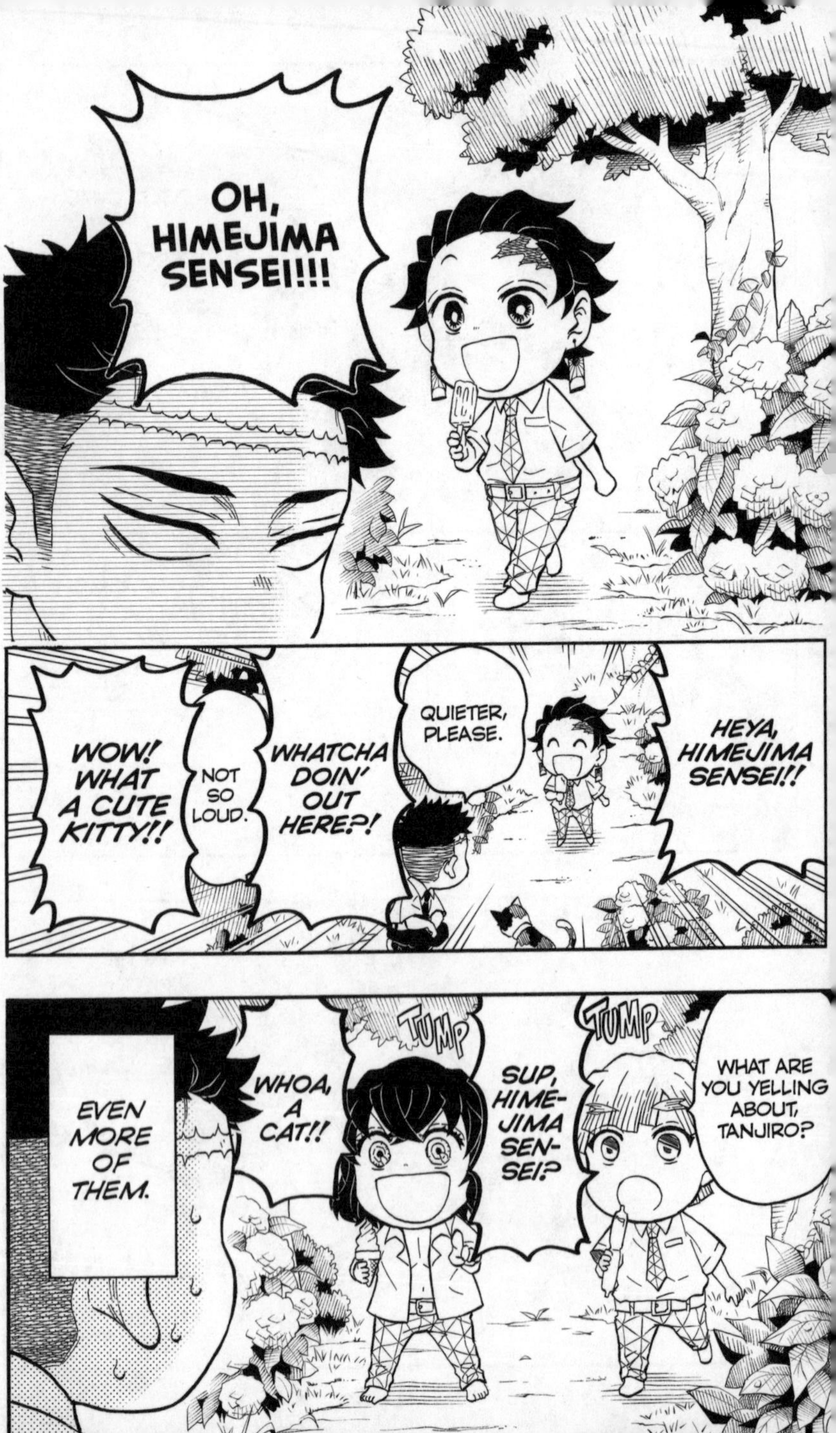
OH, HIMEJIMA SENSEI!!!
HEYA, HIMEJIMA SENSEI!!
QUIETER, PLEASE.
WHATCHA DOIN' OUT HERE?!
NOT SO LOUD.
WOW! WHAT A CUTE KITTY!!
TUMP
TUMP
WHAT ARE YOU YELLING ABOUT, TANJIRO?
SUP, HIME-JIMA SEN-SEI?
WHOA, A CAT!!
EVEN MORE OF THEM.

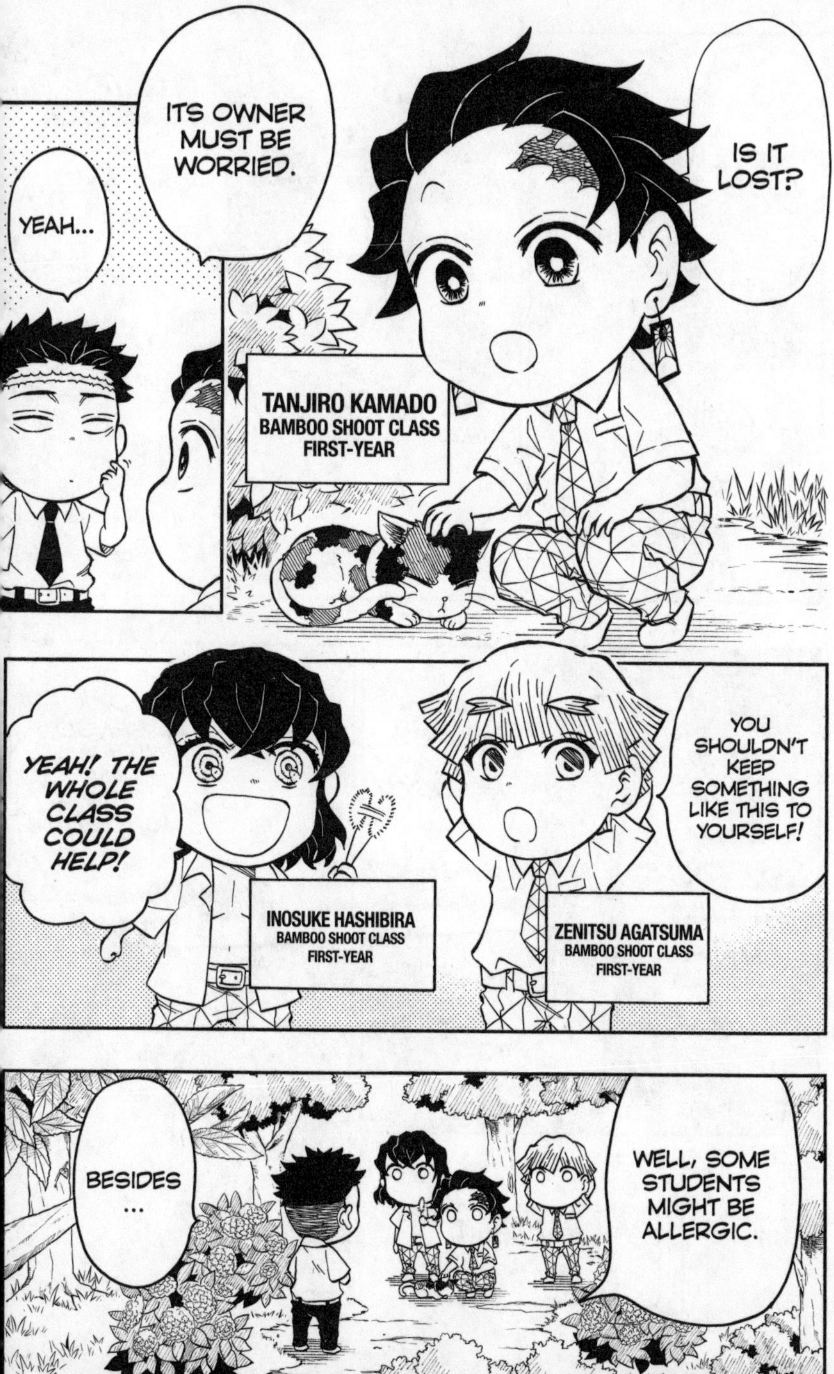
IS IT LOST?
TANJIRO KAMADO BAMBOO SHOOT CLASS FIRST-YEAR
ITS OWNER MUST BE WORRIED.
YEAH...
YOU SHOULDN'T KEEP SOMETHING LIKE THIS TO YOURSELF!
ZENITSU AGATSUMA BAMBOO SHOOT CLASS FIRST-YEAR
YEAH! THE WHOLE CLASS COULD HELP!
INOSUKE HASHIBIRA BAMBOO SHOOT CLASS FIRST-YEAR
WELL, SOME STUDENTS MIGHT BE ALLERGIC.
BESIDES ...

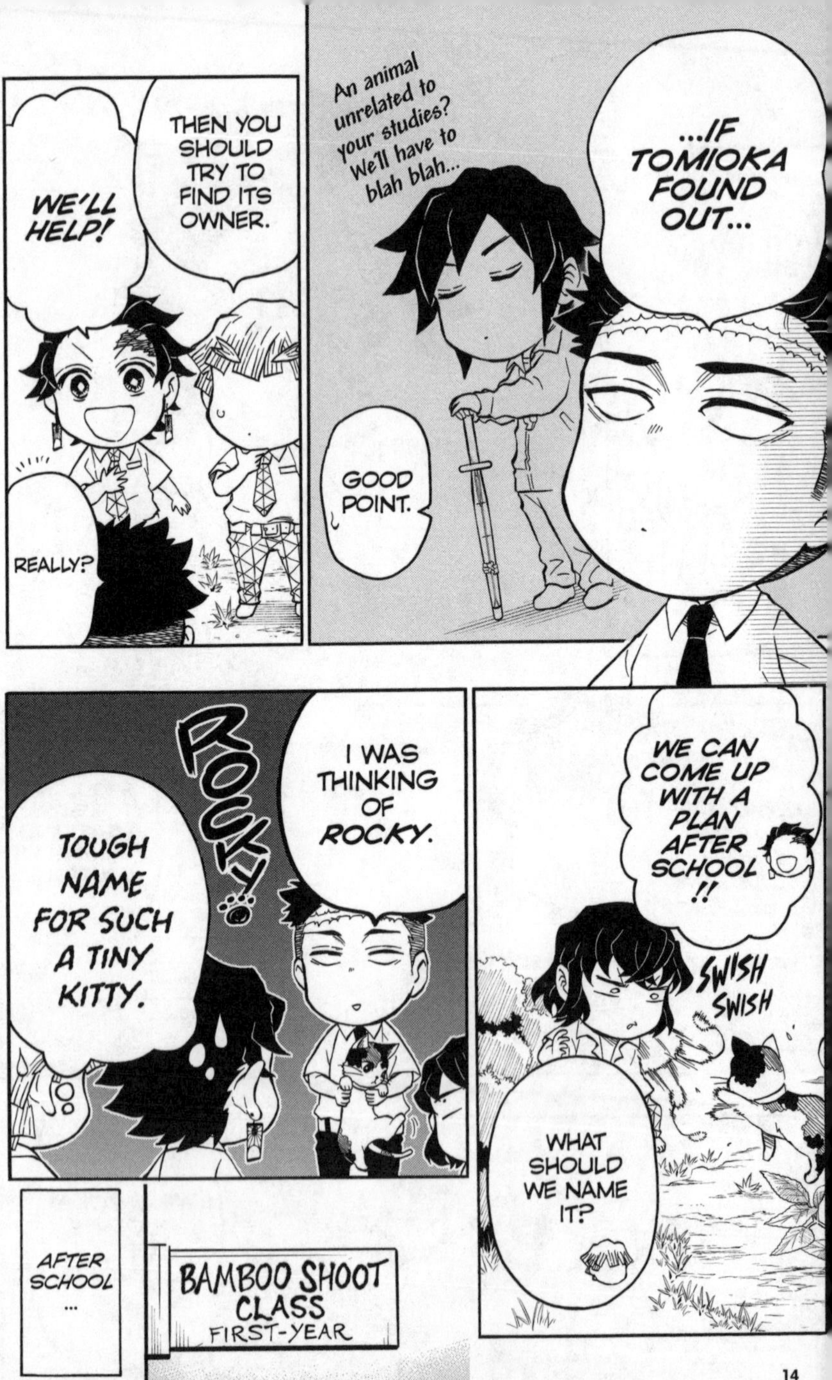
...IF TOMIOKA FOUND OUT...
An animal unrelated to your studies? We'll have to blah blah...
GOOD POINT.
THEN YOU SHOULD TRY TO FIND ITS OWNER.
WE'LL HELP!
REALLY?
WE CAN COME UP WITH A PLAN AFTER SCHOOL!!
SWISH SWISH
WHAT SHOULD WE NAME IT?
I WAS THINKING OF ROCKY.
ROCKY!
TOUGH NAME FOR SUCH A TINY KITTY.
AFTER SCHOOL ...
BAMBOO SHOOT CLASS FIRST-YEAR

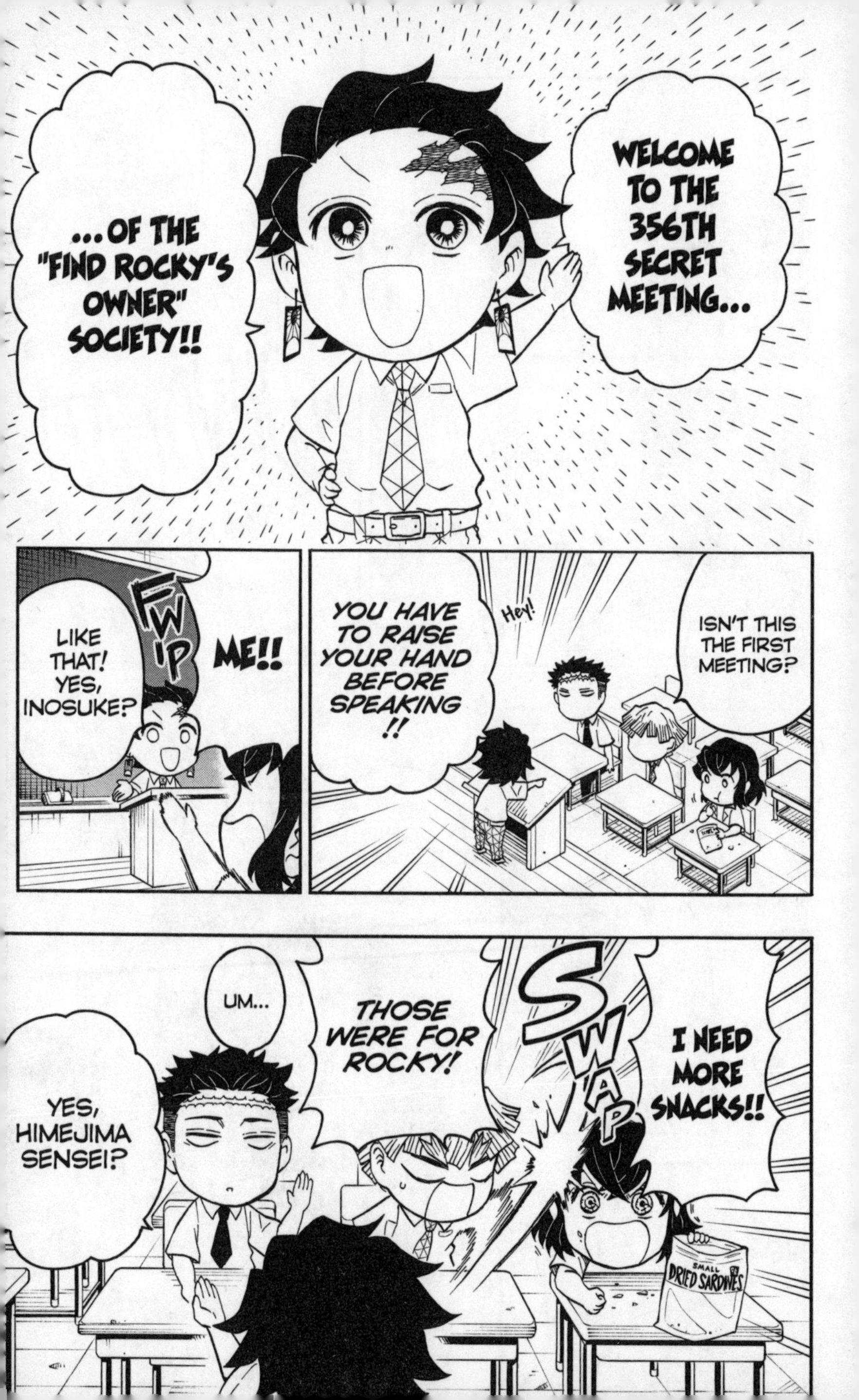
WELCOME TO THE 356TH SECRET MEETING...
...OF THE "FIND ROCKY'S OWNER" SOCIETY!!
ISN'T THIS THE FIRST MEETING?
Hey!
YOU HAVE TO RAISE YOUR HAND BEFORE SPEAKING!!
ME!!
FWIP
LIKE THAT! YES, INOSUKE?
I NEED MORE SNACKS!!
SWAP
SMALL DRIED SARDINES
THOSE WERE FOR ROCKY!
UM...
YES, HIMEJIMA SENSEI?

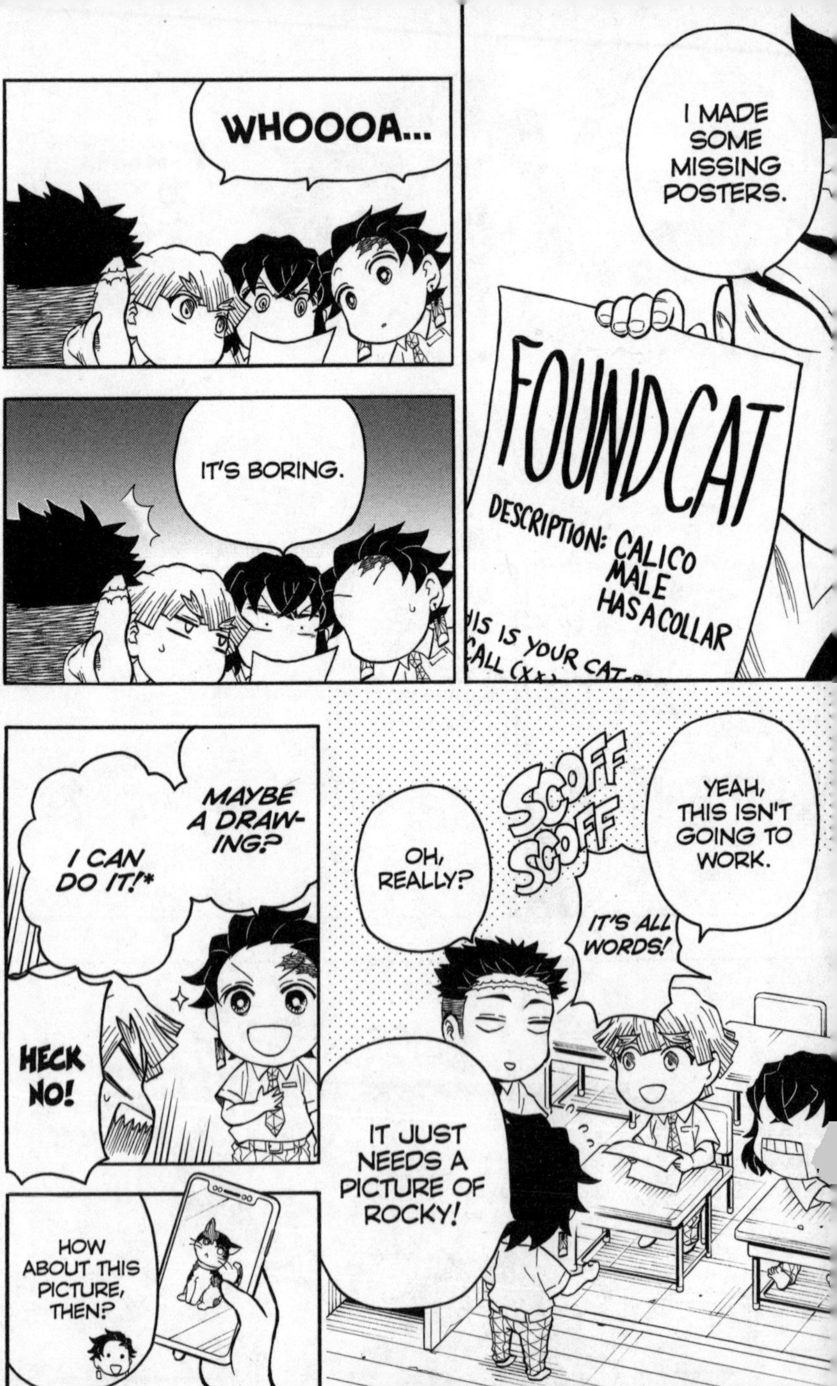
I MADE SOME MISSING POSTERS.
FOUND CAT
DESCRIPTION: CALICO MALE HAS A COLLAR
WHOOOA...
IT'S BORING.
YEAH, THIS ISN'T GOING TO WORK.
SCOFF SCOFF
OH, REALLY?
IT'S ALL WORDS!
IT JUST NEEDS A PICTURE OF ROCKY!
MAYBE A DRAWING?
I CAN DO IT!*
HECK NO!
HOW ABOUT THIS PICTURE, THEN?

*CHECK VOLUME 1 TO SEE TANJIRO'S ARTISTIC "SKILLS."

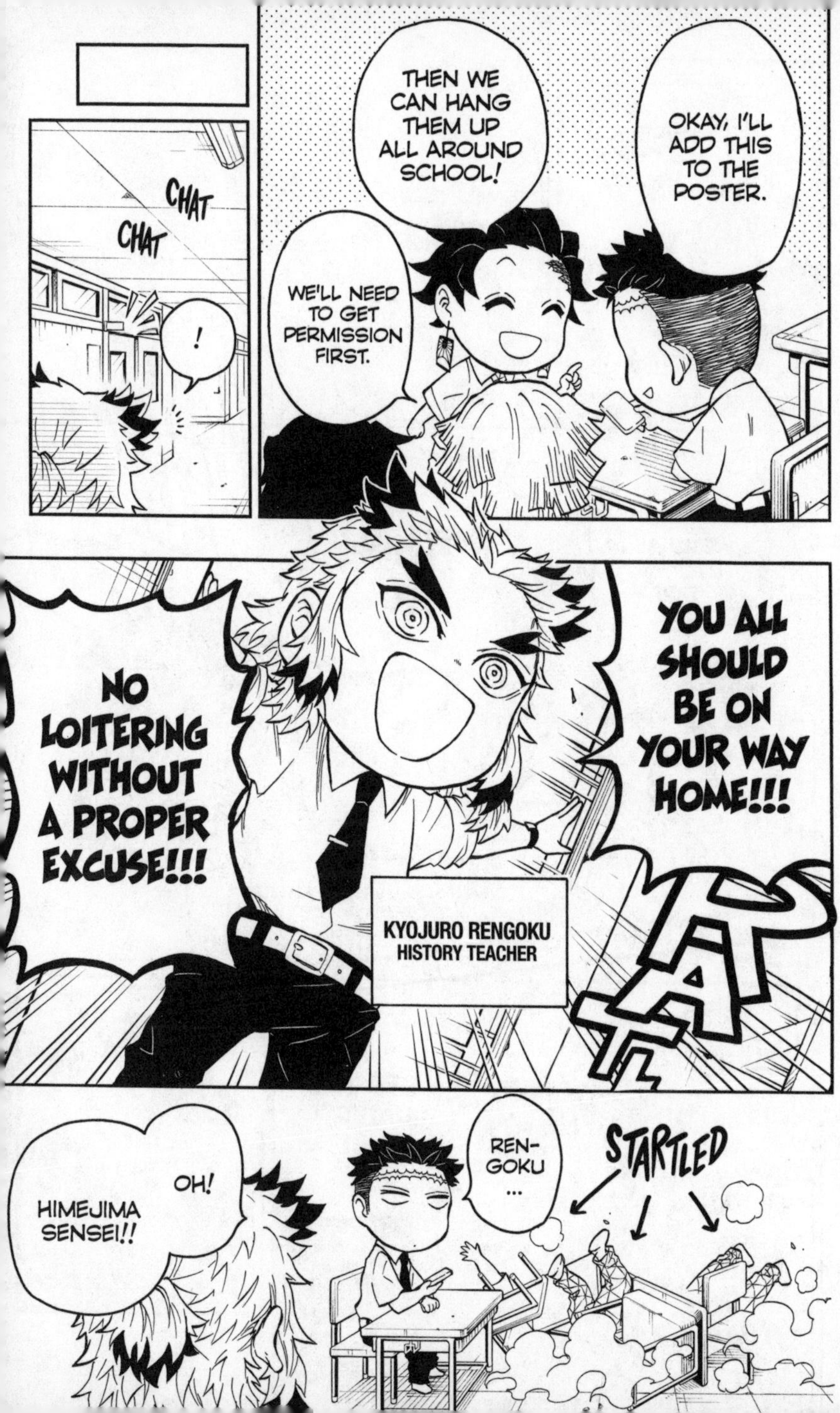
OKAY, I'LL ADD THIS TO THE POSTER.
THEN WE CAN HANG THEM UP ALL AROUND SCHOOL!
WE'LL NEED TO GET PERMISSION FIRST.
CHAT
CHAT
!
YOU ALL SHOULD BE ON YOUR WAY HOME!!!
NO LOITERING WITHOUT A PROPER EXCUSE!!!
KYOJURO RENGOKU
HISTORY TEACHER
STARTLED
REN-GOKU ...
OH!
HIMEJIMA SENSEI!!

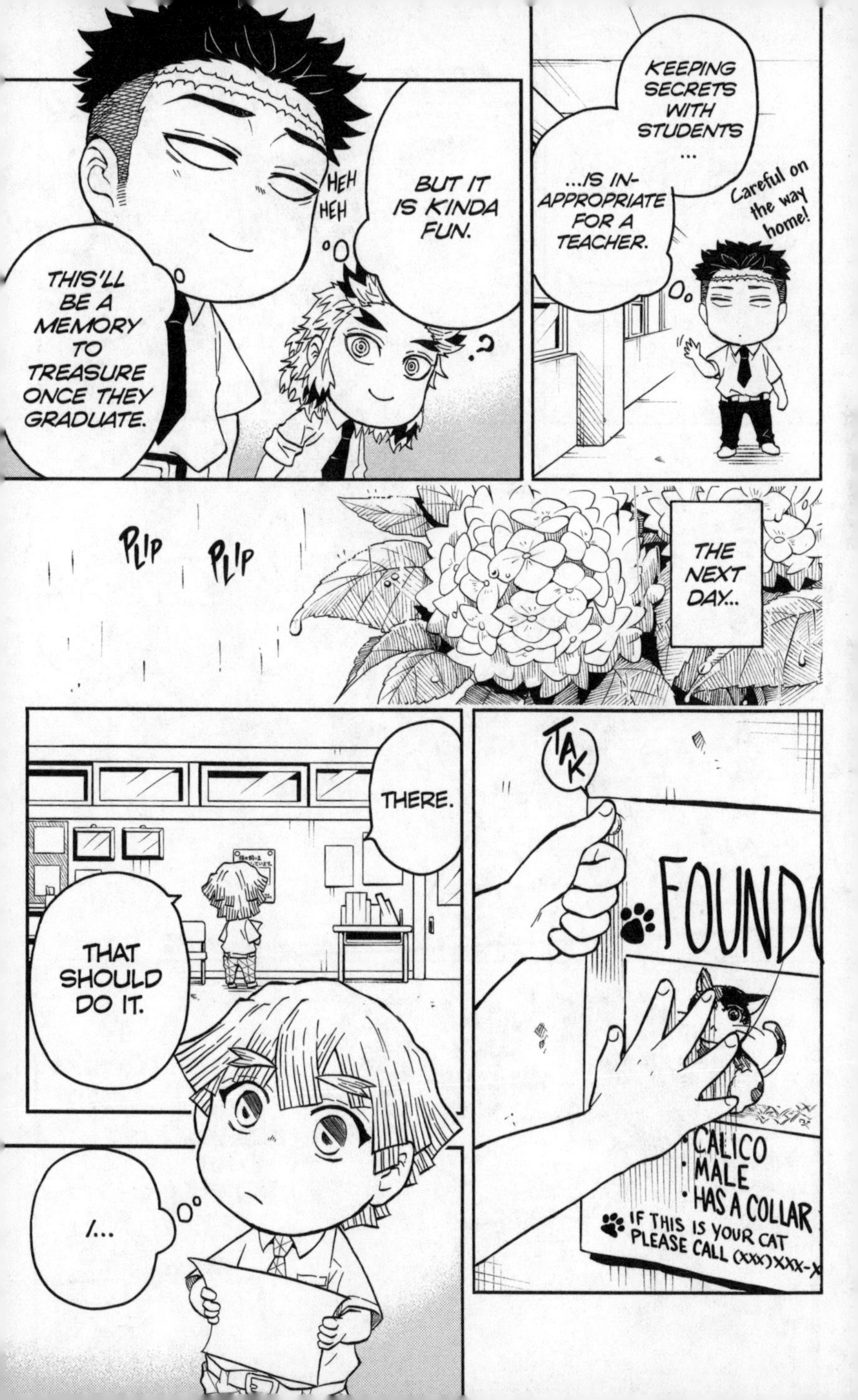
KEEPING SECRETS WITH STUDENTS ...
...IS IN-APPROPRIATE FOR A TEACHER.
Careful on the way home!
HEH HEH
BUT IT IS KINDA FUN.
THIS'LL BE A MEMORY TO TREASURE ONCE THEY GRADUATE.
THE NEXT DAY...
PLIP
PLIP
TAK
FOUND
CALICO
MALE
HAS A COLLAR
IF THIS IS YOUR CAT PLEASE CALL (XXX)XXX-X
THERE.
THAT SHOULD DO IT.
!...

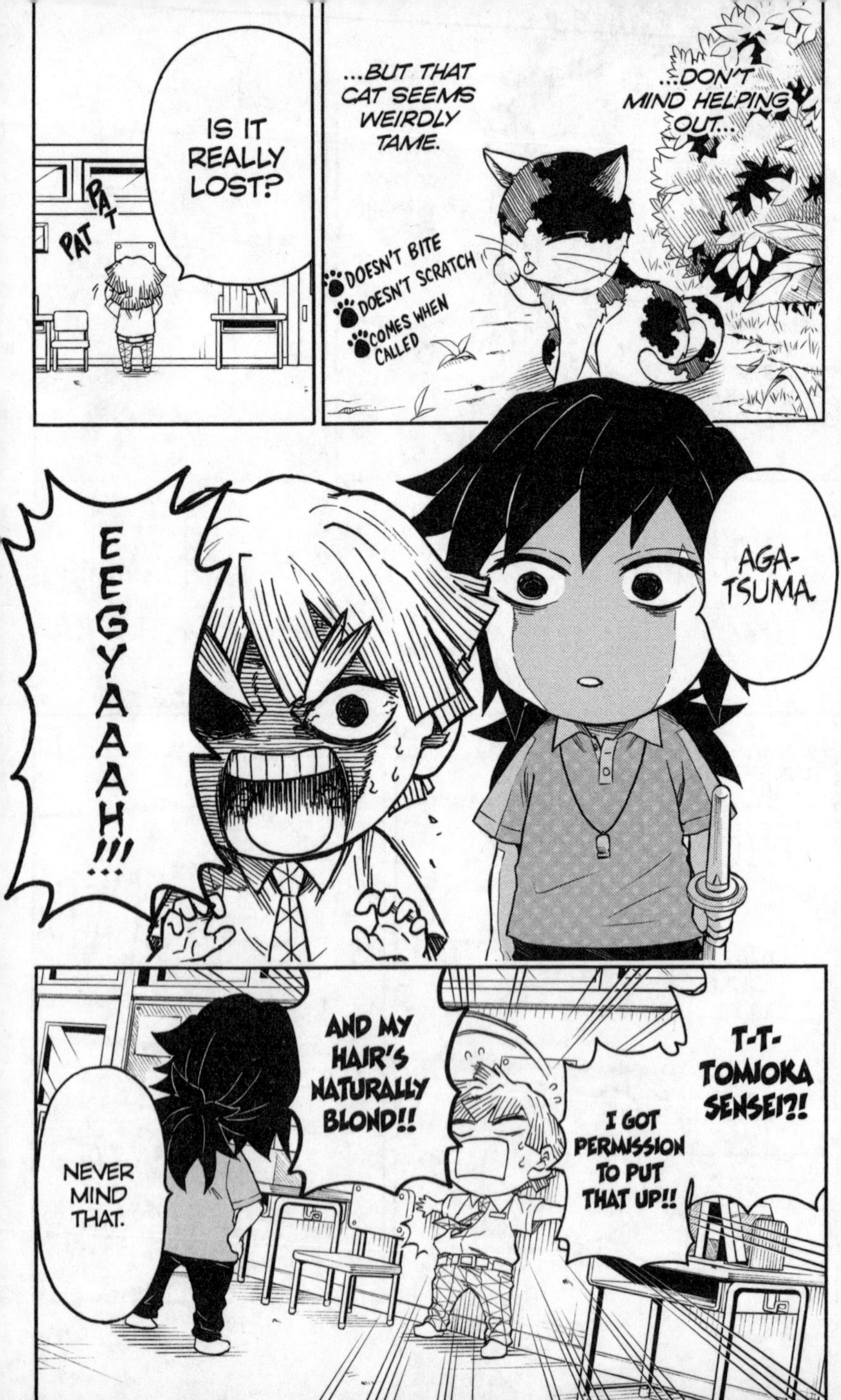
...DON'T MIND HELPING OUT...
...BUT THAT CAT SEEMS WEIRDLY TAME.
DOESN'T BITE
DOESN'T SCRATCH
COMES WHEN CALLED
IS IT REALLY LOST?
PAT
PAT
AGA-TSUMA.
EEGYAAAAH!!!
T-T-TOMIOKA SENSEI?!
I GOT PERMISSION TO PUT THAT UP!!
AND MY HAIR'S NATURALLY BLOND!!
NEVER MIND THAT.

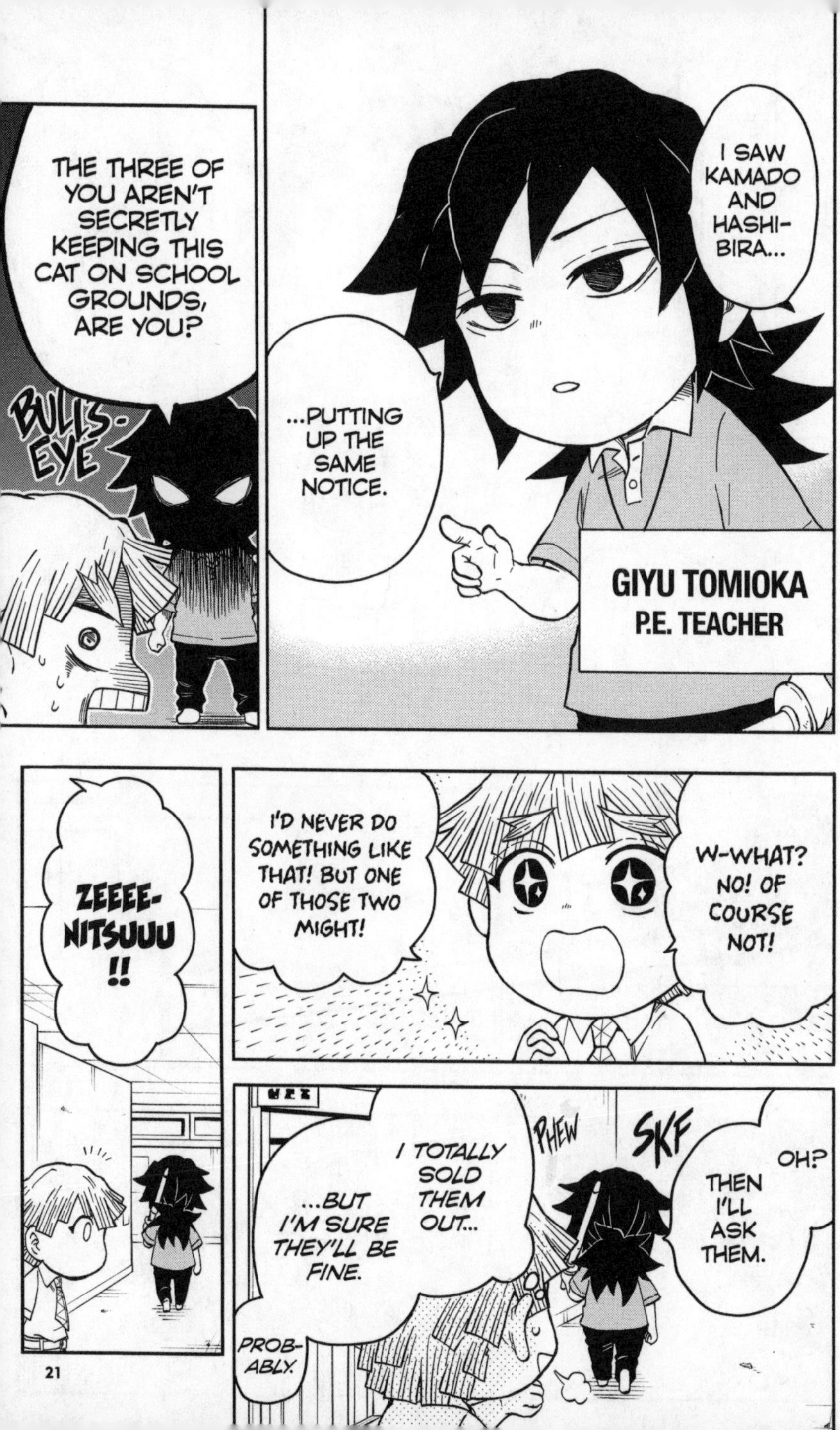
I SAW KAMADO AND HASHIBIRA...
...PUTTING UP THE SAME NOTICE.
GIYU TOMIOKA
P.E. TEACHER
THE THREE OF YOU AREN'T SECRETLY KEEPING THIS CAT ON SCHOOL GROUNDS, ARE YOU?
BULLS-EYE
W-WHAT? NO! OF COURSE NOT!
I'D NEVER DO SOMETHING LIKE THAT! BUT ONE OF THOSE TWO MIGHT!
OH?
THEN I'LL ASK THEM.
SKF
PHEW
I TOTALLY SOLD THEM OUT...
...BUT I'M SURE THEY'LL BE FINE.
PROB-ABLY.
ZEEEE-NITSUUU!!

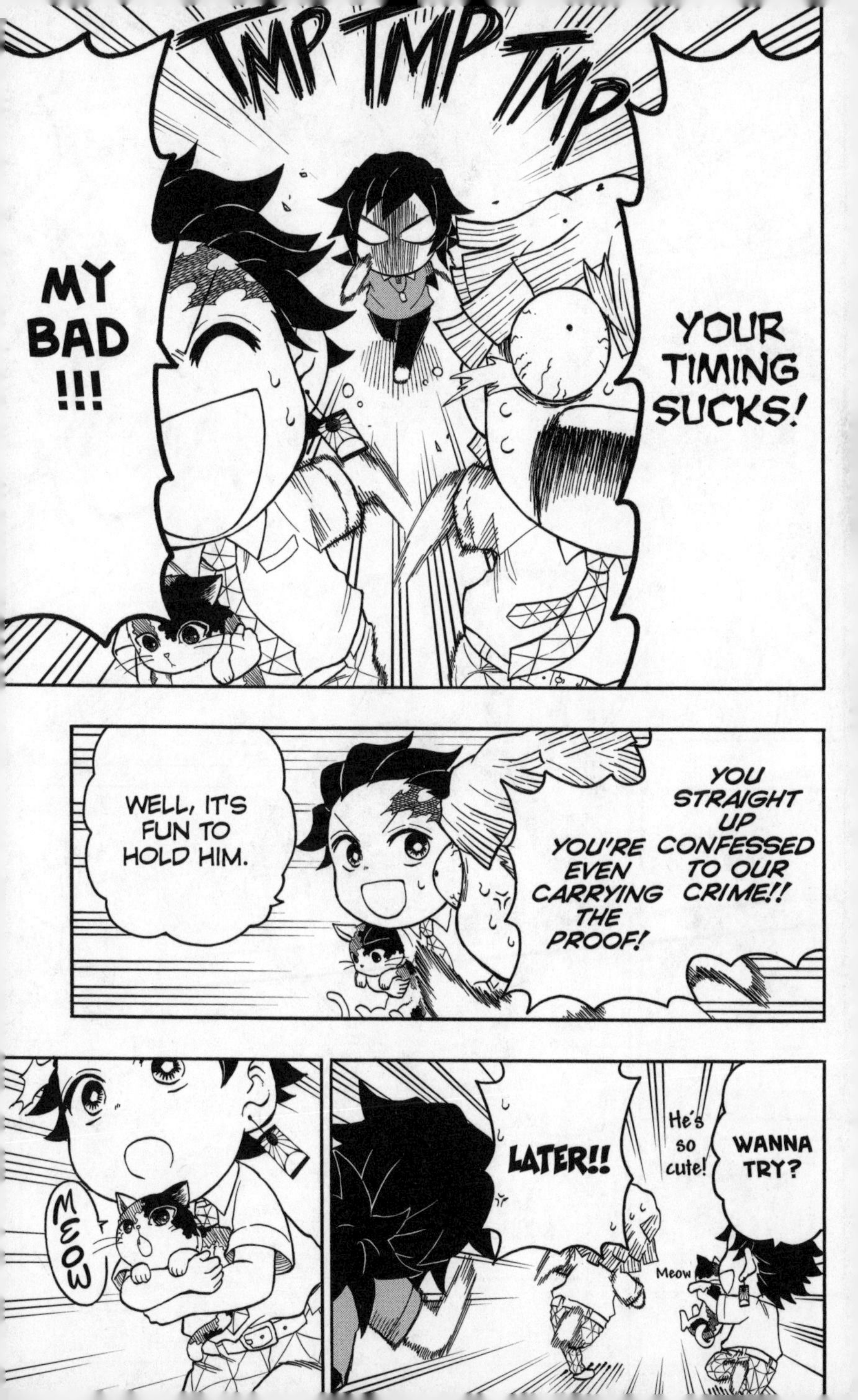
TMP TMP TMP
YOUR TIMING SUCKS!
MY BAD!!!
YOU STRAIGHT UP CONFESSED TO OUR CRIME!!
YOU'RE EVEN CARRYING THE PROOF!
WELL, IT'S FUN TO HOLD HIM.
WANNA TRY?
He's so cute!
LATER!!
Meow
MEOW

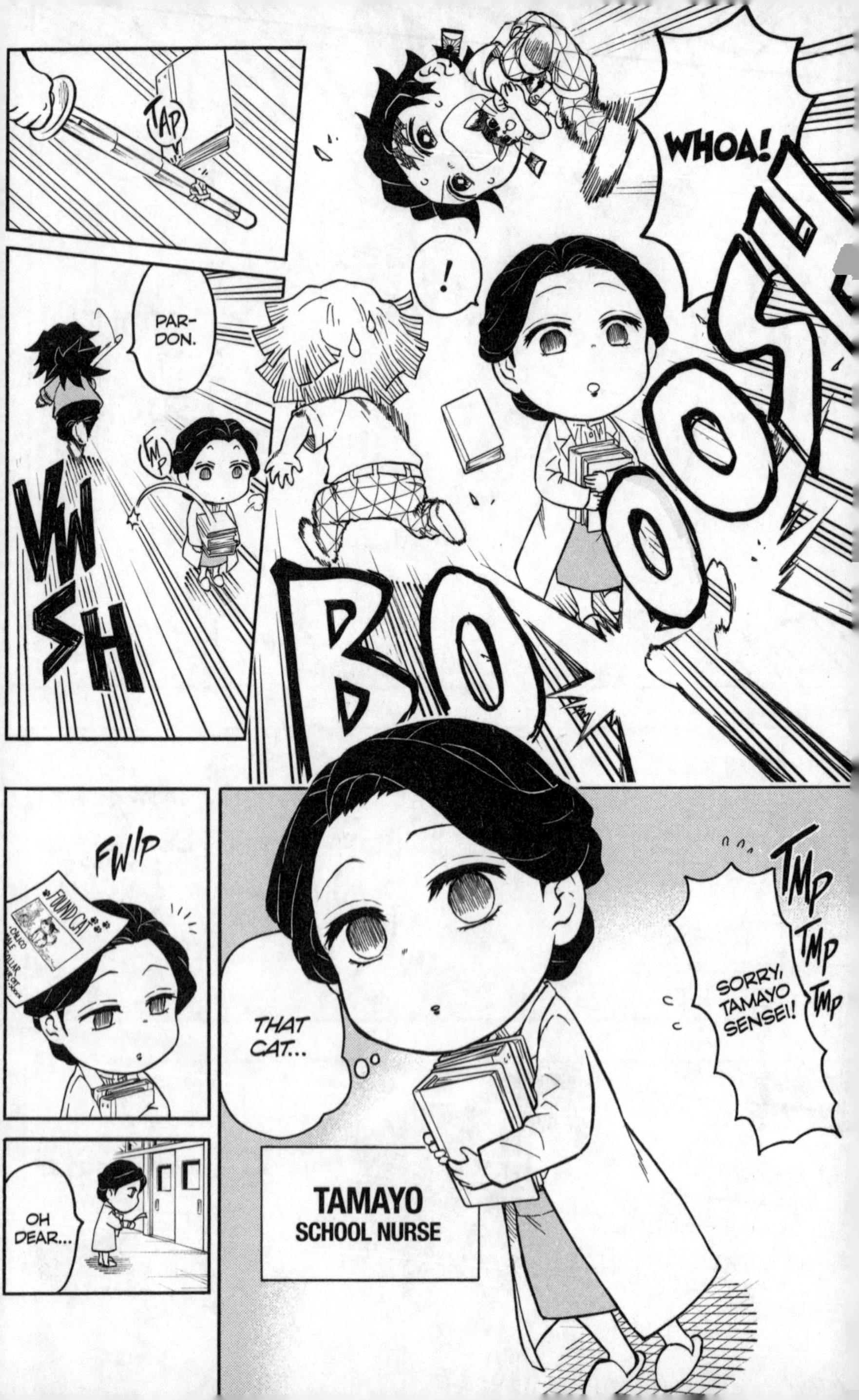
WHOA!
!
BOOOOSH
TAP
PAR-DON.
VWSH
FMP
SORRY, TAMAYO SENSEI!
TMP TMP TMP
THAT CAT...
TAMAYO
SCHOOL NURSE
FWIP
FOUND CAT
OH DEAR...

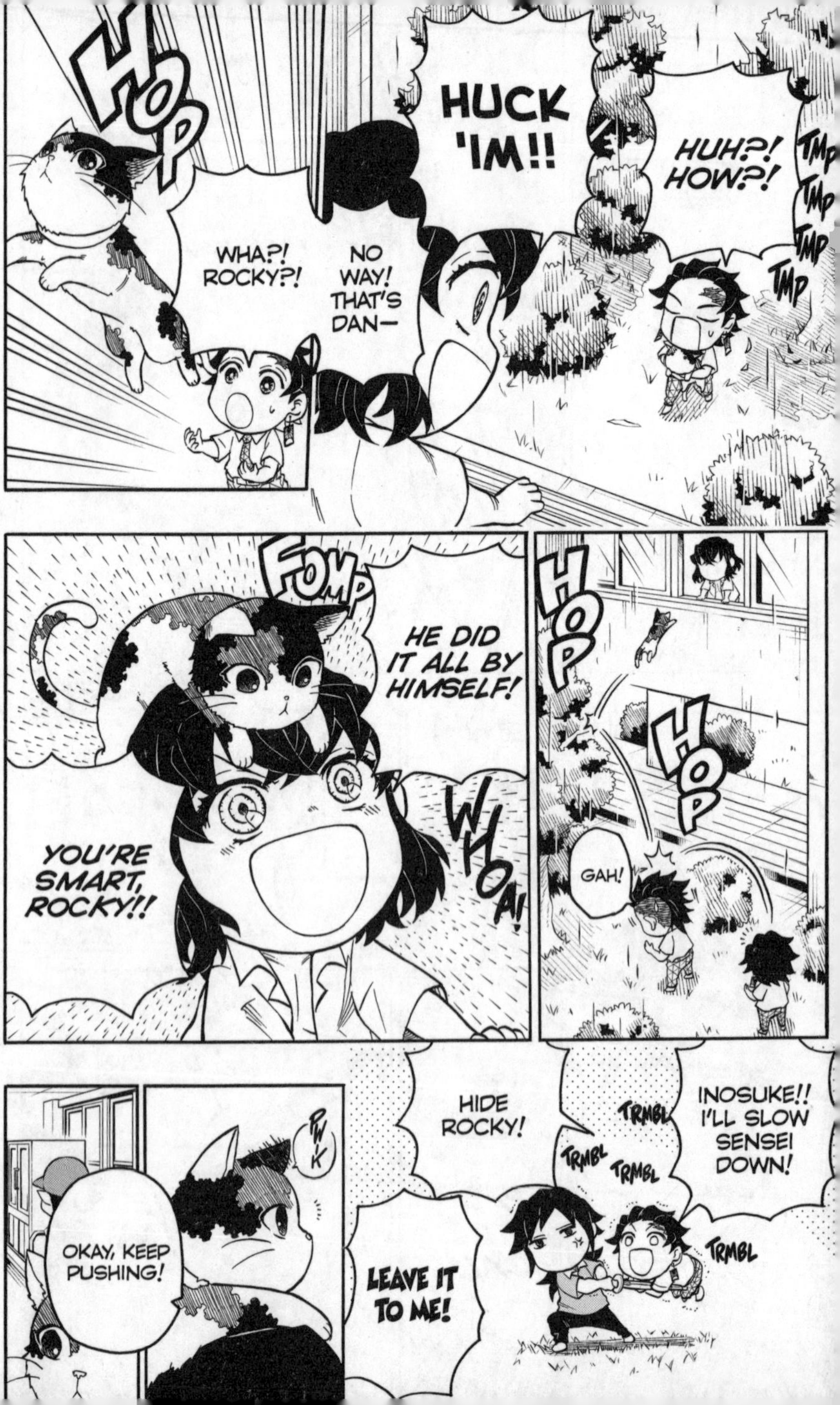
HUH?! HOW?!
TMP TMP TMP TMP
HUCK 'IM!!
NO WAY! THAT'S DAN—
WHA?! ROCKY?!
HOP
HOP
HOP
GAH!
FOMP
HE DID IT ALL BY HIMSELF!
WHOA!
YOU'RE SMART, ROCKY!!
INOSUKE!! I'LL SLOW SENSEI DOWN!
TRMBL
TRMBL TRMBL
HIDE ROCKY!
TRMBL
LEAVE IT TO ME!
PWIK
OKAY, KEEP PUSHING!

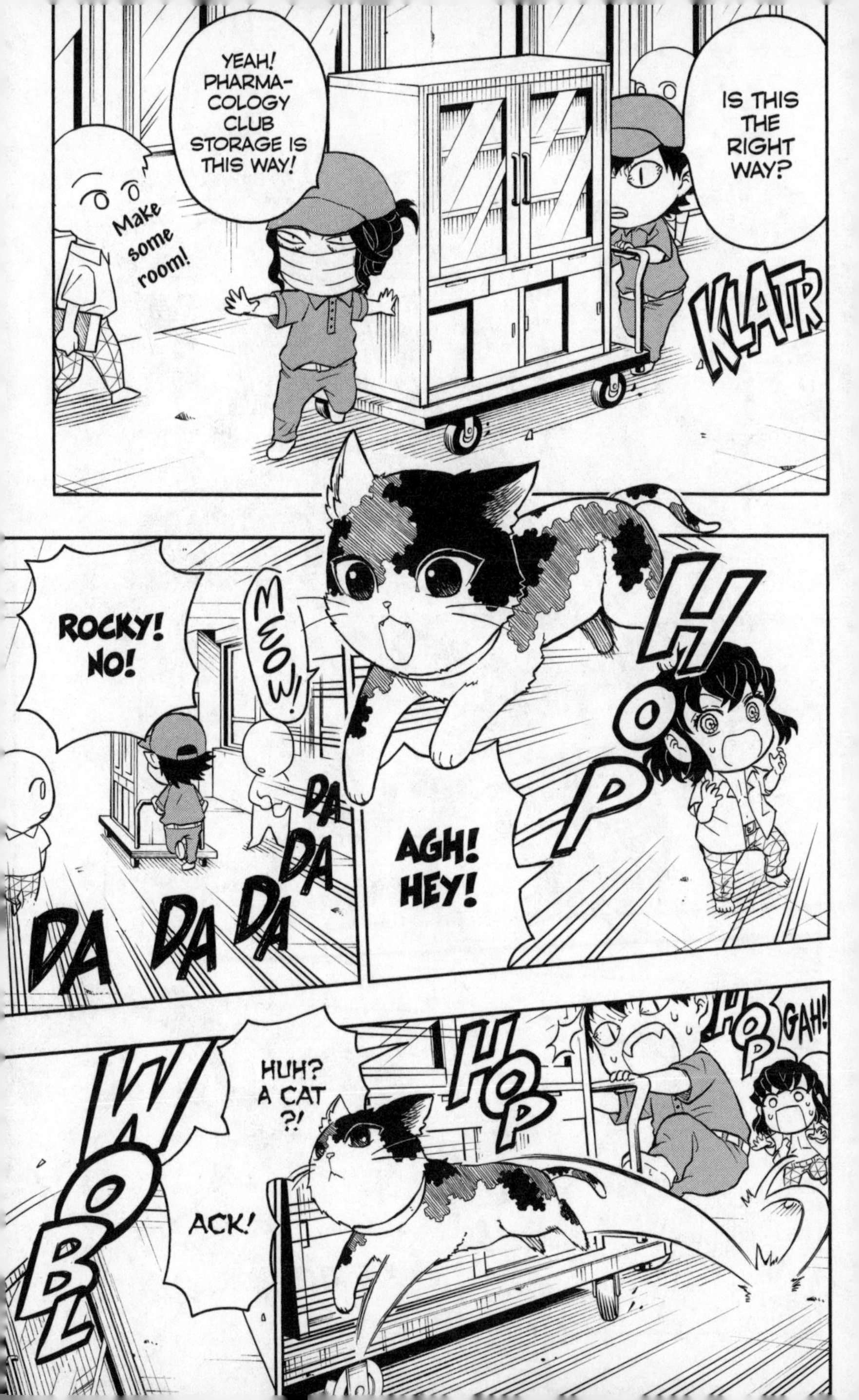
IS THIS THE RIGHT WAY?
YEAH! PHARMA-COLOGY CLUB STORAGE IS THIS WAY!
Make some room!
KLATR
HOP
AGH! HEY!
MEOW!
ROCKY! NO!
DA DA DA DA DA
GAH!
HOP
HOP
HUH? A CAT?!
ACK!
WOBL

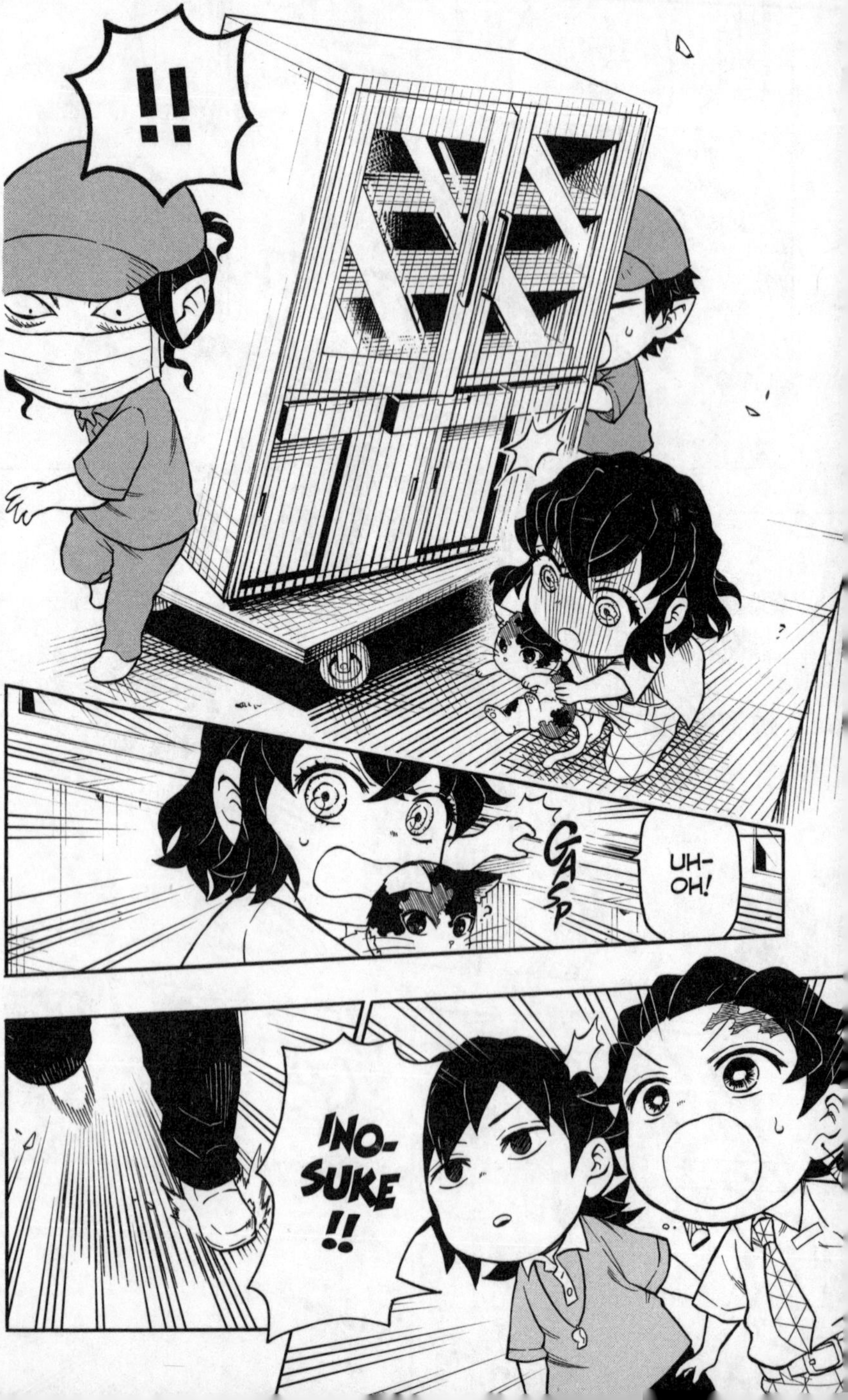
!!
UH-OH!
GASP
INO-SUKE!!

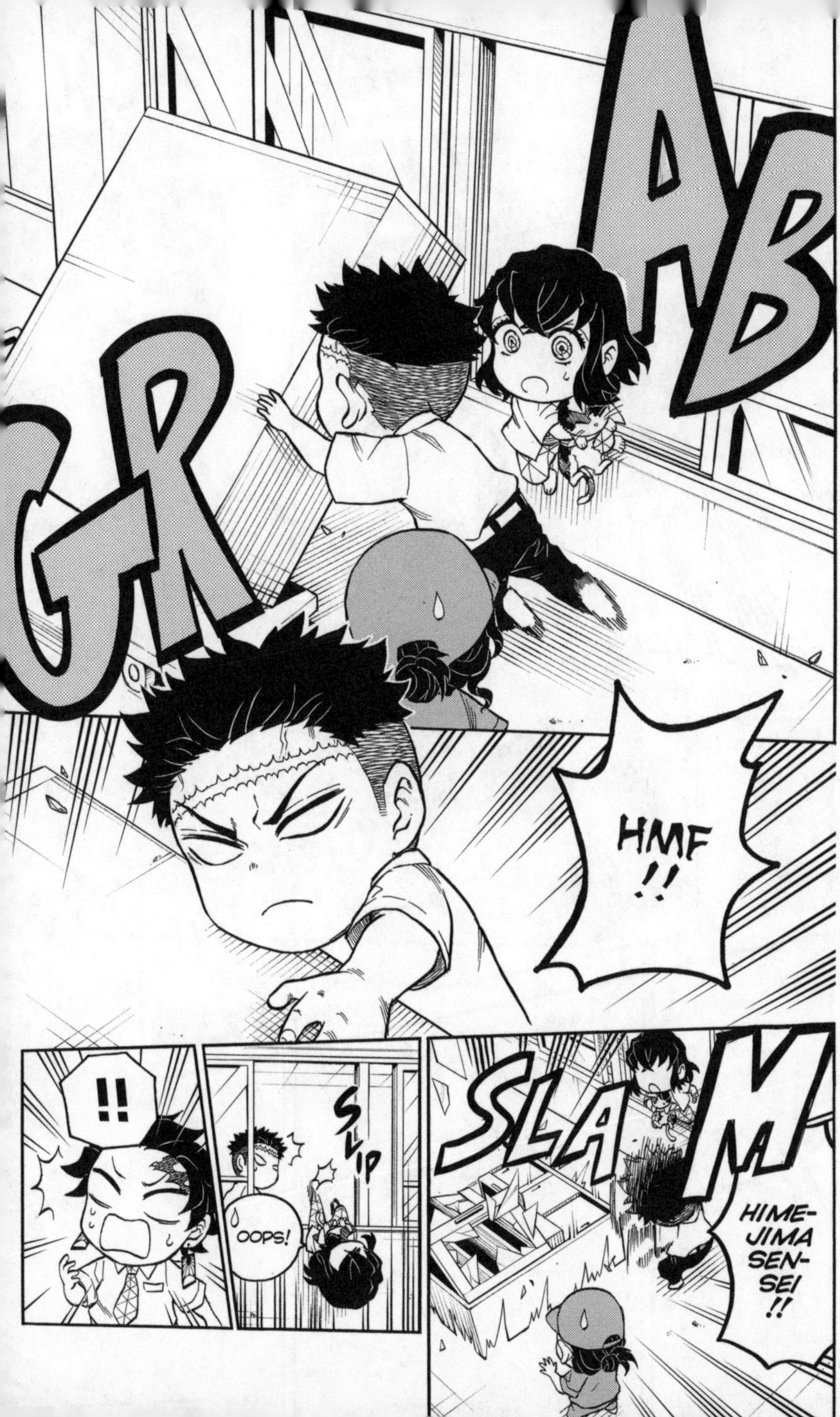

GRAB
HMF !!
SLAM
HIMEJIMA SENSEI!!
SLIP
OOPS!
!!

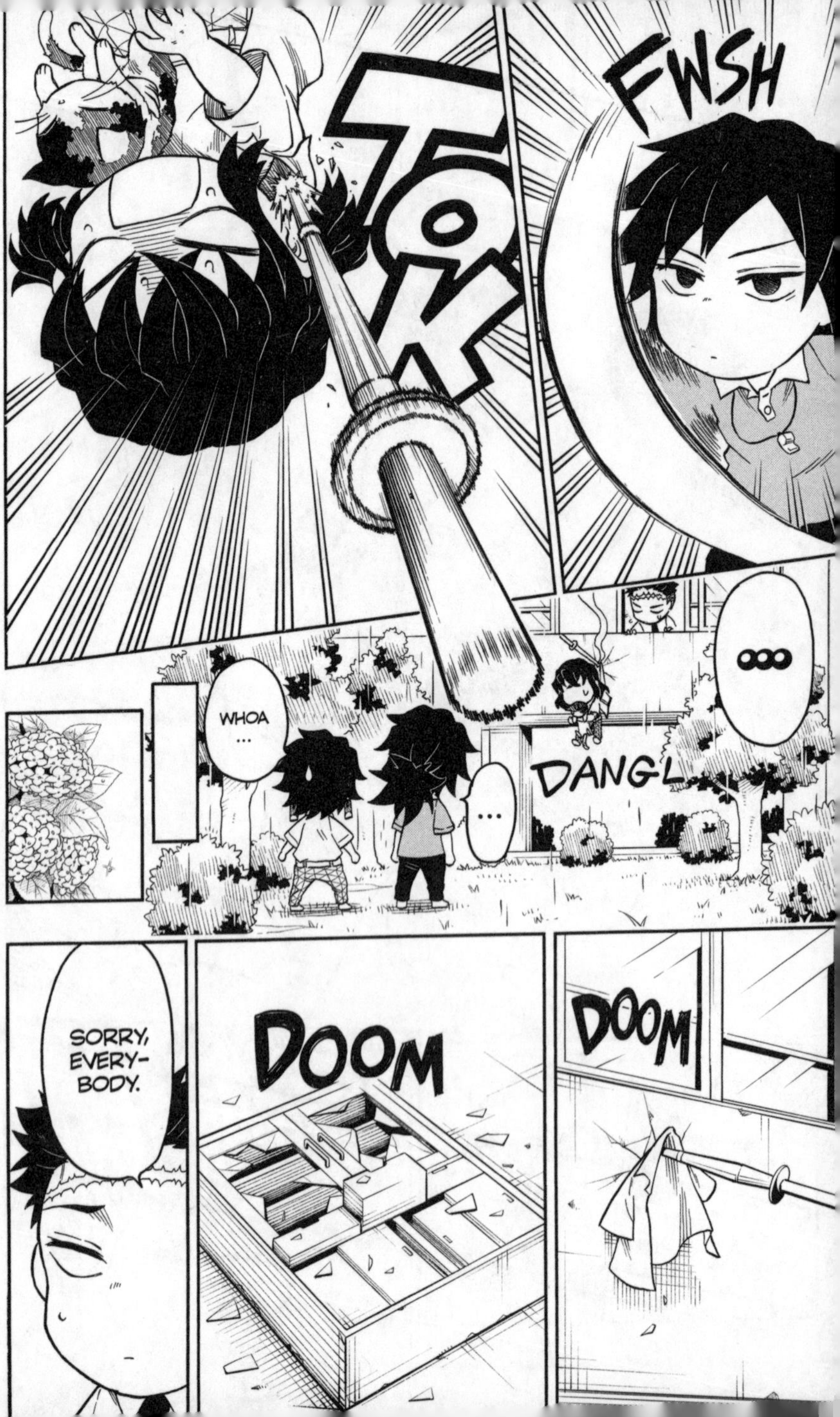
FWSH
TOK
...
DANGL
...
WHOA ...
DOOM
DOOM
SORRY, EVERY-BODY.

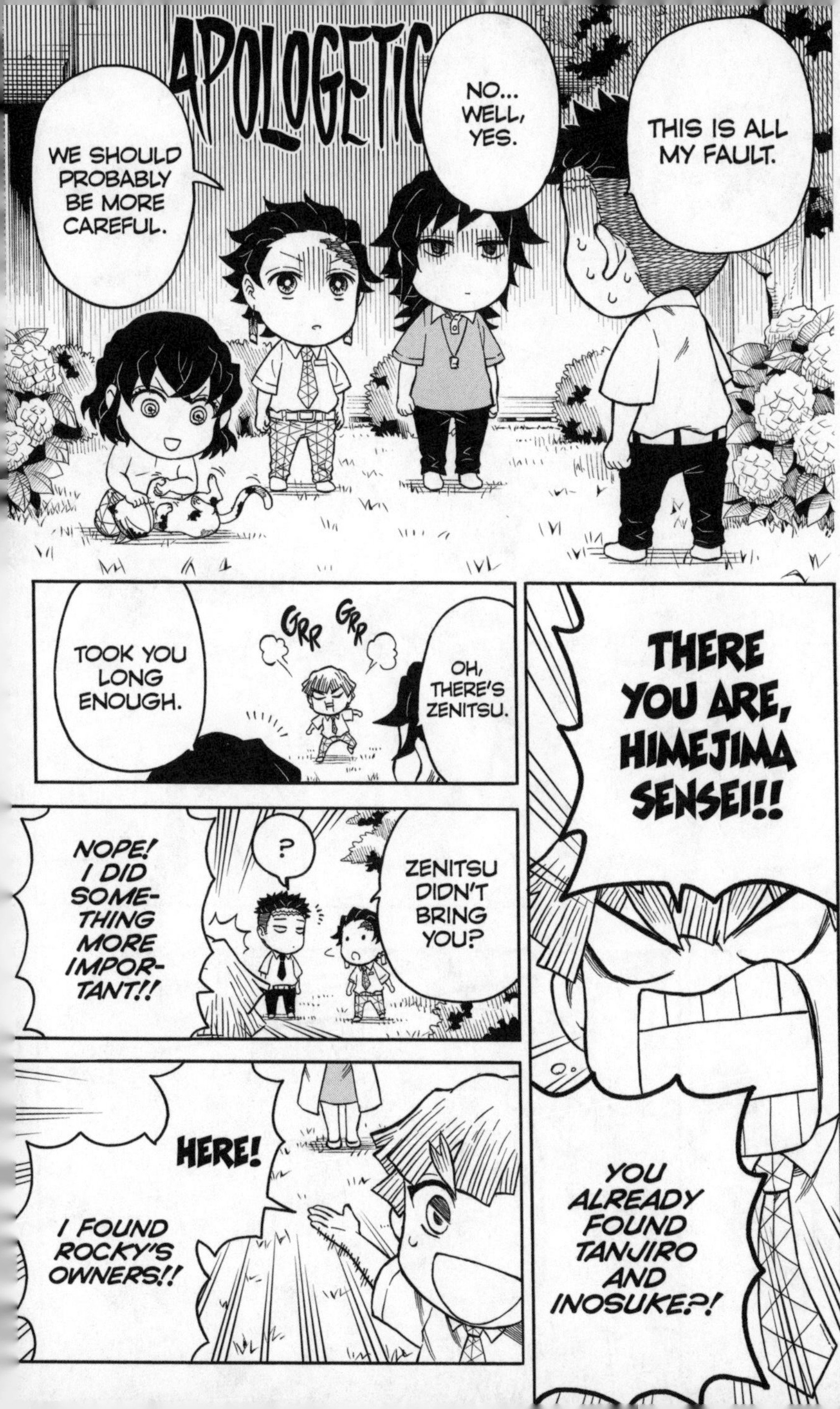
THIS IS ALL MY FAULT.
NO... WELL, YES.
APOLOGETIC
WE SHOULD PROBABLY BE MORE CAREFUL.
THERE YOU ARE, HIMEJIMA SENSEI!!
YOU ALREADY FOUND TANJIRO AND INOSUKE?!
OH, THERE'S ZENITSU.
GRR GRR
TOOK YOU LONG ENOUGH.
ZENITSU DIDN'T BRING YOU?
?
NOPE! I DID SOME-THING MORE IMPOR-TANT!!
HERE!
I FOUND ROCKY'S OWNERS!!

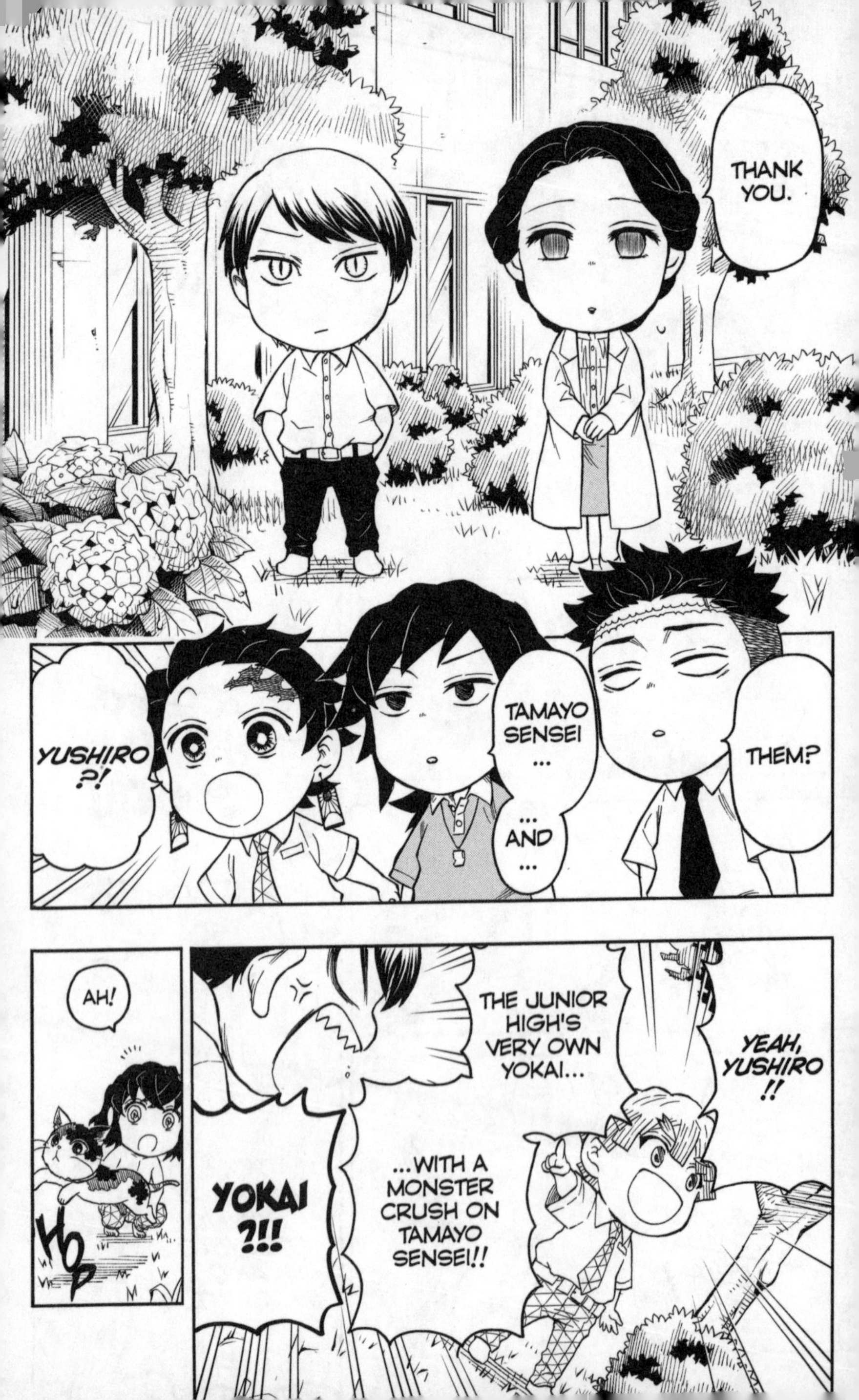
THANK YOU.
THEM?
TAMAYO SENSEI ...
... AND ...
YUSHIRO ?!
YEAH, YUSHIRO !!
THE JUNIOR HIGH'S VERY OWN YOKAI...
...WITH A MONSTER CRUSH ON TAMAYO SENSEI!!
YOKAI ?!!
AH!
HOP

WELL, UM...

IS THIS CAT YOURS?

CHACHAMARU'S MY CAT.

I SAW YOUR POSTERS.

RUB RUB

...SO HE STARTED COMING EVERY DAY.

...AND HE TOOK A LIKING TO TAMAYO SENSEI...

I BROUGHT HIM TO SCHOOL ONE TIME...

YUSHIRO
GINKGO CLASS
JUNIOR HIGH, SECOND-YEAR

SO HIS NAME ISN'T ROCKY?

HMM...

OH, I SEE.

Sorry for all the trouble.

I CAN'T KEEP HIM IN THE NURSE'S OFFICE, SO I LET HIM OUTSIDE.

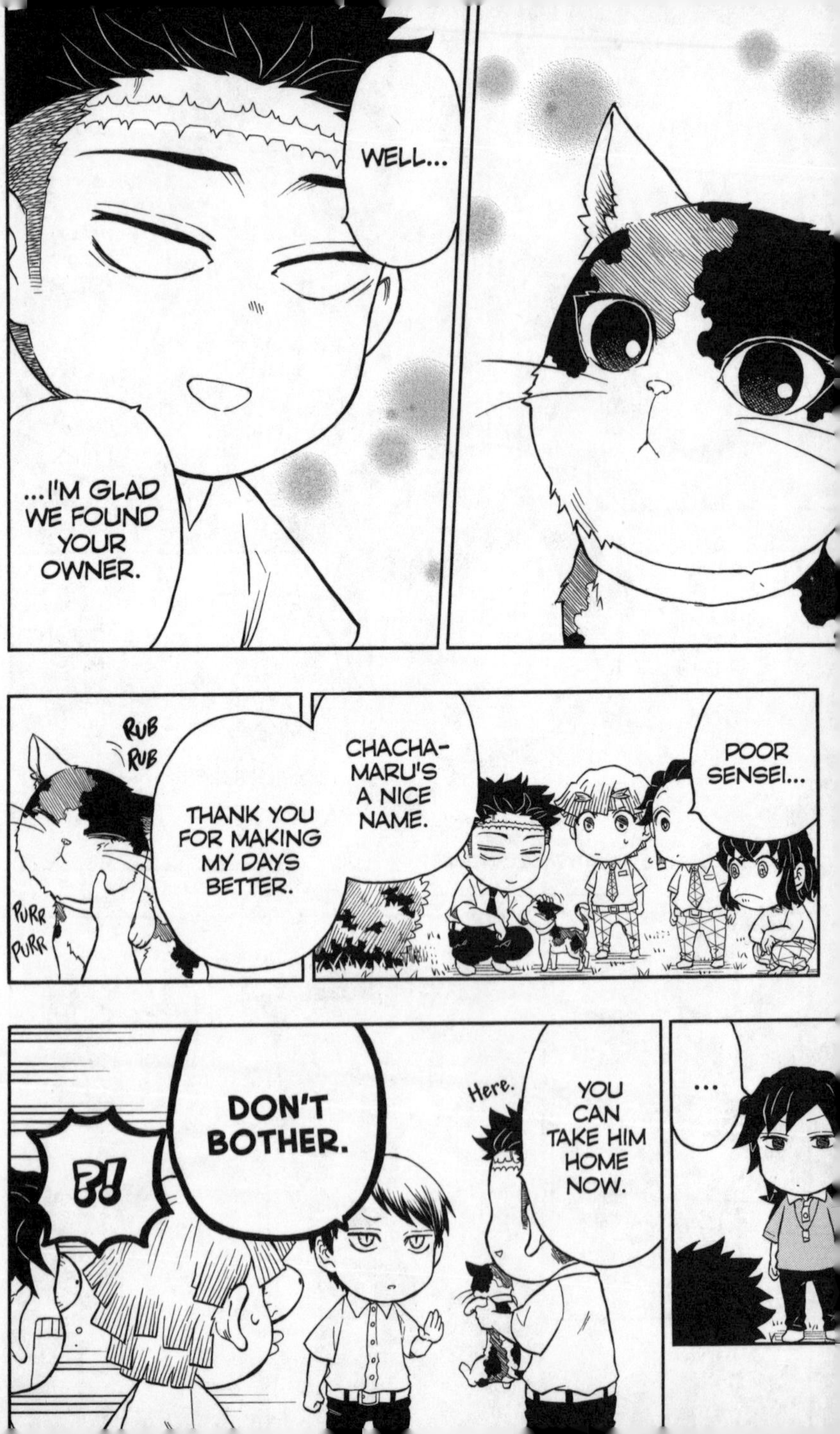
WELL...
...I'M GLAD WE FOUND YOUR OWNER.
POOR SENSEI...
CHACHA-MARU'S A NICE NAME.
THANK YOU FOR MAKING MY DAYS BETTER.
RUB RUB
PURR PURR
...
YOU CAN TAKE HIM HOME NOW.
Here.
DON'T BOTHER.
?!

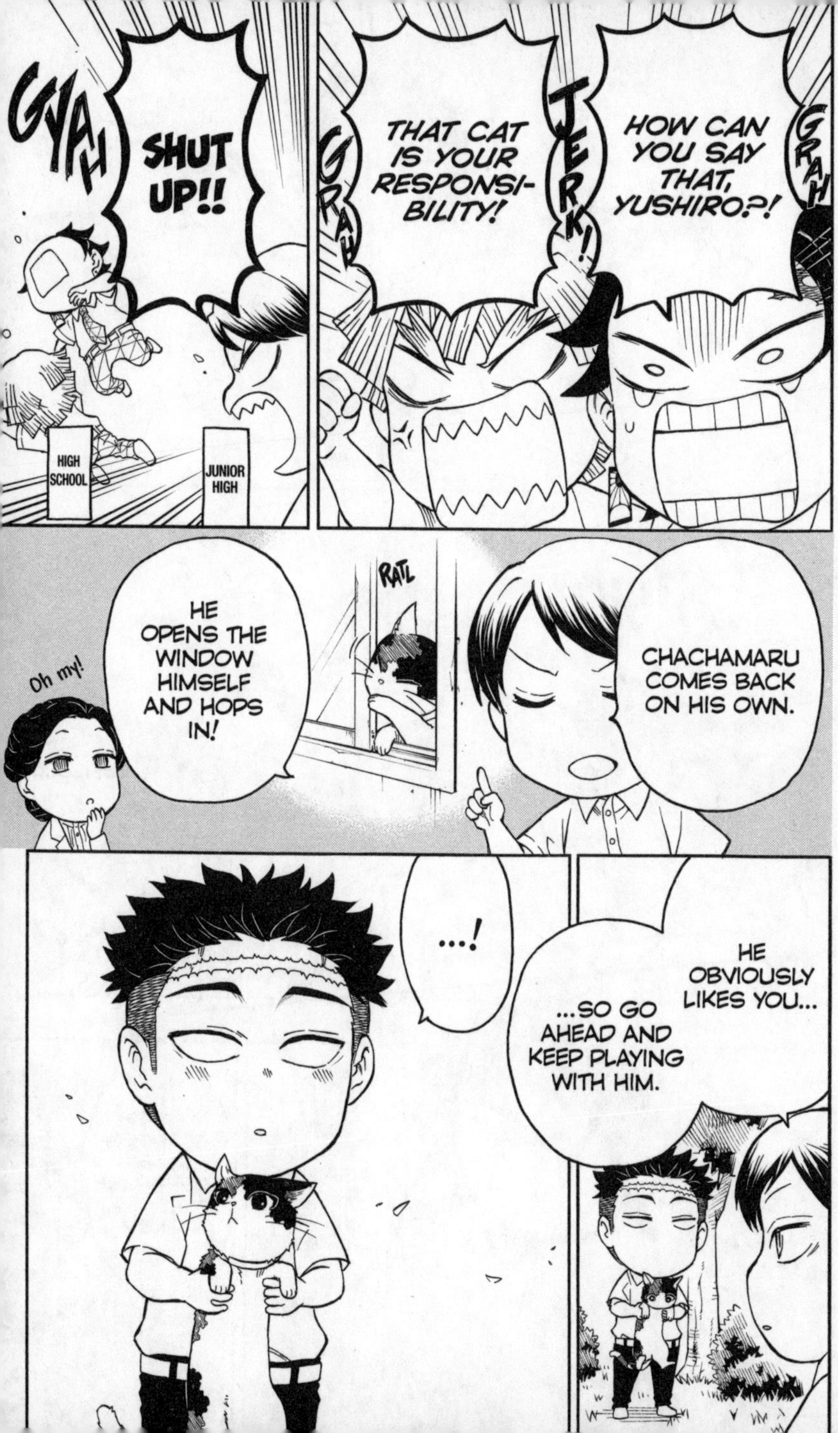
GRAH
HOW CAN YOU SAY THAT, YUSHIRO?!
JERK!
THAT CAT IS YOUR RESPONSI-BILITY!
GRAH
SHUT UP!!
GYAH
JUNIOR HIGH
HIGH SCHOOL
CHACHAMARU COMES BACK ON HIS OWN.
RATL
HE OPENS THE WINDOW HIMSELF AND HOPS IN!
Oh my!
HE OBVIOUSLY LIKES YOU...
...SO GO AHEAD AND KEEP PLAYING WITH HIM.
...!

SO WHY WERE YOU CHASING US AROUND?!

REALLY?!

TOMIOKA WAS LENIENT (FOR ONCE).

LOOK THIS WAY, SENSEI!

SNAP

...HIMEJIMA PLAYING WITH CHACHAMARU AT SCHOOL.

...THE STUDENTS OFTEN SAW...

AFTER THAT...

No thanks.

Wanna pet him?

AND THAT'S WHY I KEEP TELLING YOU NOT TO RUN IN THE HALLS!

...COST QUITE A FEW BAGS OF DRIED SARDINES.

THAT SAID, REPLACING THE PHARMA-COLOGY CLUB'S SHELVES...

AWESOME ACADEMY

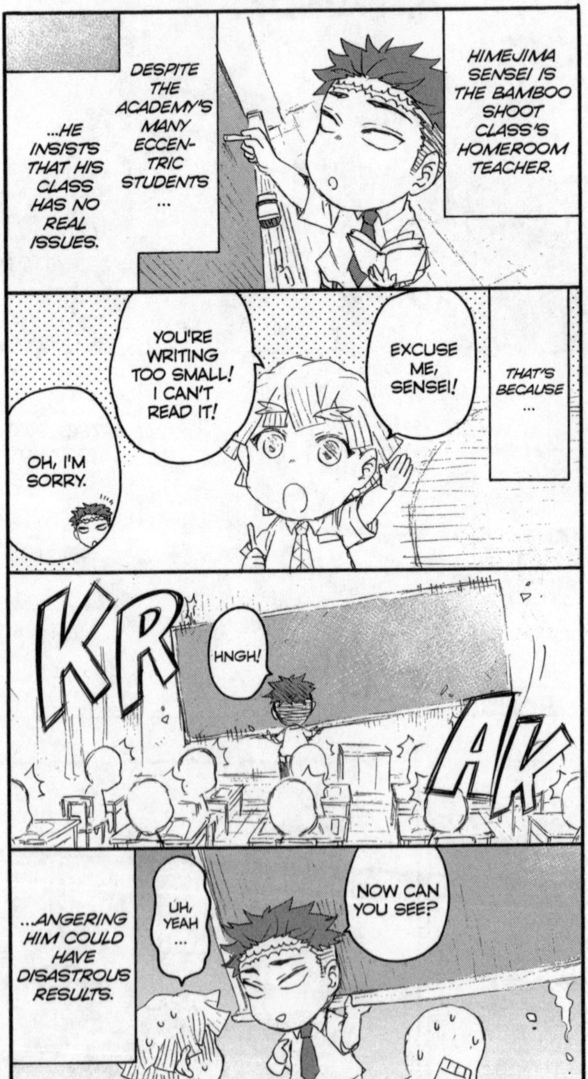
HIMEJIMA SENSEI IS THE BAMBOO SHOOT CLASS'S HOMEROOM TEACHER.
DESPITE THE ACADEMY'S MANY ECCEN-TRIC STUDENTS...
...HE INSISTS THAT HIS CLASS HAS NO REAL ISSUES.
THAT'S BECAUSE...
EXCUSE ME, SENSEI!
YOU'RE WRITING TOO SMALL! I CAN'T READ IT!
OH, I'M SORRY.
KR
HNGH!
AK
NOW CAN YOU SEE?
UH, YEAH...
...ANGERING HIM COULD HAVE DISASTROUS RESULTS.

But no one has ever seen him angry.

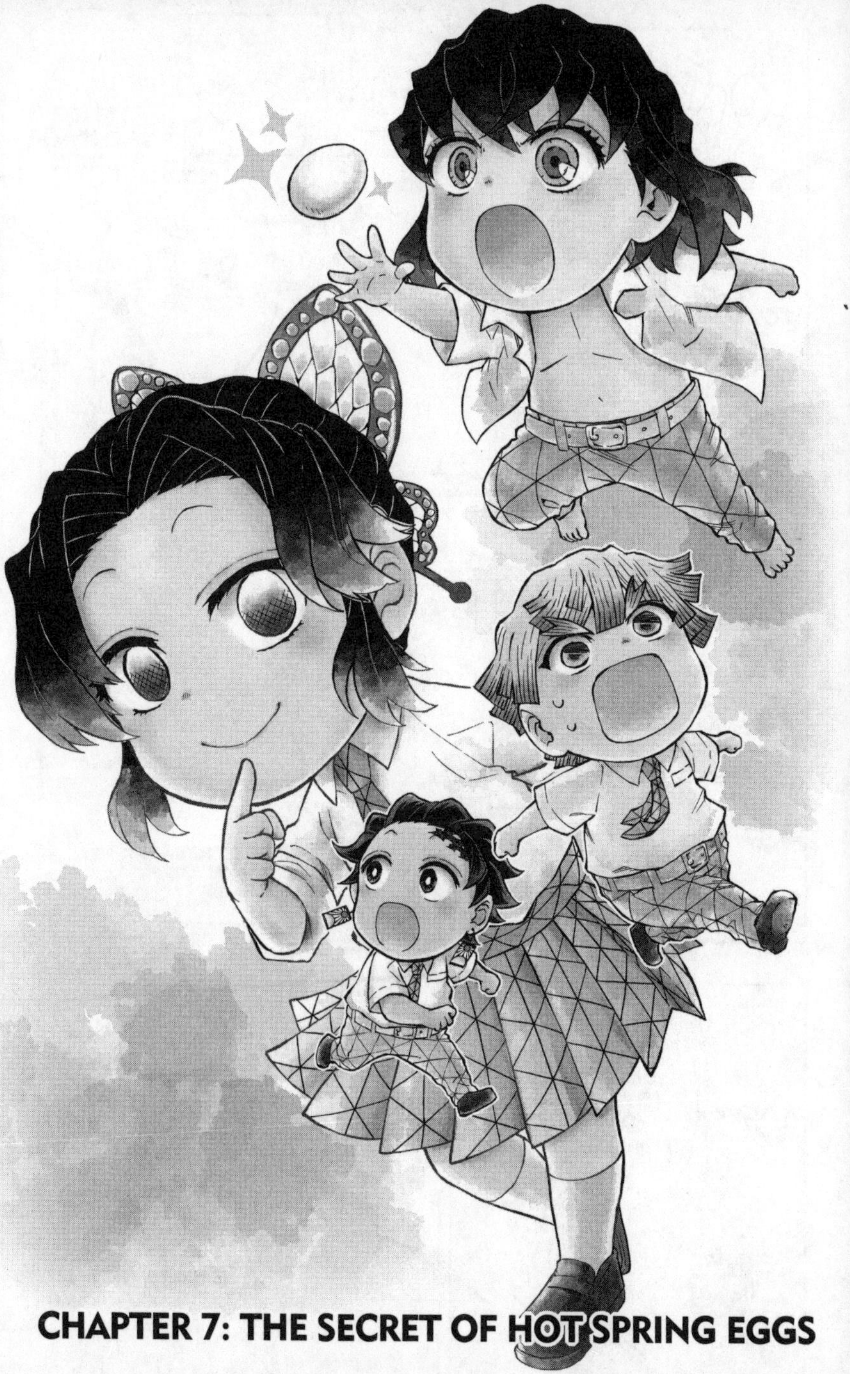

CHAPTER 7: THE SECRET OF HOT SPRING EGGS

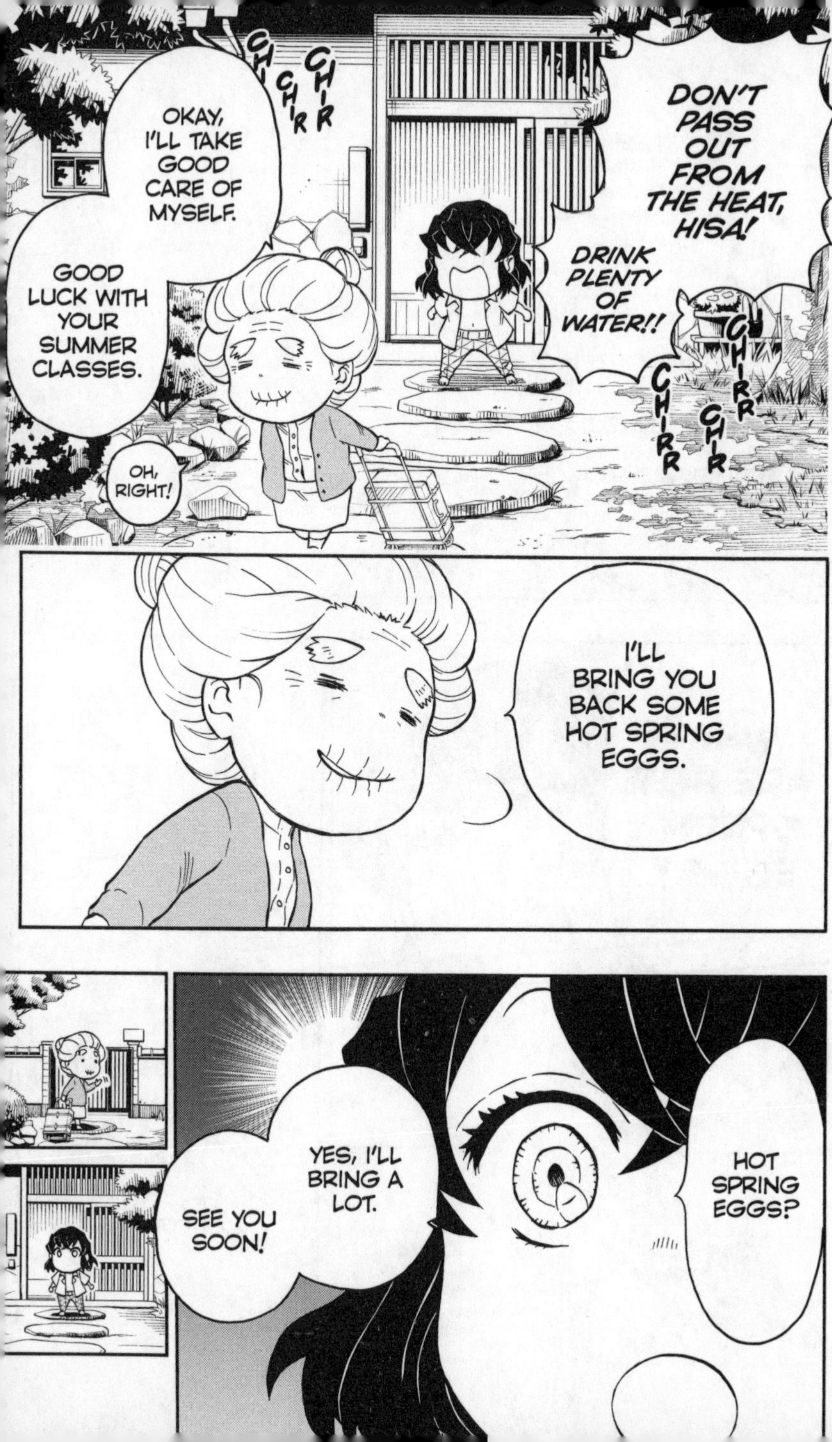
DON'T PASS OUT FROM THE HEAT, HISA!
DRINK PLENTY OF WATER!!
CHIRR CHIRR CHIRR
CHIRR CHIRR
OKAY, I'LL TAKE GOOD CARE OF MYSELF.
GOOD LUCK WITH YOUR SUMMER CLASSES.
OH, RIGHT!
I'LL BRING YOU BACK SOME HOT SPRING EGGS.
HOT SPRING EGGS?
YES, I'LL BRING A LOT.
SEE YOU SOON!

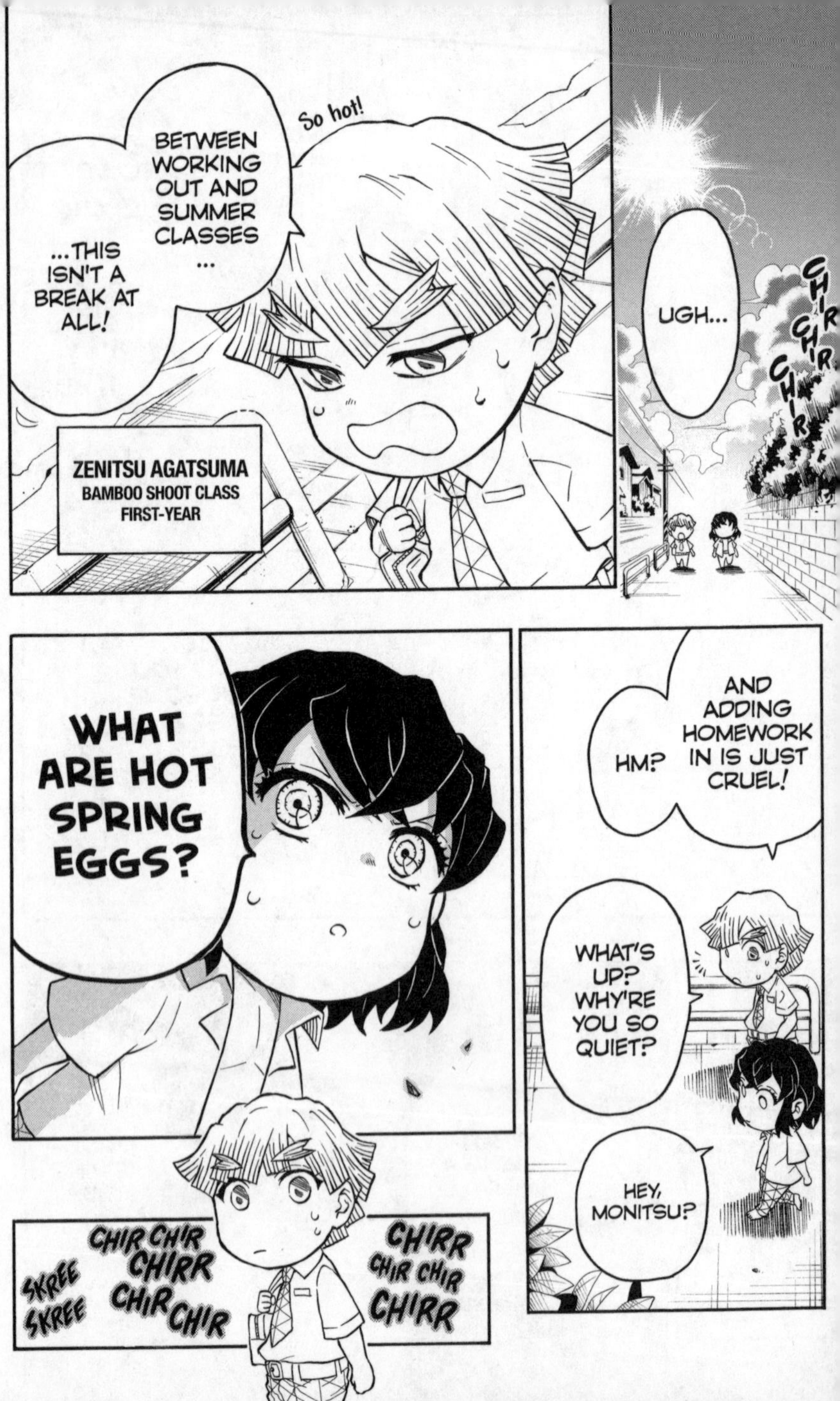
UGH...
CHIR CHIR CHIRR CHIR
So hot!
BETWEEN WORKING OUT AND SUMMER CLASSES ...
...THIS ISN'T A BREAK AT ALL!
ZENITSU AGATSUMA
BAMBOO SHOOT CLASS
FIRST-YEAR
AND ADDING HOMEWORK IN IS JUST CRUEL!
HM?
WHAT'S UP? WHY'RE YOU SO QUIET?
HEY, MONITSU?
WHAT ARE HOT SPRING EGGS?
CHIRR CHIR CHIR CHIRR
CHIR CHIR CHIRR CHIR CHIR
SKREE SKREE

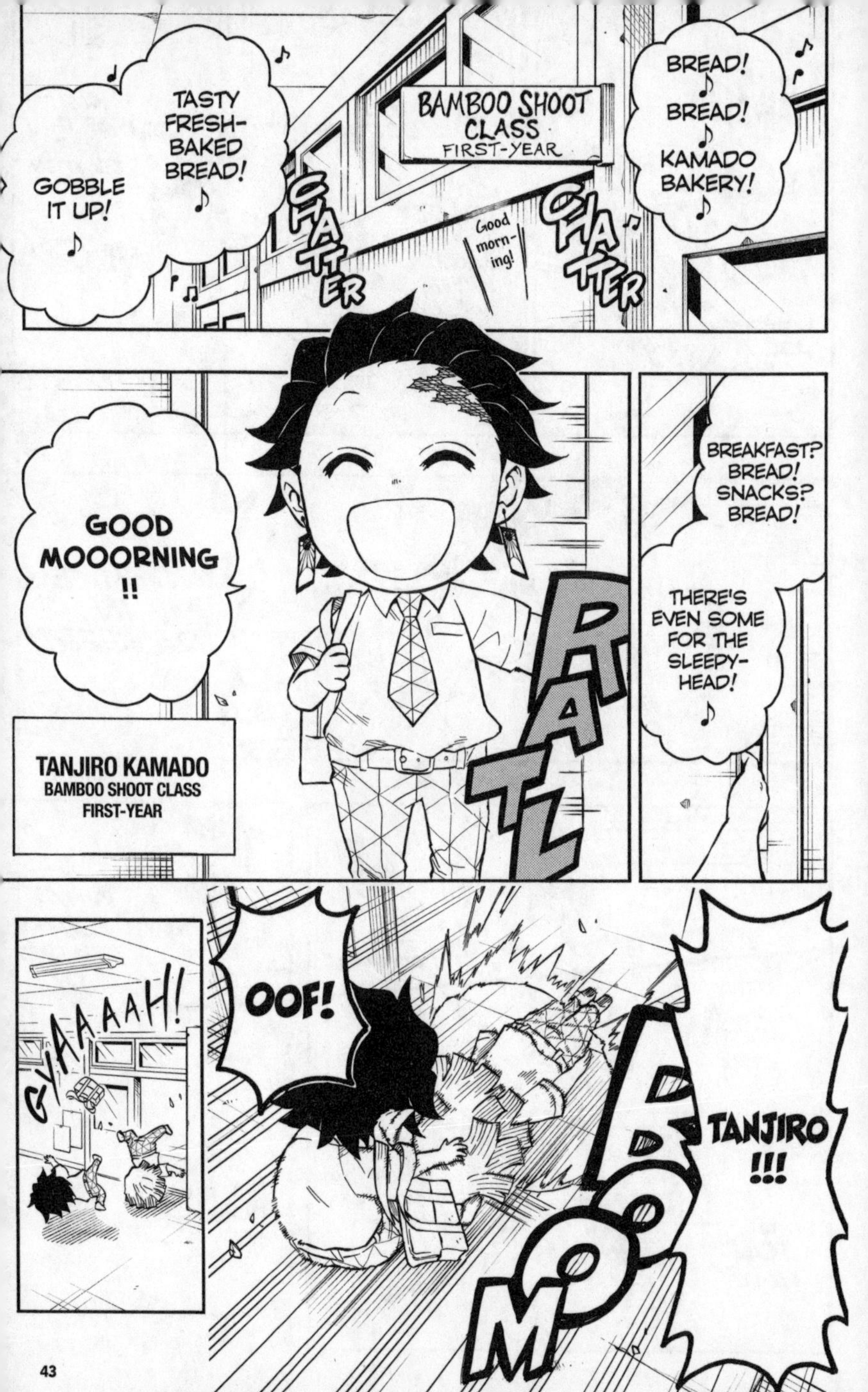
BREAD! ♪ BREAD! ♪ KAMADO BAKERY! ♪
CHATTER
Good morn-ing!
BAMBOO SHOOT CLASS FIRST-YEAR
CHATTER
TASTY FRESH-BAKED BREAD! ♪
GOBBLE IT UP! ♪
BREAKFAST? BREAD! SNACKS? BREAD!
THERE'S EVEN SOME FOR THE SLEEPY-HEAD! ♪
RATTL
GOOD MOOORNING !!
TANJIRO KAMADO
BAMBOO SHOOT CLASS
FIRST-YEAR
TANJIRO !!!
BOOM
OOF!
GYAAAAAH!

TMP TMP TMP

WHY?!

CLASS IS ABOUT TO—

FORGET ABOUT CLASS!

NO QUESTIONS!! JUST COME OUT BACK WITH ME!!

WHAT WAS THAT FOR, ZENITSU?!

HE IS?!

INOSUKE'S IN DANGER!!

BUT INOSUKE DIDN'T KNOW WHAT THEY WERE...

...AND SAID SHE'D BRING BACK HOT SPRING EGGS!

TMP TMP TMP TMP TMP TMP

W-WHAT HAP-PENED?!

HISA'S TAKING A TRIP TO A HOT SPRING...

...SO I TOLD HIM!!

"WHAT ARE HOT SPRING EGGS?"

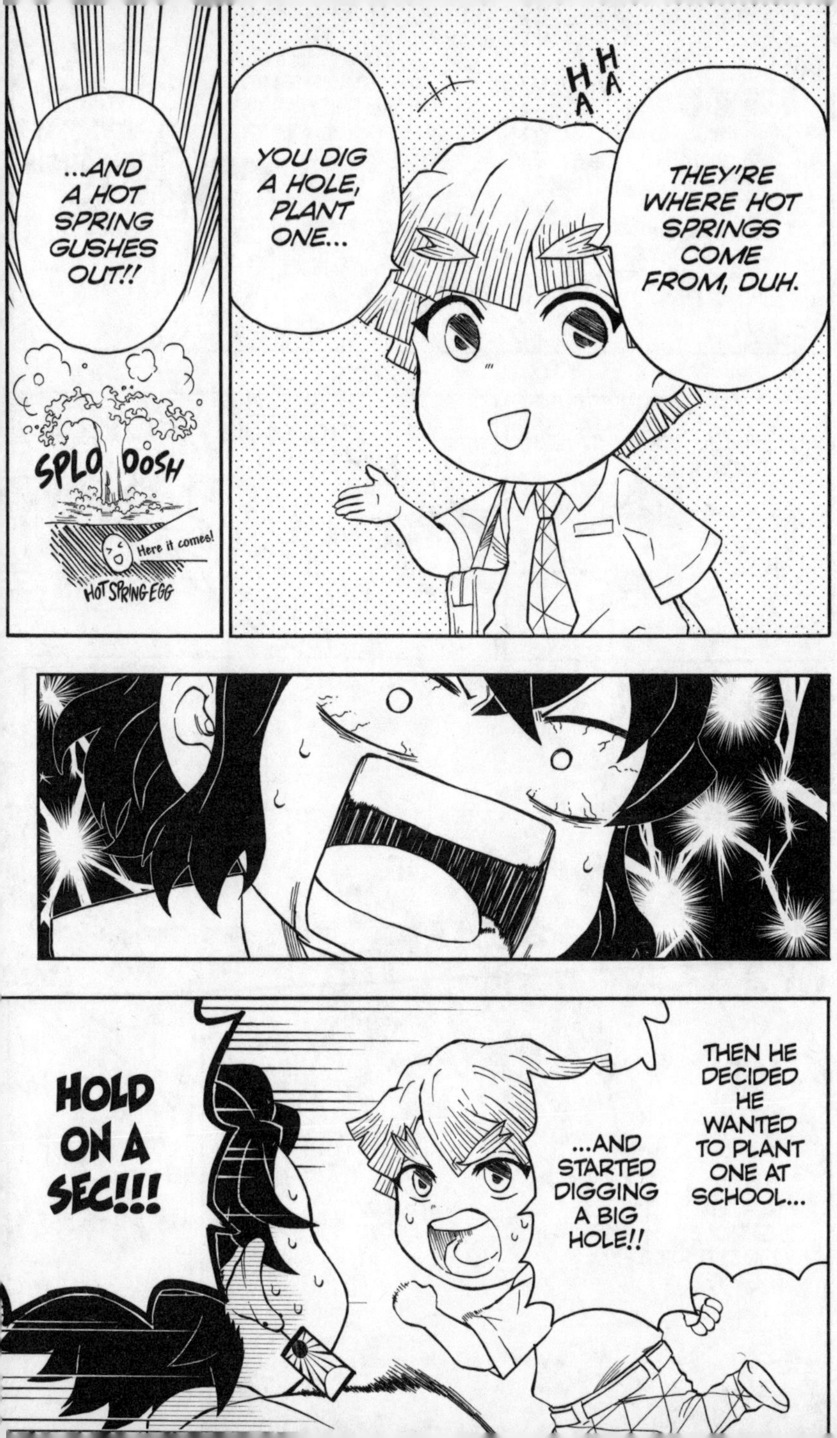
HAHA
THEY'RE WHERE HOT SPRINGS COME FROM, DUH.
YOU DIG A HOLE, PLANT ONE...
...AND A HOT SPRING GUSHES OUT!!
SPLOOOSH
Here it comes!
HOT SPRING EGG
THEN HE DECIDED HE WANTED TO PLANT ONE AT SCHOOL...
...AND STARTED DIGGING A BIG HOLE!!
HOLD ON A SEC!!!

...

HOT SPRING EGGS! HOT SPRING EGGS!

SHNK SHNK

BY THE TIME HISA GETS BACK...

...I'LL HAVE A GIANT HOT SPRING ALL READY FOR HER!

WHAT DO YOU MEAN?

NOW WHAT, TANJIRO?

YOU WERE THE ONE WHO LIED TO HIM!!

DOES HE EVEN HAVE A BRAIN?

I THINK I'M GONNA CRY...

HE'S ACTUALLY DIGGING.

I'LL NEVER ASK ANOTHER FAVOR!

...BUT I NEED YOU TO BE THE ONE TO TELL HIM THE TRUTH.

I'LL APOLO-GIZE LATER...

Listen...

URGH...

HOP TO IT!

NOW YOU GO APOLO-GIZE!

WHAT?! HE'LL KILL ME!

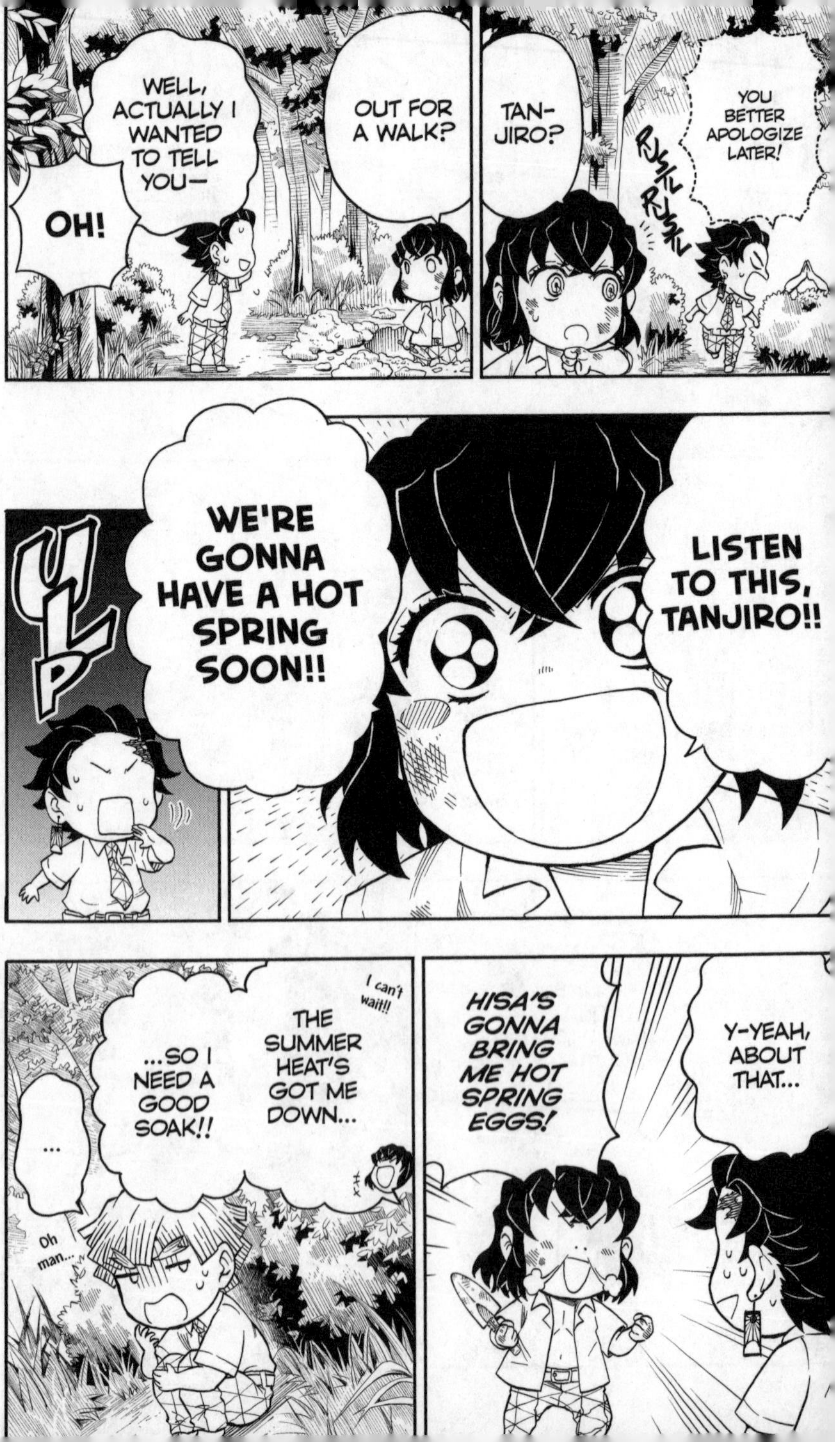
YOU BETTER APOLOGIZE LATER!
TAN-JIRO?
OUT FOR A WALK?
WELL, ACTUALLY I WANTED TO TELL YOU—
OH!
LISTEN TO THIS, TANJIRO!!
WE'RE GONNA HAVE A HOT SPRING SOON!!
ULP
Y-YEAH, ABOUT THAT...
HISA'S GONNA BRING ME HOT SPRING EGGS!
I can't wait!!
THE SUMMER HEAT'S GOT ME DOWN...
...SO I NEED A GOOD SOAK!!
...
Oh man...

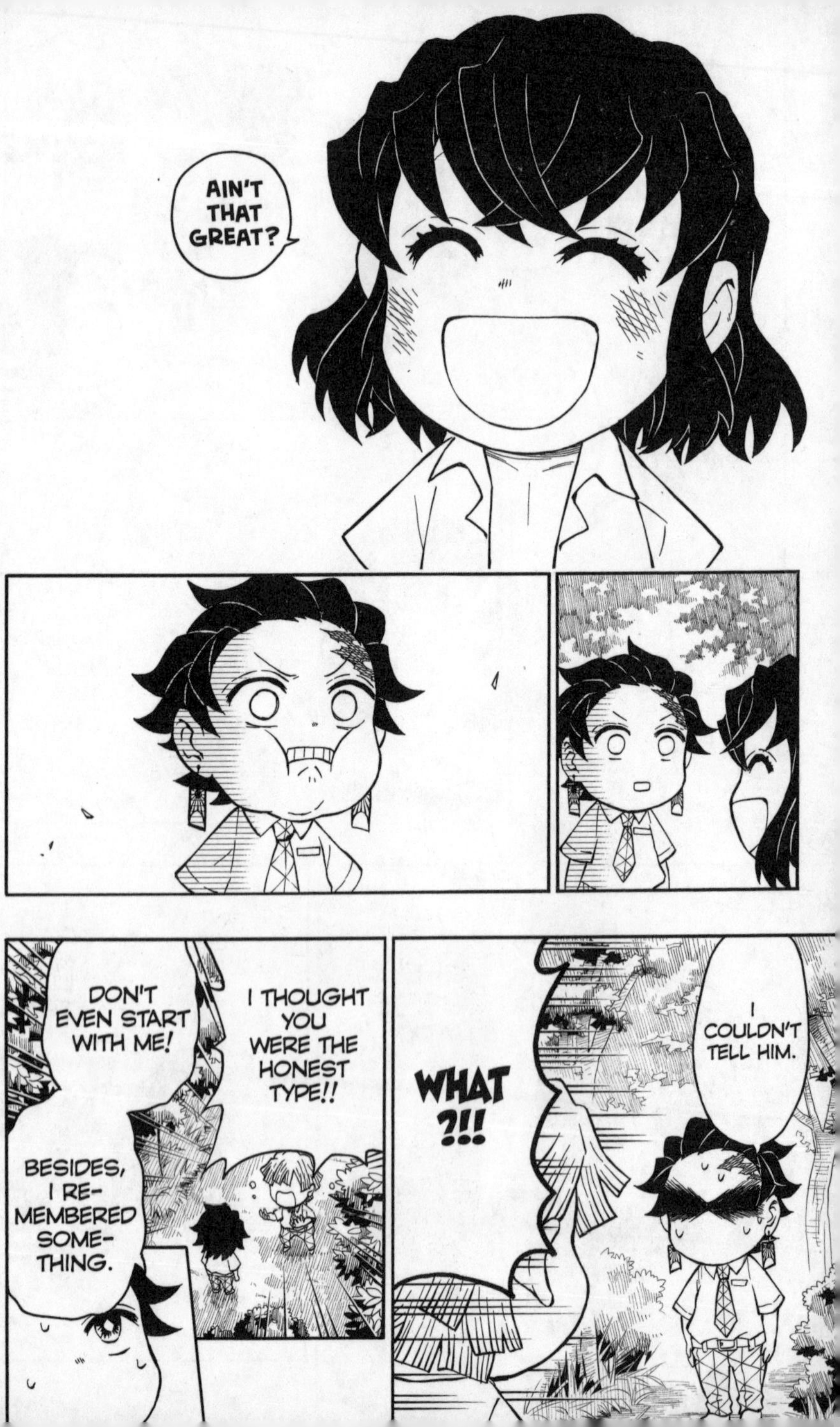
AIN'T THAT GREAT?
I COULDN'T TELL HIM.
WHAT ?!!
I THOUGHT YOU WERE THE HONEST TYPE!!
DON'T EVEN START WITH ME!
BESIDES, I RE-MEMBERED SOME-THING.

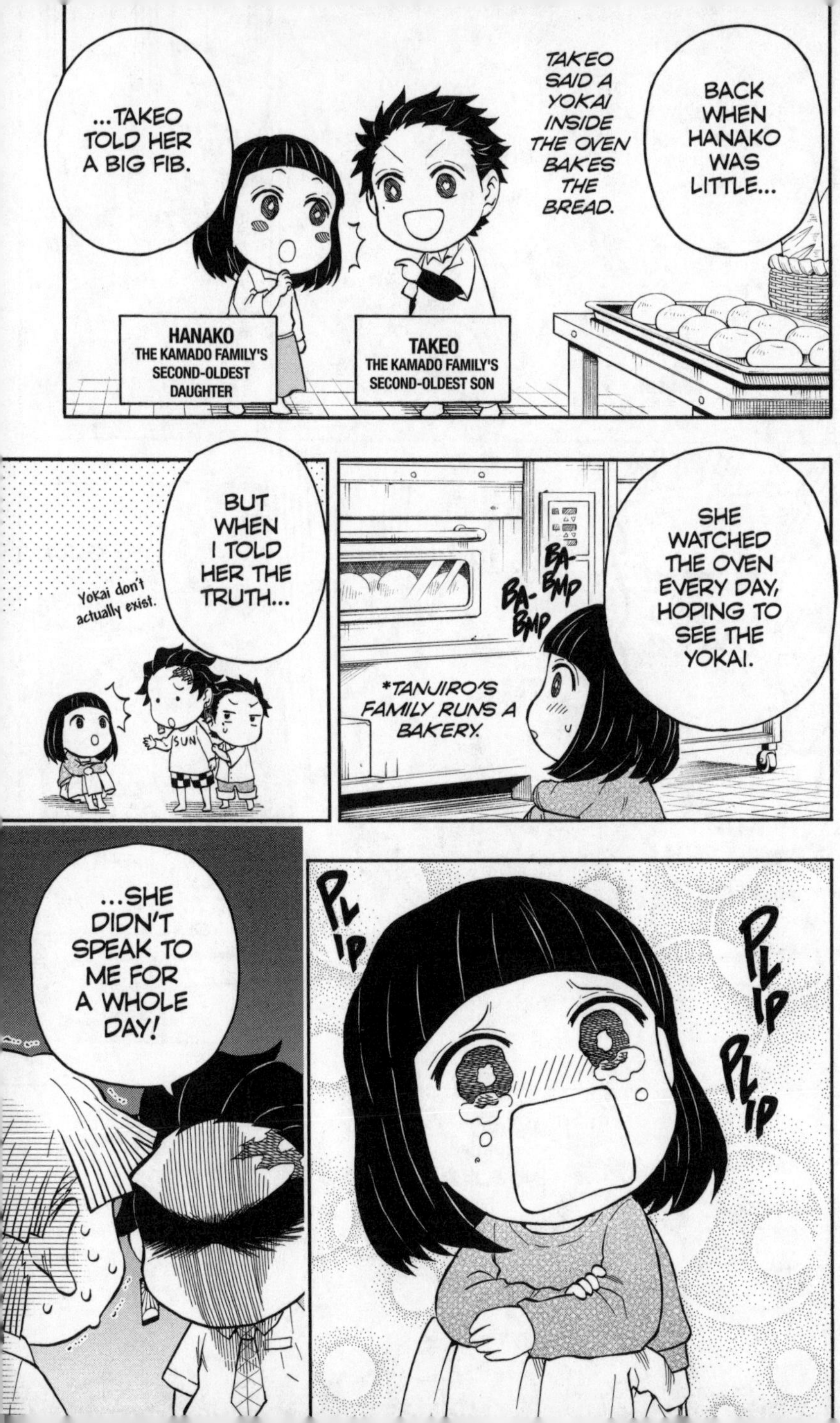
BACK WHEN HANAKO WAS LITTLE...
TAKEO SAID A YOKAI INSIDE THE OVEN BAKES THE BREAD.
...TAKEO TOLD HER A BIG FIB.
TAKEO
THE KAMADO FAMILY'S SECOND-OLDEST SON
HANAKO
THE KAMADO FAMILY'S SECOND-OLDEST DAUGHTER
SHE WATCHED THE OVEN EVERY DAY, HOPING TO SEE THE YOKAI.
BA-BMP
BA-BMP
*TANJIRO'S FAMILY RUNS A BAKERY.
BUT WHEN I TOLD HER THE TRUTH...
Yokai don't actually exist.
SUN
PLIP
PLIP
PLIP
PLIP
...SHE DIDN'T SPEAK TO ME FOR A WHOLE DAY!

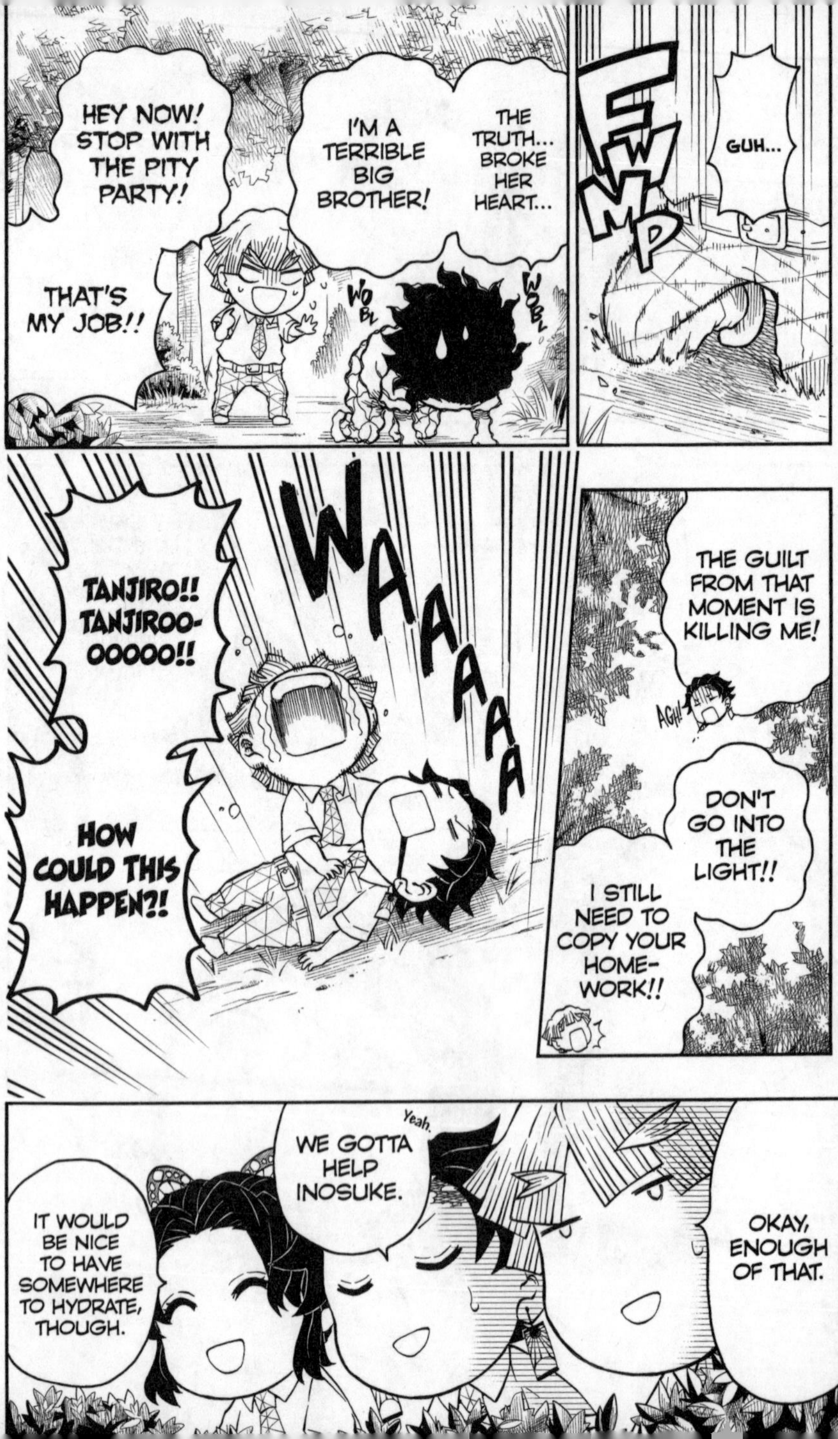
FWMP
GUH...
THE TRUTH... BROKE HER HEART...
I'M A TERRIBLE BIG BROTHER!
WOBBL
WOBBL
HEY NOW! STOP WITH THE PITY PARTY!
THAT'S MY JOB!!
THE GUILT FROM THAT MOMENT IS KILLING ME!
AGH!
DON'T GO INTO THE LIGHT!!
I STILL NEED TO COPY YOUR HOME-WORK!!
WAAAAAAA
TANJIRO!! TANJIROO-OOOOO!!
HOW COULD THIS HAPPEN?!
OKAY, ENOUGH OF THAT.
WE GOTTA HELP INOSUKE.
Yeah.
IT WOULD BE NICE TO HAVE SOMEWHERE TO HYDRATE, THOUGH.

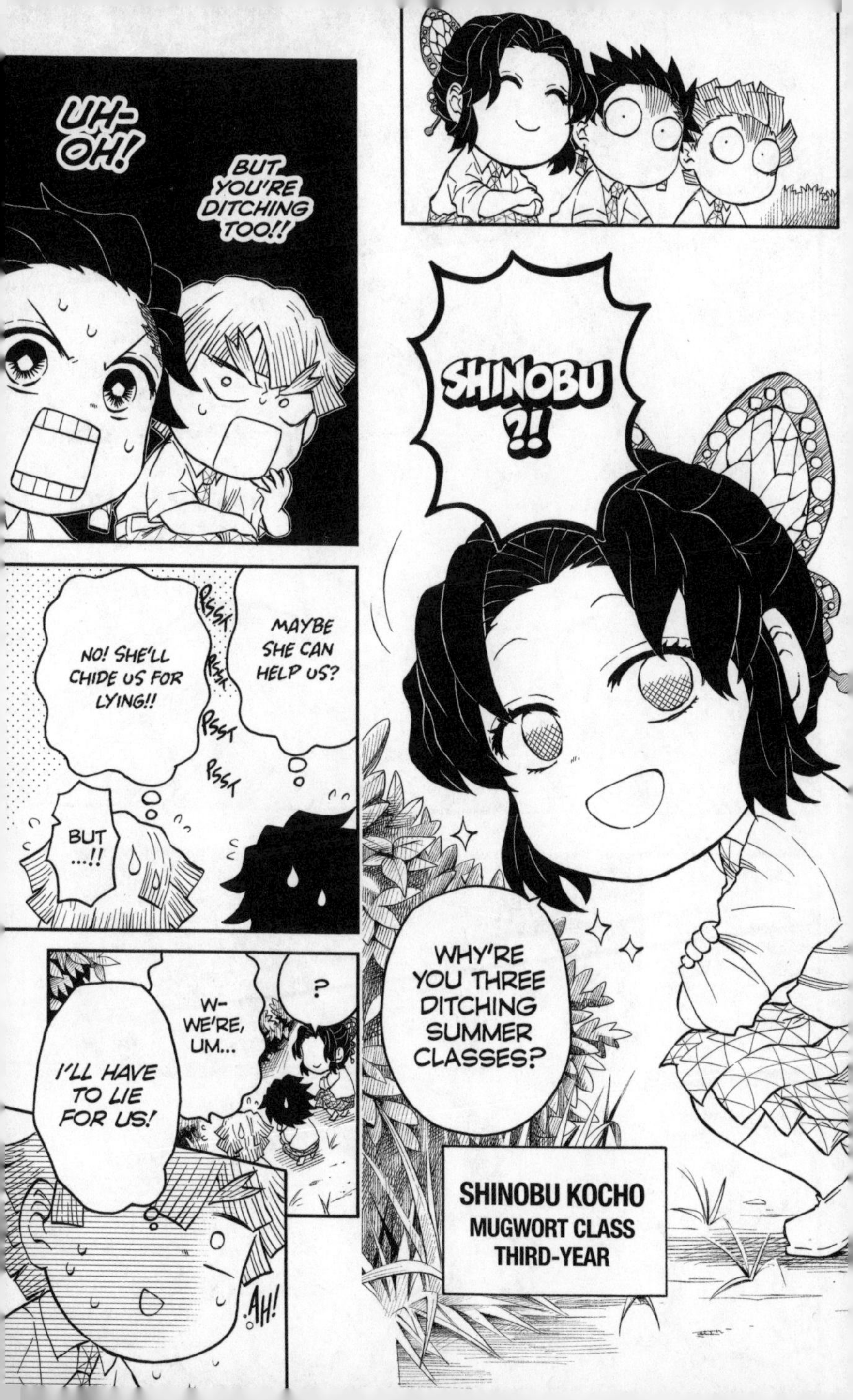
SHINOBU ?!!
WHY'RE YOU THREE DITCHING SUMMER CLASSES?
SHINOBU KOCHO
MUGWORT CLASS
THIRD-YEAR
UH-OH!
BUT YOU'RE DITCHING TOO!!
MAYBE SHE CAN HELP US?
PSSK
PSSK
NO! SHE'LL CHIDE US FOR LYING!!
PSST
PSSK
BUT ...!!
?
W-WE'RE, UM...
I'LL HAVE TO LIE FOR US!
AH!

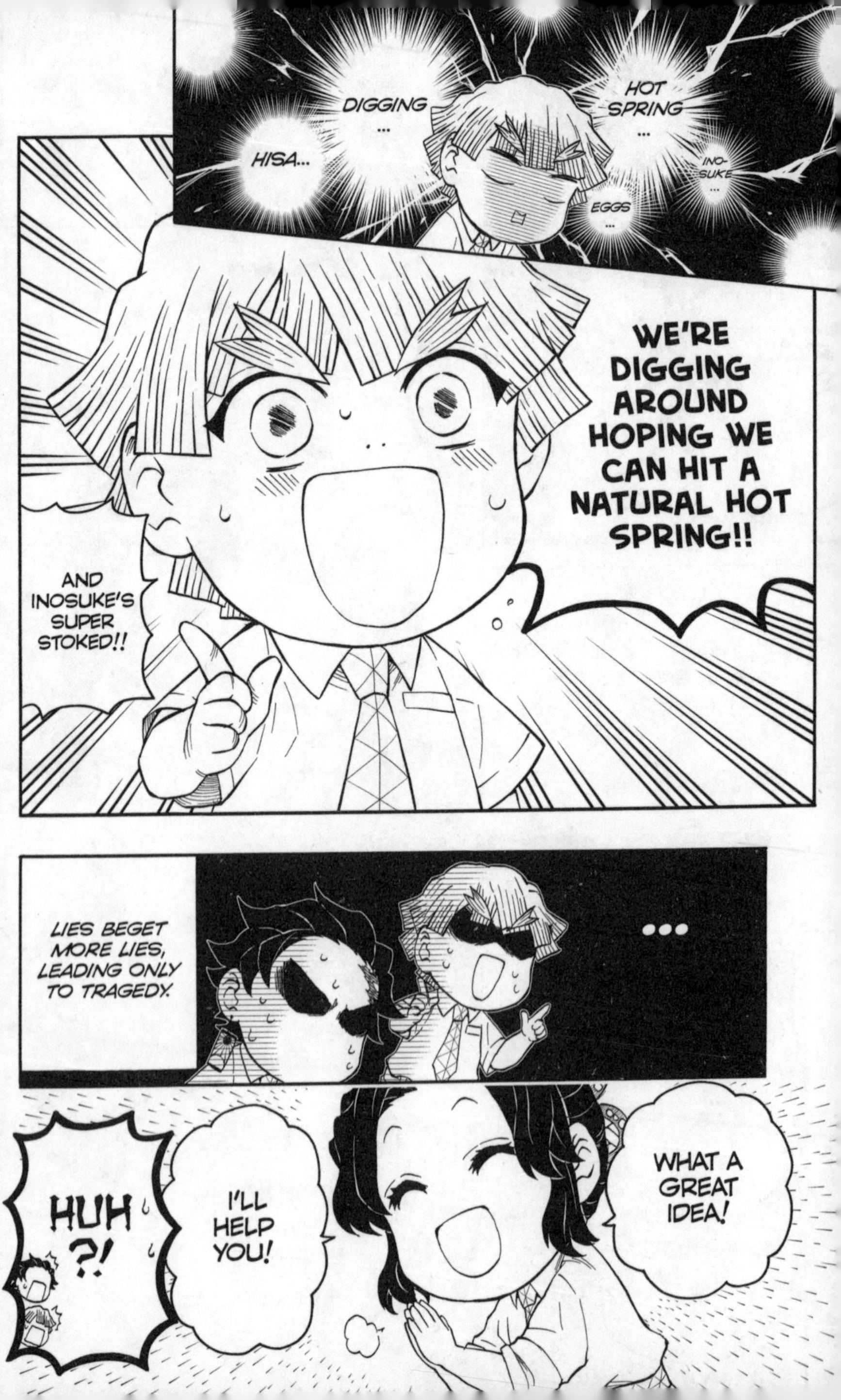
HOT SPRING...
DIGGING...
INO-SUKE...
HISA...
EGGS...
WE'RE DIGGING AROUND HOPING WE CAN HIT A NATURAL HOT SPRING!!
AND INOSUKE'S SUPER STOKED!!
...
LIES BEGET MORE LIES, LEADING ONLY TO TRAGEDY.
WHAT A GREAT IDEA!
I'LL HELP YOU!
HUH?!

WANNA KNOW SOMETHING NEAT?

I DOUBT THAT!

HUH? NO, UM...

MAYBE WE'LL GET LUCKY AND ACTUALLY FIND ONE!

IT'S ENTIRELY POSSIBLE THERE COULD STILL BE SOME HIDING UNDERGROUND.

...THIS AREA WAS KNOWN FOR ITS HOT SPRINGS.

BEFORE THEY BUILT THE SCHOOL...

?!

AND VISIT A HOT SPRING AT SCHOOL?!

WE COULD ACTUALLY SUCCEED?!

KIMETSU HOT SPRING?!

THAT MEANS...

WAIT, REALLY?!

YOU'VE NEVER HEARD OF...

...KIMETSU HOT SPRING?

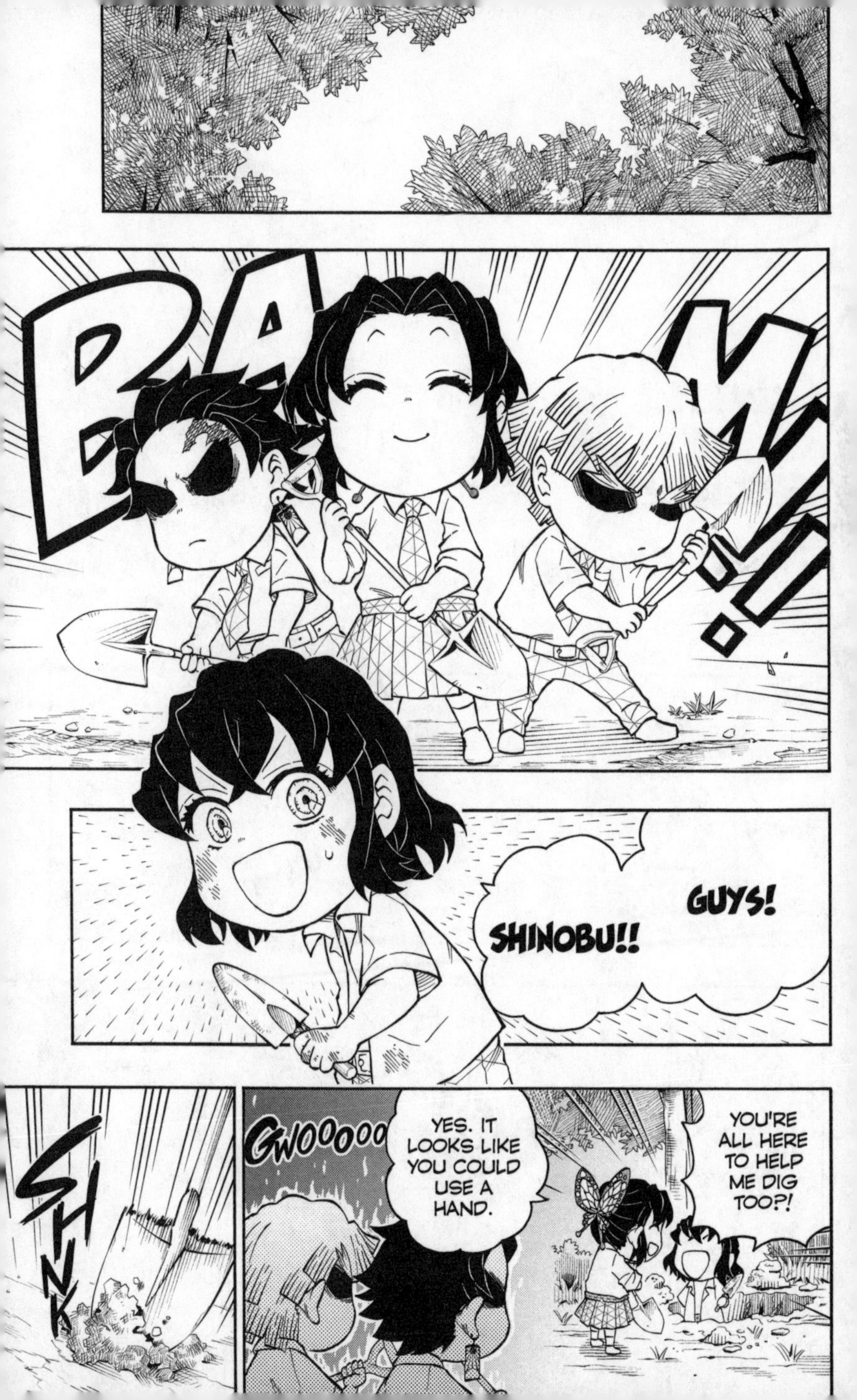
BAM!!
GUYS!
SHINOBU!!
YOU'RE ALL HERE TO HELP ME DIG TOO?!
YES. IT LOOKS LIKE YOU COULD USE A HAND.
GWOOOOO
SHINK

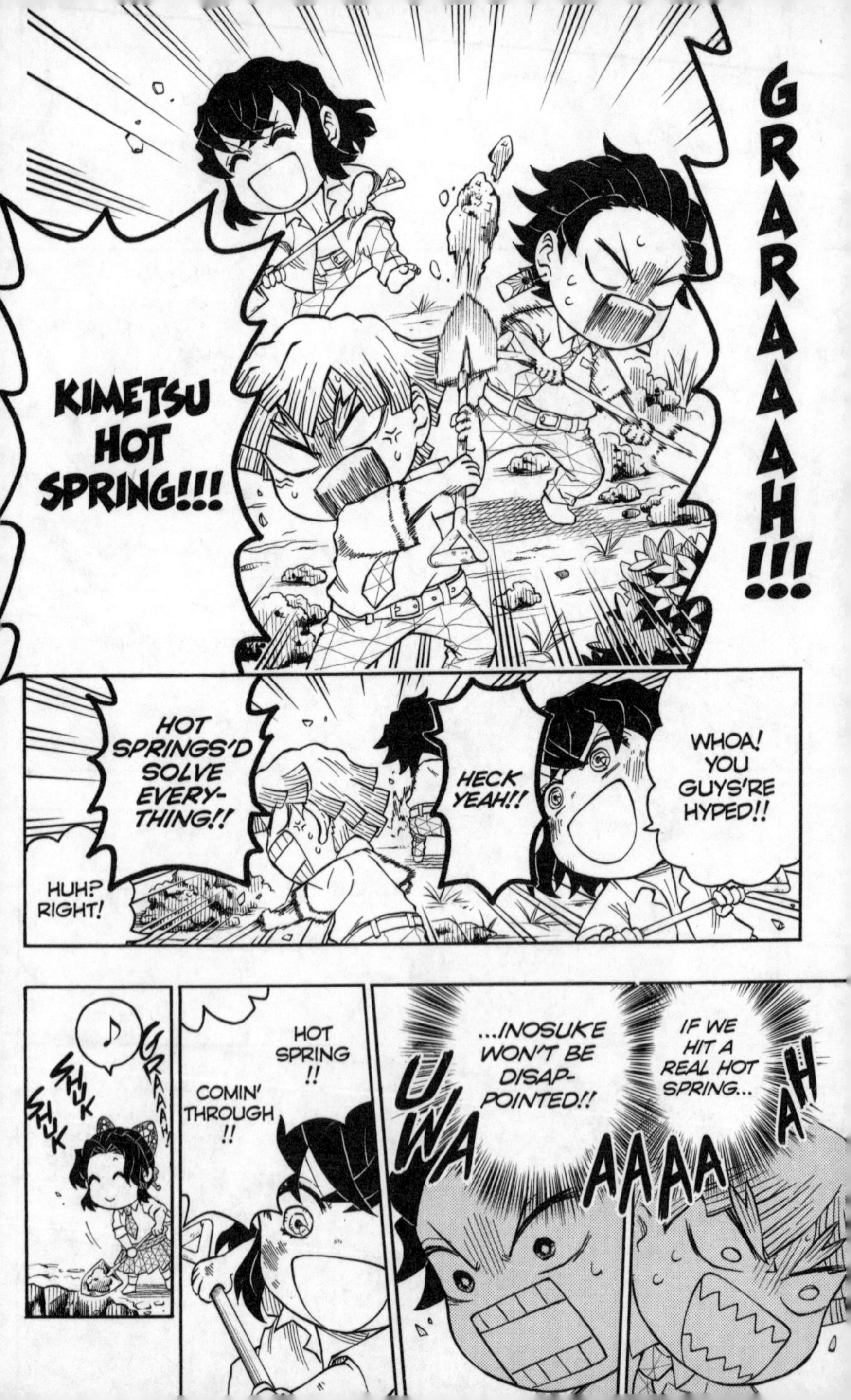
GRAAAAH!!!
KIMETSU HOT SPRING!!!
WHOA! YOU GUYS'RE HYPED!!
HECK YEAH!!
HOT SPRINGS'D SOLVE EVERY-THING!!
HUH? RIGHT!
IF WE HIT A REAL HOT SPRING...
...INOSUKE WON'T BE DISAP-POINTED!!
UWAAAAAAH
HOT SPRING!!
COMIN' THROUGH!!
♪
GRAAAAH!
SHUK SHUK

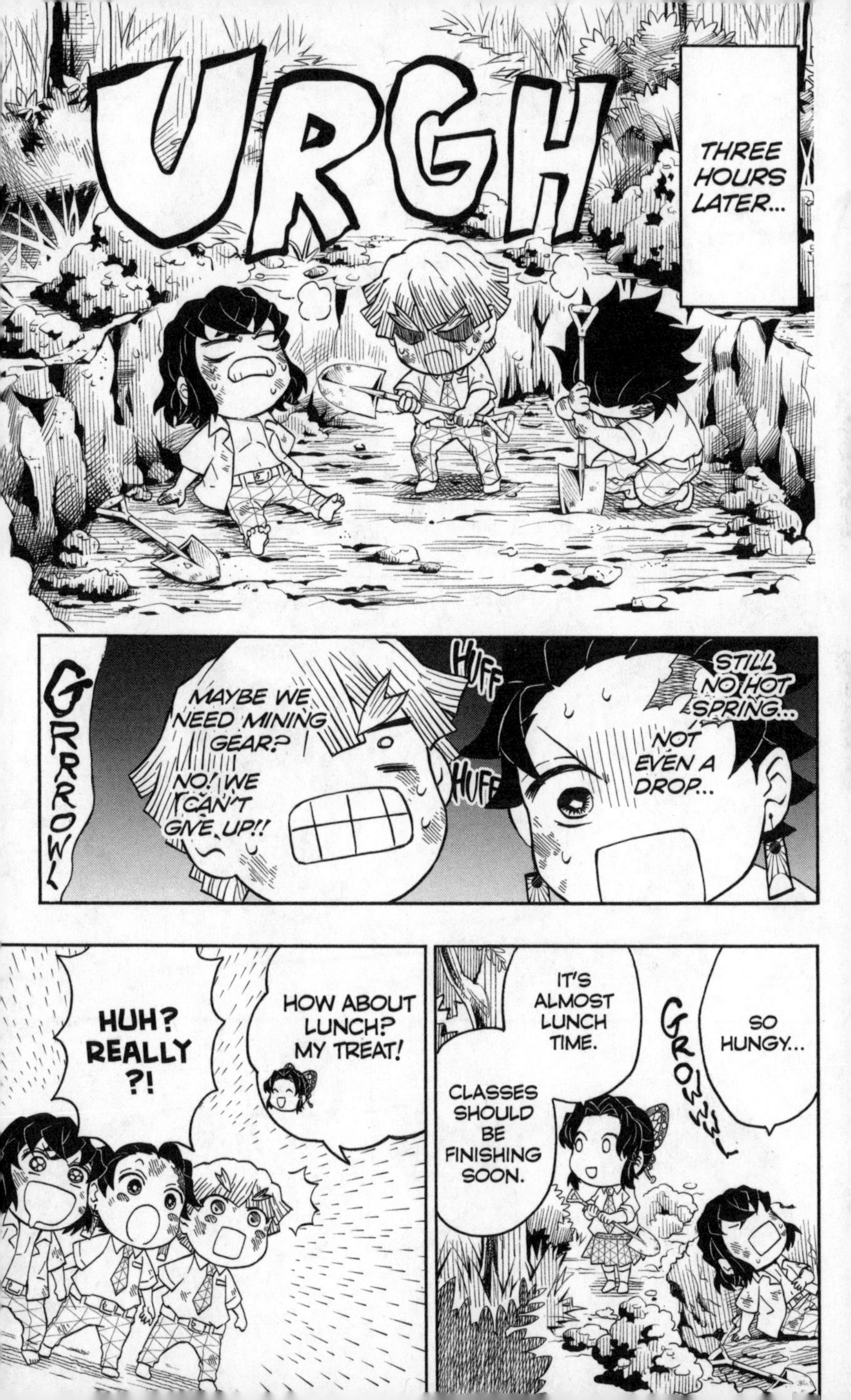
THREE HOURS LATER...
URGH
STILL NO HOT SPRING...
NOT EVEN A DROP...
HUFF
HUFF
MAYBE WE NEED MINING GEAR?
NO! WE CAN'T GIVE UP!!
GRRROWL
SO HUNGY...
GROWWL
IT'S ALMOST LUNCH TIME.
CLASSES SHOULD BE FINISHING SOON.
HOW ABOUT LUNCH? MY TREAT!
HUH? REALLY?!

THEM

WHAT'S THAT SUP- POSED TO MEAN ?!

WHEW! AT LEAST YOU FOUND US...

...AND NOT THEM.

GAH! THERE YOU ARE!!

FORGOT ABOUT THAT.

Oops.

YOU'VE BEEN DITCHING CLASS!!

I'LL GO GET US SOME DRINKS!

CHIRR CHIRR CHIRR

WELL, IF YOU SAY SO.

Really?

SORRY. I NEEDED THEIR HELP WITH SOMETHING.

I'LL CLEAR IT LATER.

NOW LET'S EAT!!

A HOT SPRING WILL MAKE HER HAPPY TOO!

Pssst Pssk Psst

I FEEL BAD ABOUT THIS, BUT...

OKAY!!

FEEL FREE TO EAT!

PWOK

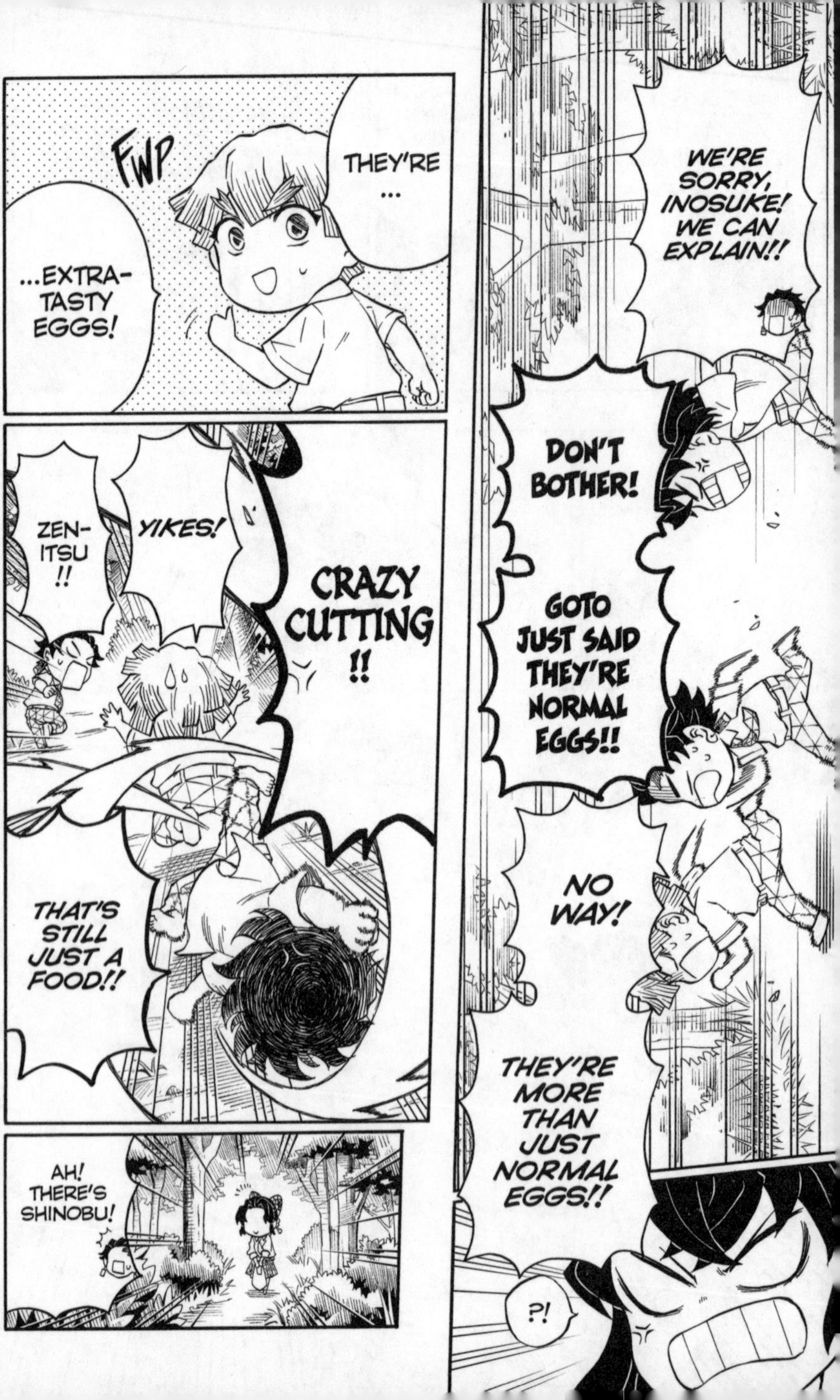
WE'RE SORRY, INOSUKE! WE CAN EXPLAIN!!
DON'T BOTHER!
GOTO JUST SAID THEY'RE NORMAL EGGS!!
NO WAY!
THEY'RE MORE THAN JUST NORMAL EGGS!!
?!
FWP
THEY'RE ...
...EXTRA-TASTY EGGS!
YIKES!
ZEN-ITSU !!
CRAZY CUTTING !!
THAT'S STILL JUST A FOOD!!
AH! THERE'S SHINOBU!

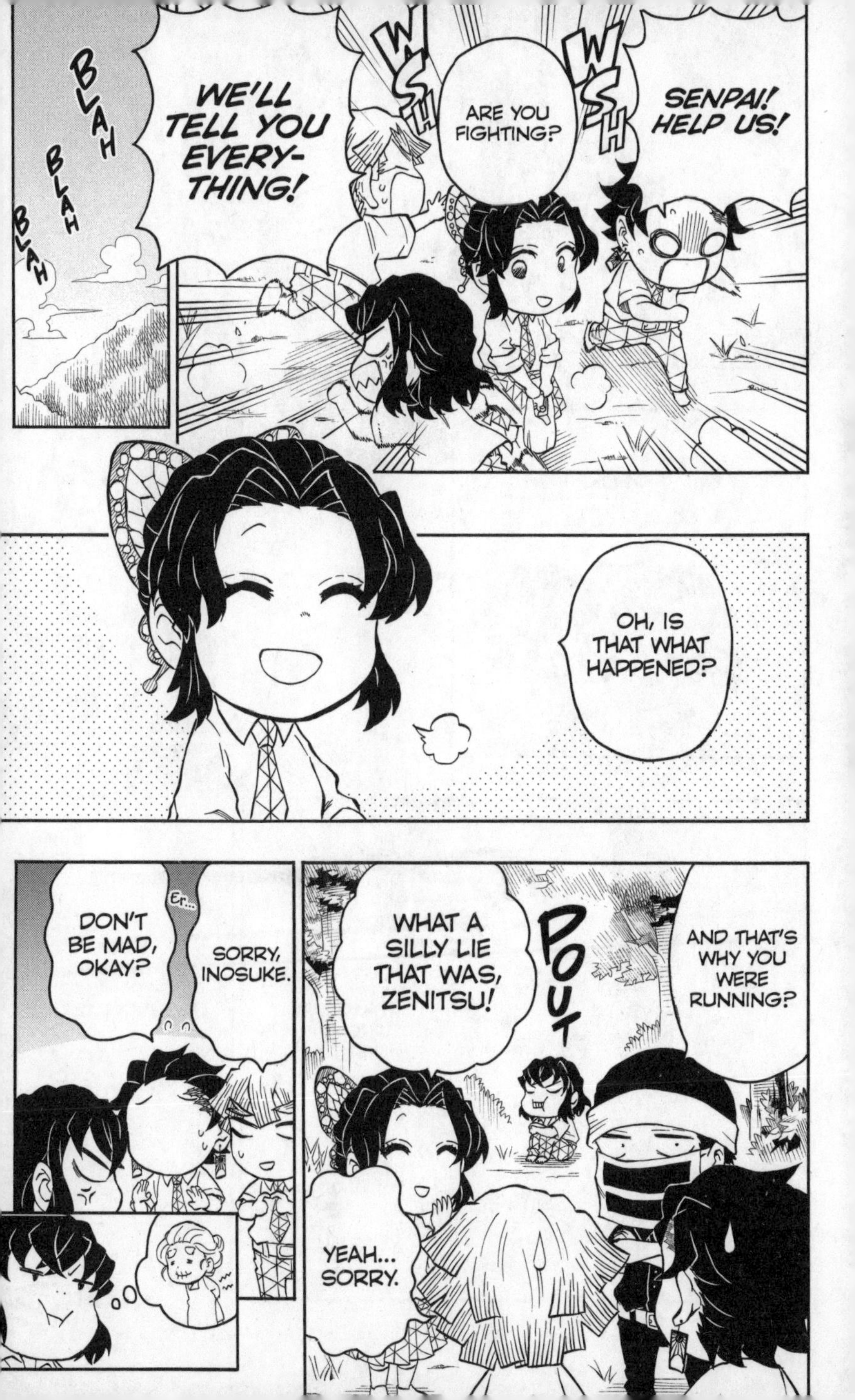
SENPAI! HELP US!
WSH
ARE YOU FIGHTING?
WSH
WE'LL TELL YOU EVERY-THING!
BLAH BLAH BLAH
OH, IS THAT WHAT HAPPENED?
AND THAT'S WHY YOU WERE RUNNING?
POUT
WHAT A SILLY LIE THAT WAS, ZENITSU!
YEAH... SORRY.
SORRY, INOSUKE.
Er...
DON'T BE MAD, OKAY?

WE'RE REALLY, REALLY ... SORRY !!

INOSUKE ...

COLD

MO TEA

THEY'RE A NATURAL OCCUR-ANCE...

...THAT ONLY APPEAR IN CERTAIN PLACES.

THAT'S WHY THEY'RE SO VALUABLE.

...HOT SPRINGS OCCUR...

...WHEN GEOTHERMAL ACTIVITY HEATS GROUNDWATER.

HOT SPRING

AH♥

GROUNDWATER

HERE YOU GO!!

MAGMA

THEY'RE GOOD FOR BACK PAIN!

Club prez ↓

BATH SALTS THE PHARMACOLOGY CLUB MADE!

WHAT'S INSIDE?

REALLY?!

TAKE THIS AS THANKS!

BUTTERFLY BRAND

SWUP

SHE KNEW WE WERE LYING?!

No way!

HUH?

I'LL BE GOING NOW.

SHE HAD THAT PREPARED.

...

WHAT ABOUT KIMETSU HOT SPRING?

We'll help!

DON'T YOU WANT TO FIND A HOT SPRING?

ARE YOU GOING TO KEEP DIGGING?

NO. I'M LEAVING AFTER I EAT.

WHAT'RE YOU TALKING ABOUT?

WHAT?!

DON'T LEAVE IT TO HER

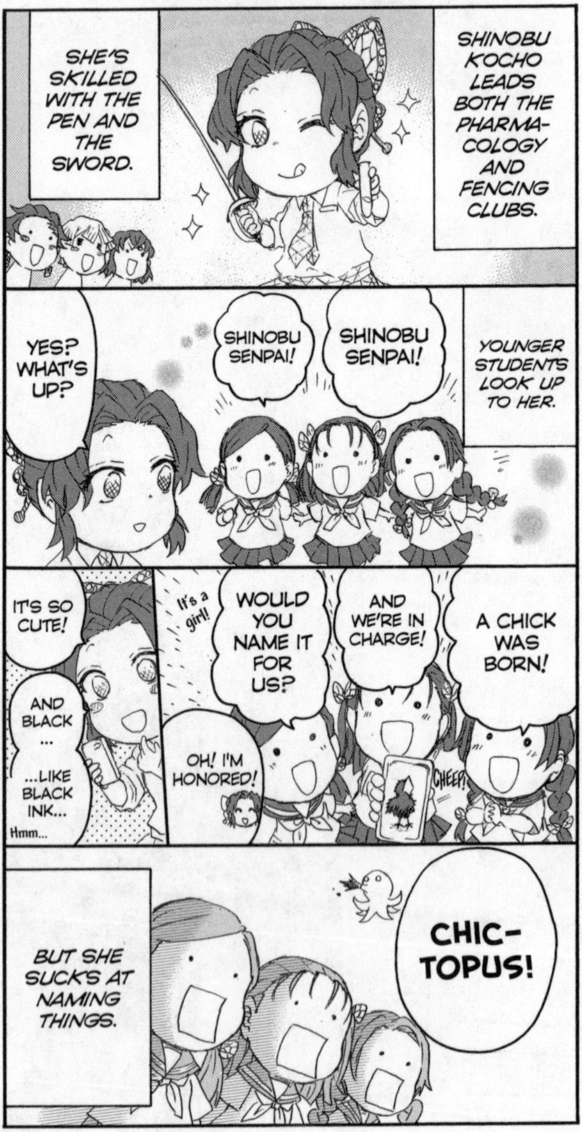

SHINOBU KOCHO LEADS BOTH THE PHARMACOLOGY AND FENCING CLUBS.
SHE'S SKILLED WITH THE PEN AND THE SWORD.
YOUNGER STUDENTS LOOK UP TO HER.
SHINOBU SENPAI!
SHINOBU SENPAI!
YES? WHAT'S UP?
A CHICK WAS BORN!
AND WE'RE IN CHARGE!
WOULD YOU NAME IT FOR US?
It's a girl!
CHEEP!
IT'S SO CUTE!
OH! I'M HONORED!
AND BLACK...
...LIKE BLACK INK...
Hmm...
CHIC-TOPUS!
BUT SHE SUCKS AT NAMING THINGS.

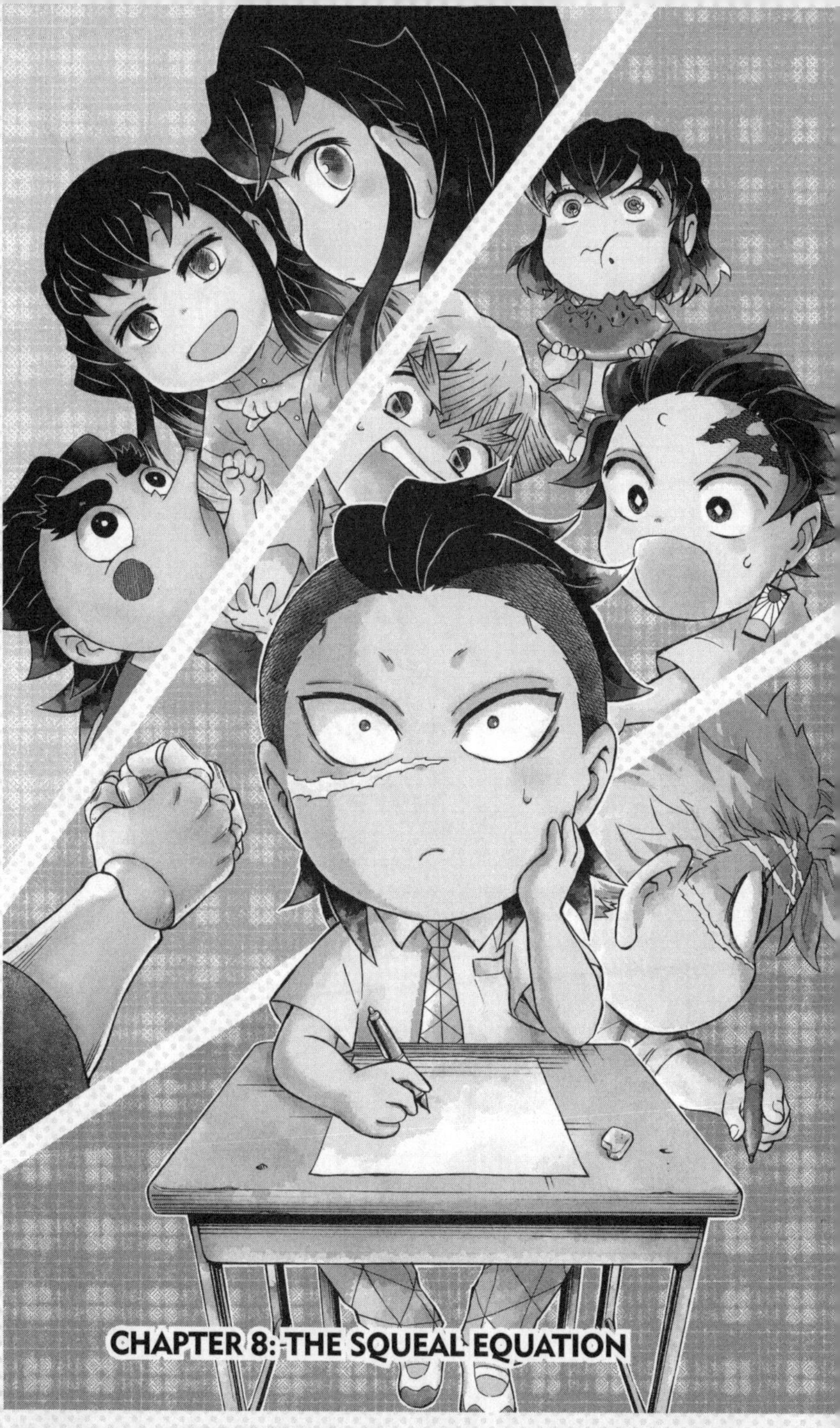
CHAPTER 8: THE SQUEAL EQUATION

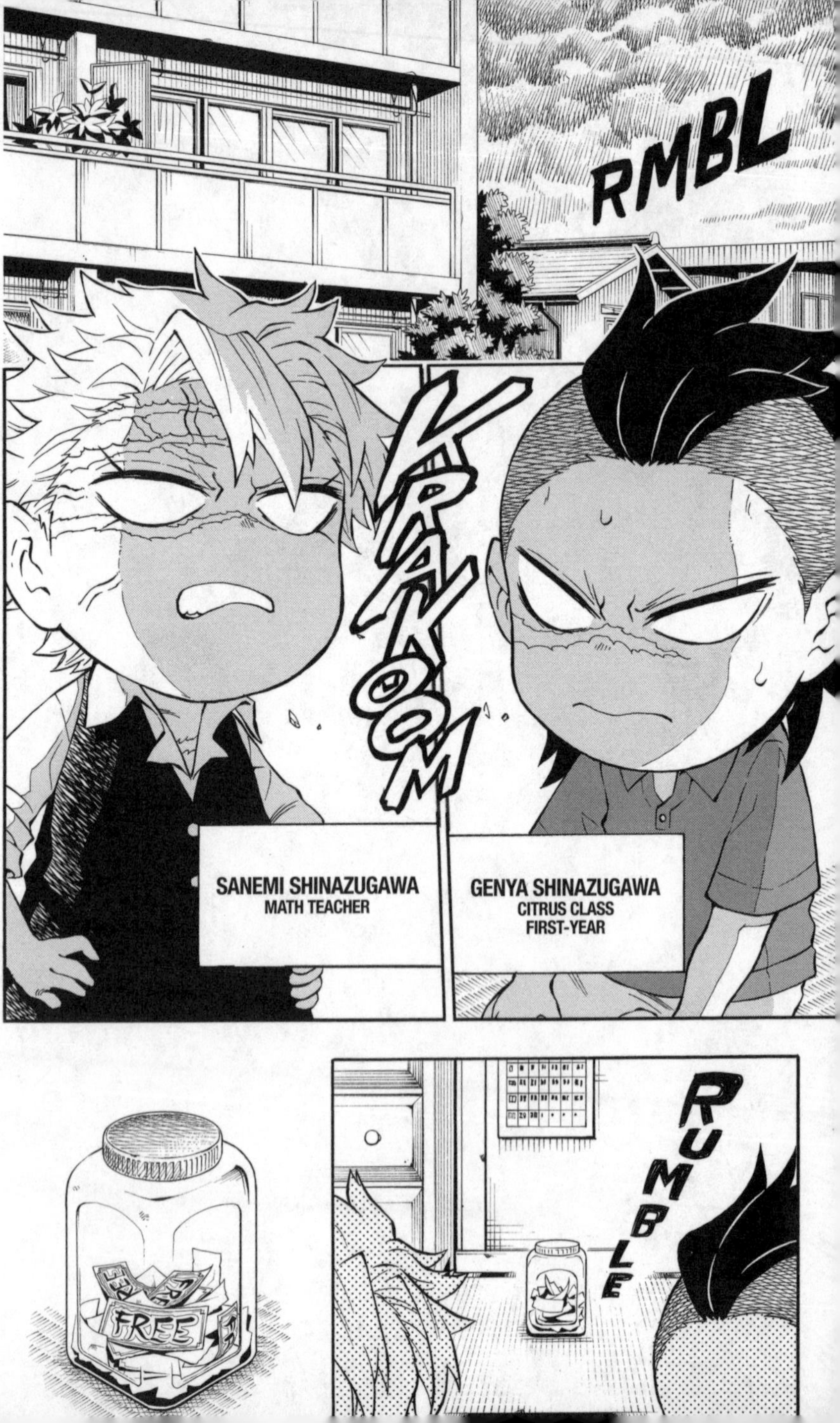
RMBL
VRAKOOM
GENYA SHINAZUGAWA
CITRUS CLASS
FIRST-YEAR
SANEMI SHINAZUGAWA
MATH TEACHER
RUMBLE
FREE

WE HAD A FIGHT ABOUT MY GRADES!!

I CAN'T ASK HIM!

MY FINAL EXAM SCORES SUCKED!

WHAT HAPPENED?

YOU CAN FIGHT HIM? RESPECT!

GOT THAT, GENYA?

IF YOU SCORE THIS BADLY AGAIN...

NEVER SCORE THIS LOW AGAIN!

FLASH-BACK

THE GAME'S OPERATOR WON'T LIKE THAT!

WITHOUT SPENDING ANYTHING?!

MARKS-MANSHIP CLUB ACE →

I WANT TO WIN ALL THE PRIZES AT THE MARKSMANSHIP GAME.

...BUT WHAT WAS YOUR RANK ON FINALS?

I DON'T MIND...

Well...

RIGHT?

ANYWAY, WE'LL HELP YOU.

13/90

THIRTEENTH.

SMARTY-PANTS!

HOW THE HECK ARE WE SUP-POSED TO HELP YOU?!

NO WAY!

ARE YOU FOR REAL?!

GYAH! YOU DON'T UNDER-STAND!

NOM NOM

47TH

72ND

28TH

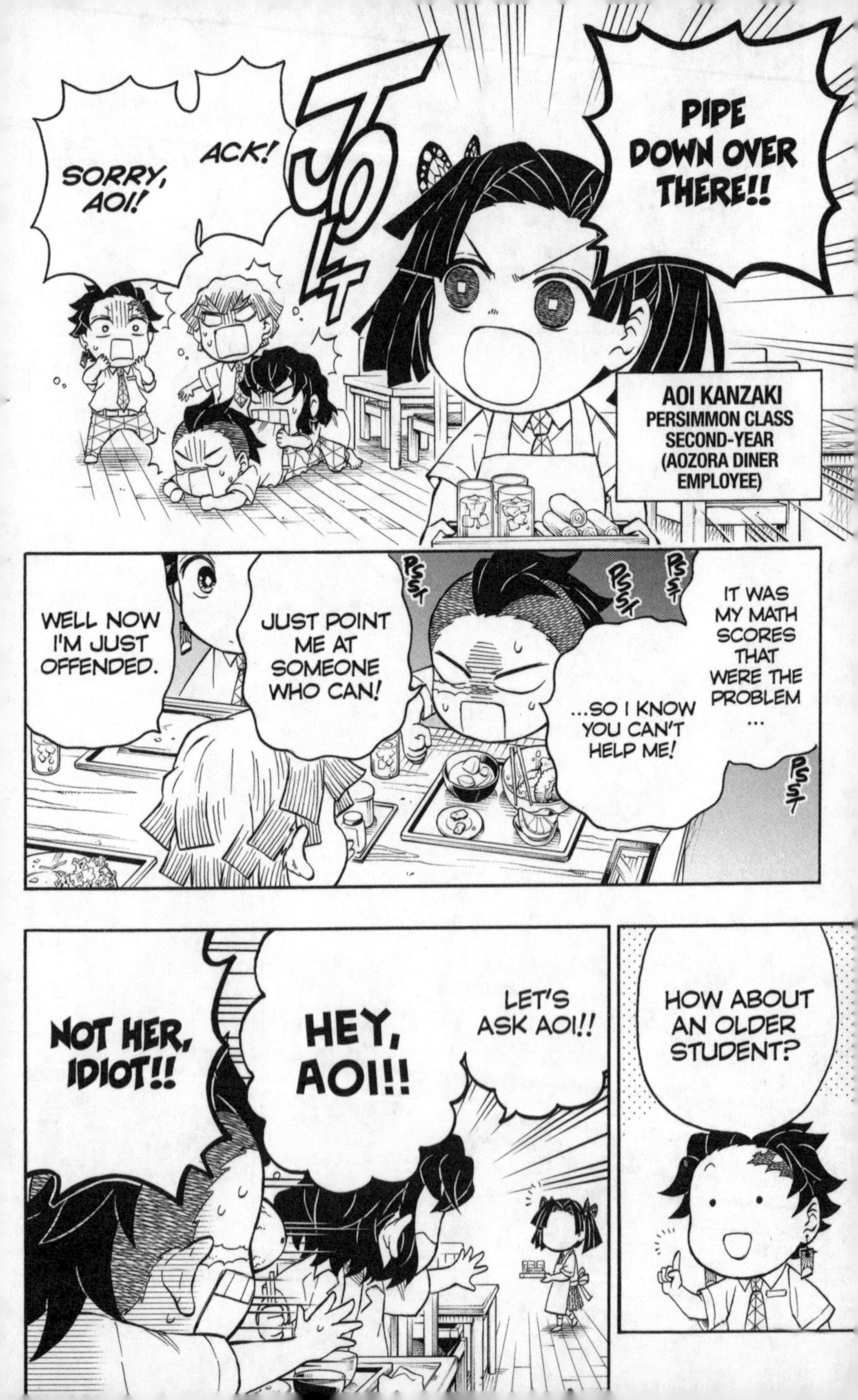
PIPE DOWN OVER THERE!!
JOLT
AOI KANZAKI
PERSIMMON CLASS SECOND-YEAR (AOZORA DINER EMPLOYEE)
ACK!
SORRY, AOI!
IT WAS MY MATH SCORES THAT WERE THE PROBLEM ...
PSST PSST PSST PSST
...SO I KNOW YOU CAN'T HELP ME!
JUST POINT ME AT SOMEONE WHO CAN!
WELL NOW I'M JUST OFFENDED.
HOW ABOUT AN OLDER STUDENT?
LET'S ASK AOI!!
HEY, AOI!!
NOT HER, IDIOT!!

REFILL PLEASE.

YES, INOSUKE?

KANAO

SHINOBU

SO...NOT KANAO OR SHINOBU?

PICK A GUY!

NO GIRLS!

NERVOUS AROUND GIRLS

HMM

HE'S AWAY AT SOCCER CAMP.

SPARKL

HOW ABOUT MURATA?

TOKITO

DING DONG

I KNOW!

IT DOESN'T HAVE TO BE AN *OLDER* STUDENT!

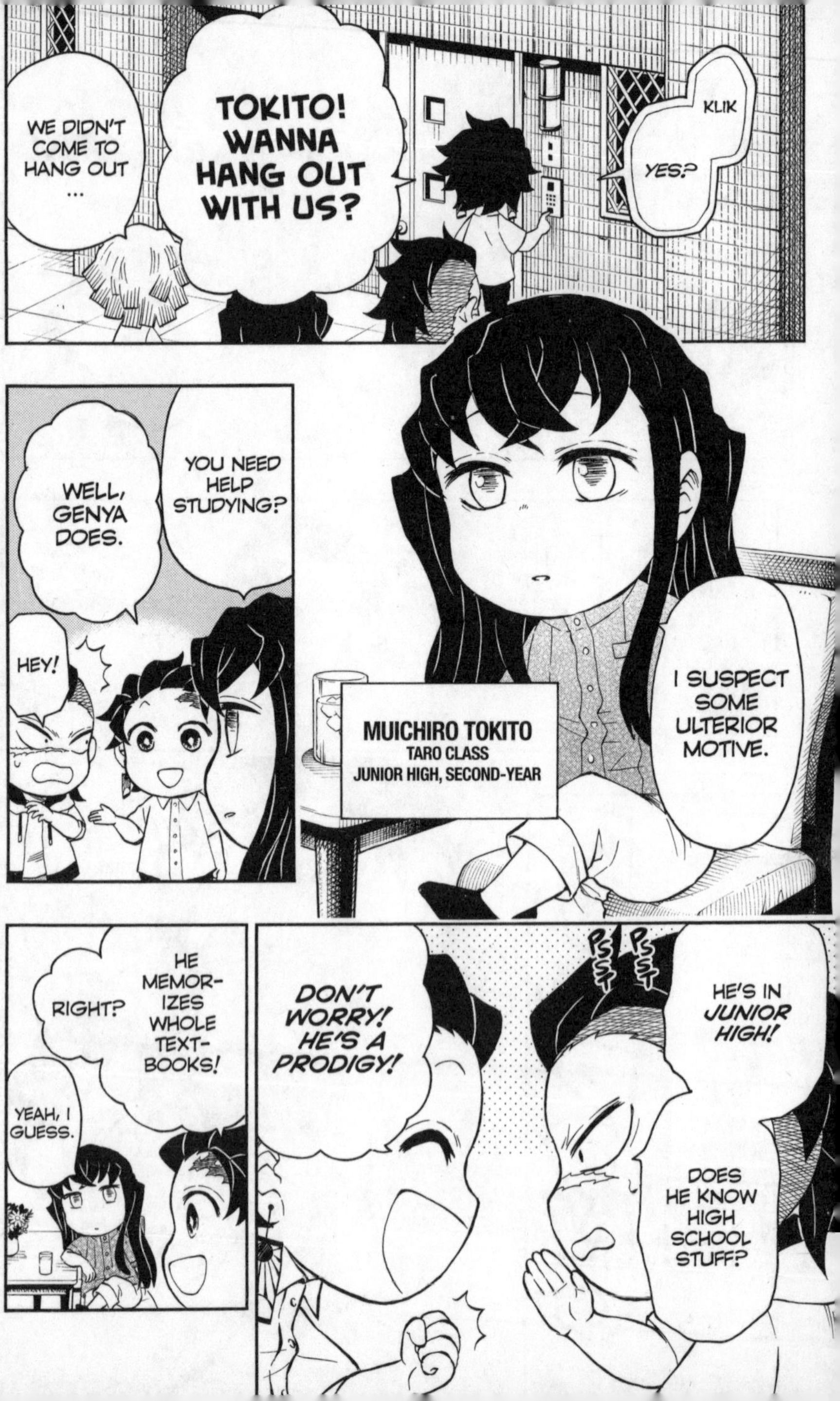
KLIK
YES?
TOKITO! WANNA HANG OUT WITH US?
WE DIDN'T COME TO HANG OUT ...
MUICHIRO TOKITO
TARO CLASS
JUNIOR HIGH, SECOND-YEAR
I SUSPECT SOME ULTERIOR MOTIVE.
YOU NEED HELP STUDYING?
WELL, GENYA DOES.
HEY!
PSST PSST
HE'S IN JUNIOR HIGH!
DOES HE KNOW HIGH SCHOOL STUFF?
DON'T WORRY! HE'S A PRODIGY!
HE MEMORIZES WHOLE TEXTBOOKS!
RIGHT?
YEAH, I GUESS.

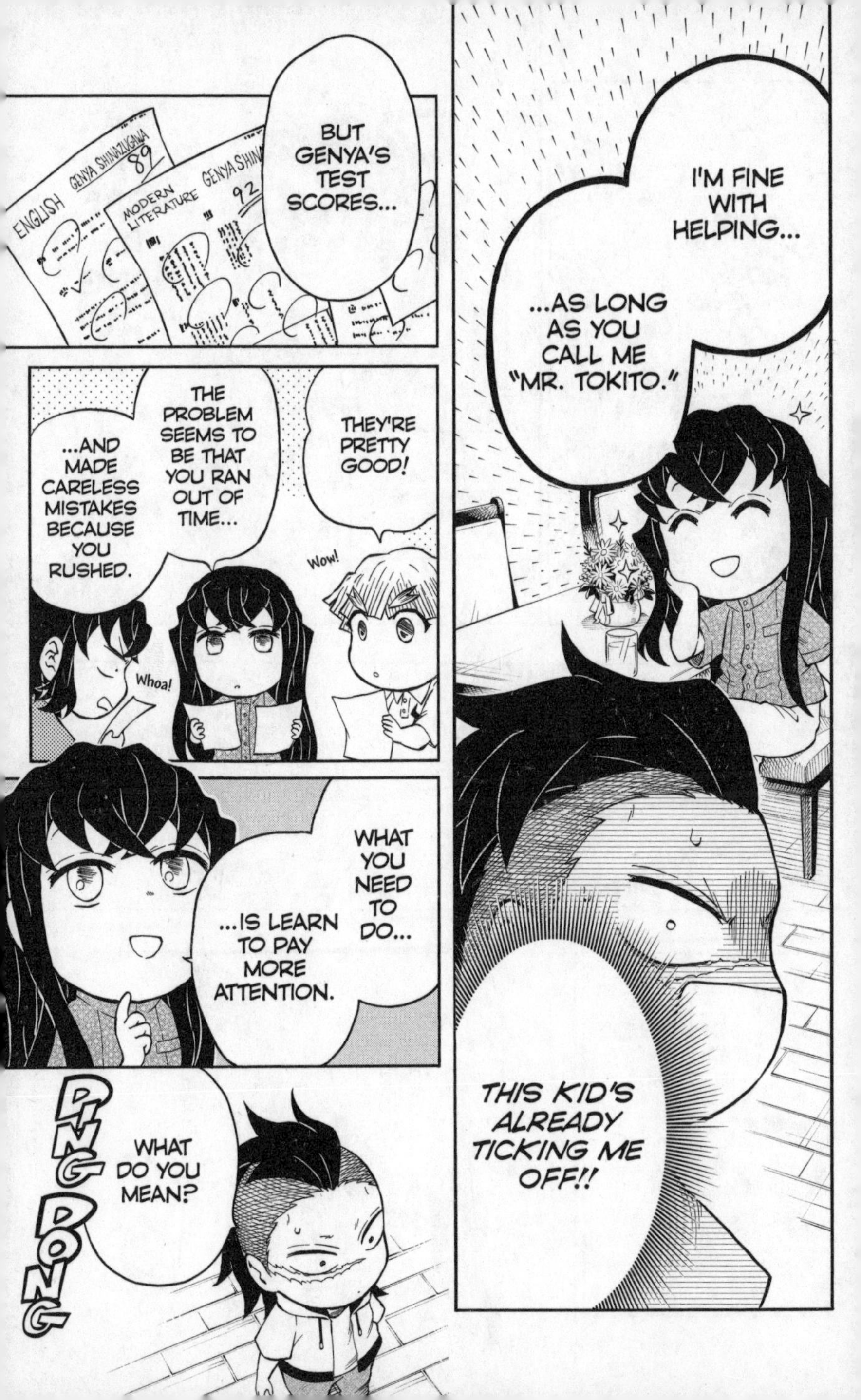
I'M FINE WITH HELPING...
...AS LONG AS YOU CALL ME "MR. TOKITO."
THIS KID'S ALREADY TICKING ME OFF!!
ENGLISH
GENYA SHINAZUGAWA
89
MODERN LITERATURE
92
BUT GENYA'S TEST SCORES...
THEY'RE PRETTY GOOD!
THE PROBLEM SEEMS TO BE THAT YOU RAN OUT OF TIME...
...AND MADE CARELESS MISTAKES BECAUSE YOU RUSHED.
Wow!
Whoa!
WHAT YOU NEED TO DO...
...IS LEARN TO PAY MORE ATTENTION.
WHAT DO YOU MEAN?
DING DONG

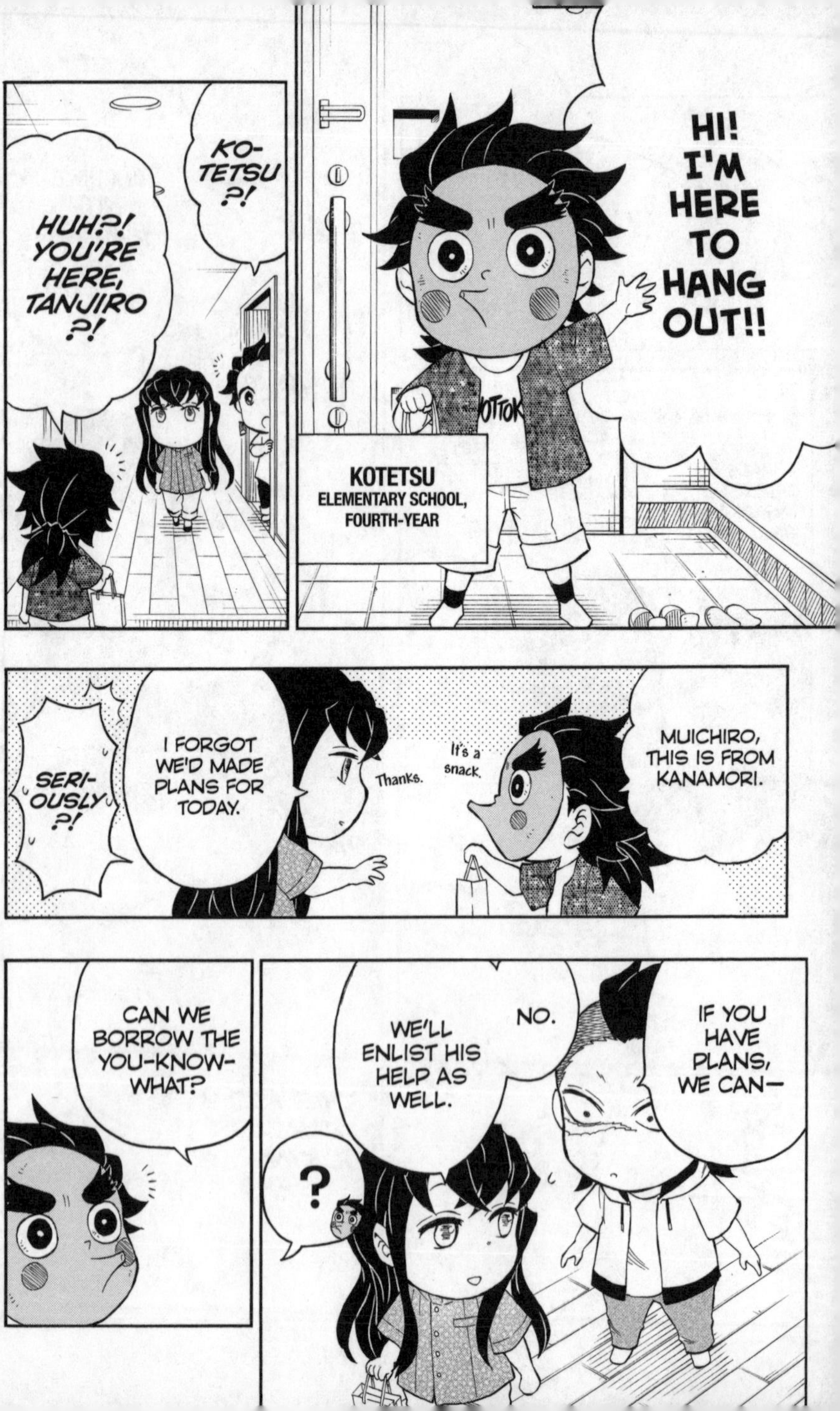
HI! I'M HERE TO HANG OUT!!
OTTOK
KOTETSU
ELEMENTARY SCHOOL, FOURTH-YEAR
KO-TETSU?!
HUH?! YOU'RE HERE, TANJIRO?!
MUICHIRO, THIS IS FROM KANAMORI.
It's a snack.
Thanks.
I FORGOT WE'D MADE PLANS FOR TODAY.
SERI-OUSLY?!
IF YOU HAVE PLANS, WE CAN—
NO.
WE'LL ENLIST HIS HELP AS WELL.
?
CAN WE BORROW THE YOU-KNOW-WHAT?

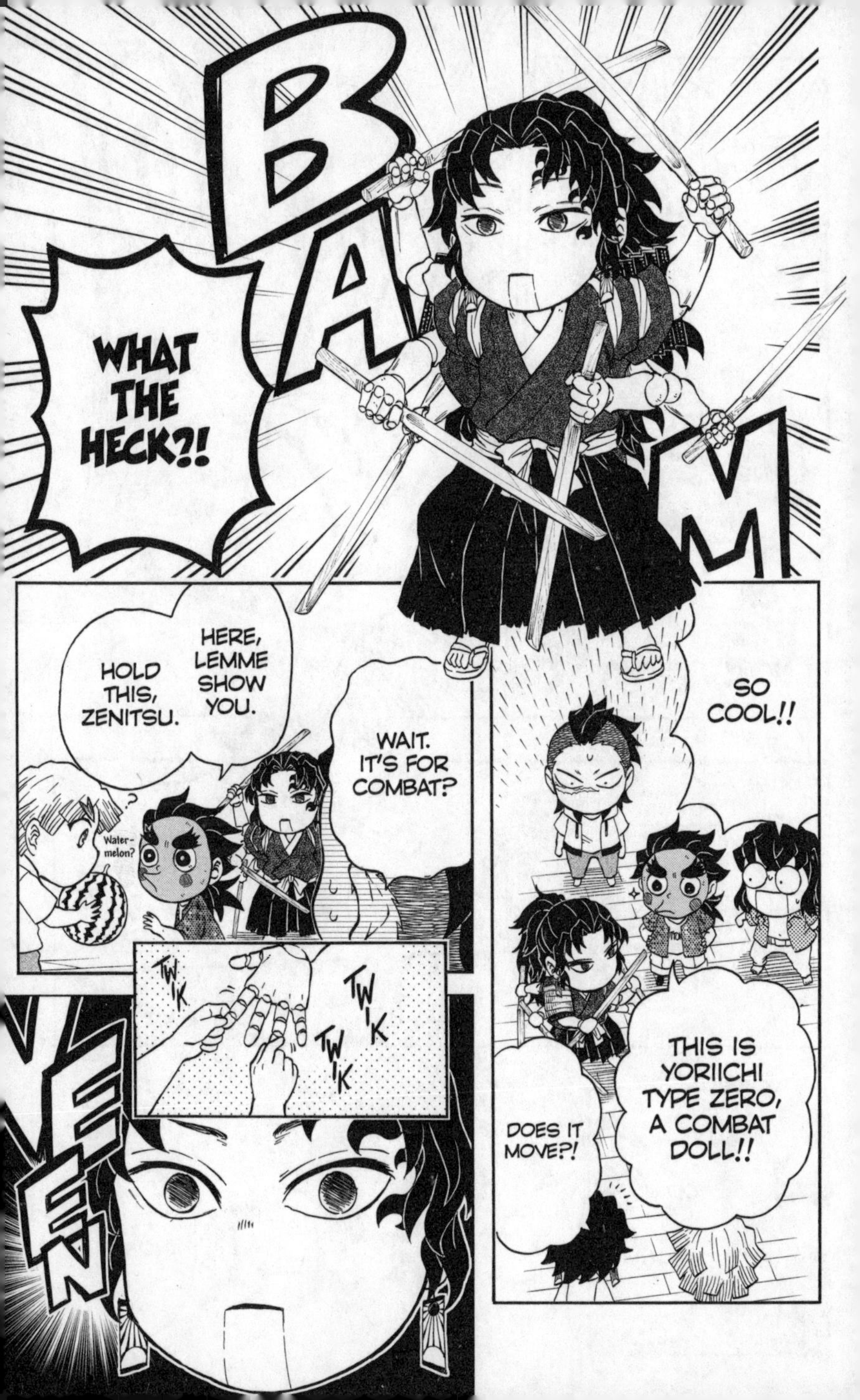
BAM
WHAT THE HECK?!
SO COOL!!
THIS IS YORIICHI TYPE ZERO, A COMBAT DOLL!!
DOES IT MOVE?!
HERE, LEMME SHOW YOU.
HOLD THIS, ZENITSU.
WAIT. IT'S FOR COMBAT?
Water-melon?
TWIK
TWIK
TWIK
VEEN

I'D BE DEAD!!!

IT'S GOOD FOR MOTI-VATION.

* WATERMELON

...THAT'LL BE YOUR HEAD.

THAT WOULD KILL ME!!

AND WHAT'D YOU DO TO ITS HANDS?!

THAT'S NOT JUST A DOLL, THEN!

YOU PROGRAM IT?!

TAK TAK TAK TAK

I'LL PROGRAM IT TO STOP FOR CORRECT ANSWERS.

HOW IS THAT GONNA MOTIVATE ME?!

I have plenty.

WE'LL JUST HAVE IT SPLIT ANOTHER WATERMELON INSTEAD.

FROM TETSUIDO

OH, OKAY.

TOKITO, I THINK THIS IS A LITTLE TOO DANGER-OUS.

...AFTER THE DOLL SPLITS THE WATERMELON...

...I'LL HAVE NO CHOICE BUT TO THROW AWAY THE LEFTOVERS.

OKAY, IN THAT CASE...

CHOMP MUNCH CHOMP

AT THAT POINT YOU'RE JUST WASTING WATERMELON!!

← LOVES WATERMELON

IF THAT'S ALL IT TAKES, WHY'RE WE EVEN USING THAT THING?!

I CAN'T LET THAT HAPPEN!!

THAT'D BE TERRIBLE!!

GRAAAAAAH

UM...

...BE STUDYING TOO?

SHOULDN'T YOU THREE...

HUH?

DOESN'T THAT WORRY YOU?

YOUR GRADES ARE WORSE THAN HIS, RIGHT?

YOU GET BAD GRADES WHEN YOU'RE LAZY.

HARSH

TICK TICK TICK

YOU HAVE 20 SECONDS !!

$$y = -3(x-1)^2 + 5$$
$$-3 \leqq x \leqq -1$$

FIND THE MAXIMUM AND MINIMUM VALUES FOR THIS EQUATION !!

FIRST QUESTION!!

W-WELL, UM...

CORRECT!

UM...X=-3 FOR A MINIMUM OF -43 AND X=-1 FOR A MAX OF -7!!!

...

BESIDES, YORIICHI IS BUSY WITH GENYA.

CHOP

GAH!

DURING SUMMER BREAK IT IS WISE TO STUDY HARD BUT WHO WOULD BOTHER?

—A SUMMER HAIKU BY THREE NINCOMPOOPS

GENYA'S DEDICATED!

TING TING

I'M NOT GETTING PUNCHED BY THAT THING!

GAH!

I DIALED IT DOWN TO GOOSE-EGG MODE.

NO WORRIES! I'VE GOT ANOTHER ONE!!

NO WAY!

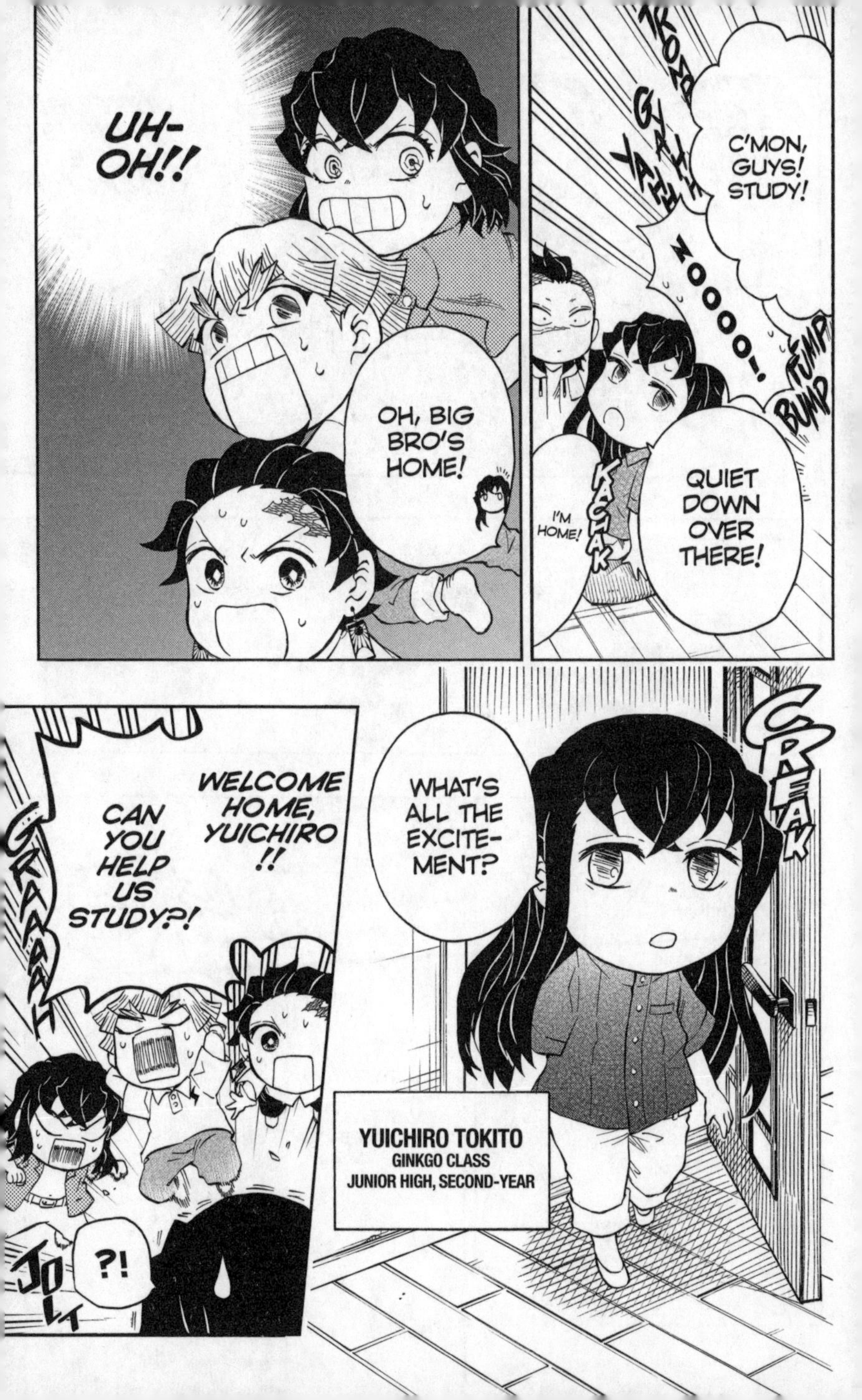
C'MON, GUYS! STUDY!
NOOOOO!!
BUMP
QUIET DOWN OVER THERE!
KACHAK
I'M HOME!
UH-OH!!
OH, BIG BRO'S HOME!
CREAK
WHAT'S ALL THE EXCITEMENT?
YUICHIRO TOKITO
GINKGO CLASS
JUNIOR HIGH, SECOND-YEAR
WELCOME HOME, YUICHIRO!!
CAN YOU HELP US STUDY?!
GRAAAAH
?!
JOLT

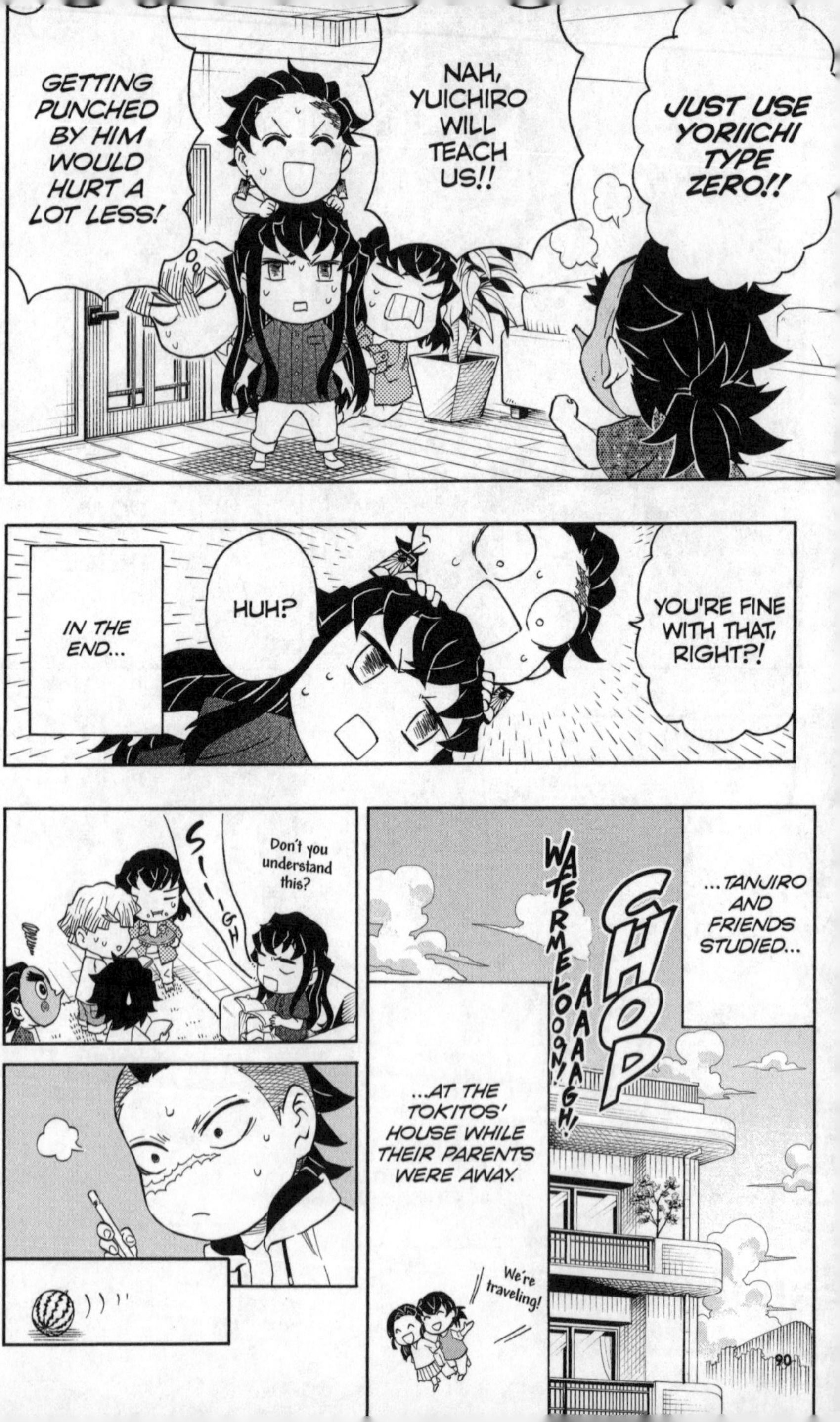
JUST USE YORIICHI TYPE ZERO!!
NAH, YUICHIRO WILL TEACH US!!
GETTING PUNCHED BY HIM WOULD HURT A LOT LESS!
YOU'RE FINE WITH THAT, RIGHT?!
HUH?
IN THE END...
...TANJIRO AND FRIENDS STUDIED...
CHOP
WATERMELOOON! AAAAGH!
...AT THE TOKITOS' HOUSE WHILE THEIR PARENTS WERE AWAY.
We're traveling!
Don't you understand this?
SIIIGH

I KNOW THAT'S THE RIGHT ATTITUDE, BUT...

Y-YEAH...

LET'S ALL DO OUR BEST!!

DON'T WORRY! YOU'LL GET YOUR VOUCHERS BACK!!

?

HE'S LIKE AN INFORMATION SPONGE.

YOU THINK SO?

...I CAN'T BELIEVE THAT TOKITO...

...ALREADY KNOWS ALL THIS.

IF I WAS GIFTED LIKE TOKITO...

GRRR

You try it!

Come on already!

STAY BACK! YIIIKES!

Goose-egg mode

CHATTER

C'mon! Just try it!

CHATTER

...THEN MY BROTHER WOULDN'T GET MAD AT ME...

...FOR BEING A LOSER.

HE MUST BE ASHAMED OF ME.

CONTEMPLATIVE

GENYA...

HIS FAVO-RITE?!

YOU'RE HIS FAVORITE!

HE GETS ANGRY BECAUSE HE CARES ABOUT YOU.

...YOU'RE NOT A LOSER.

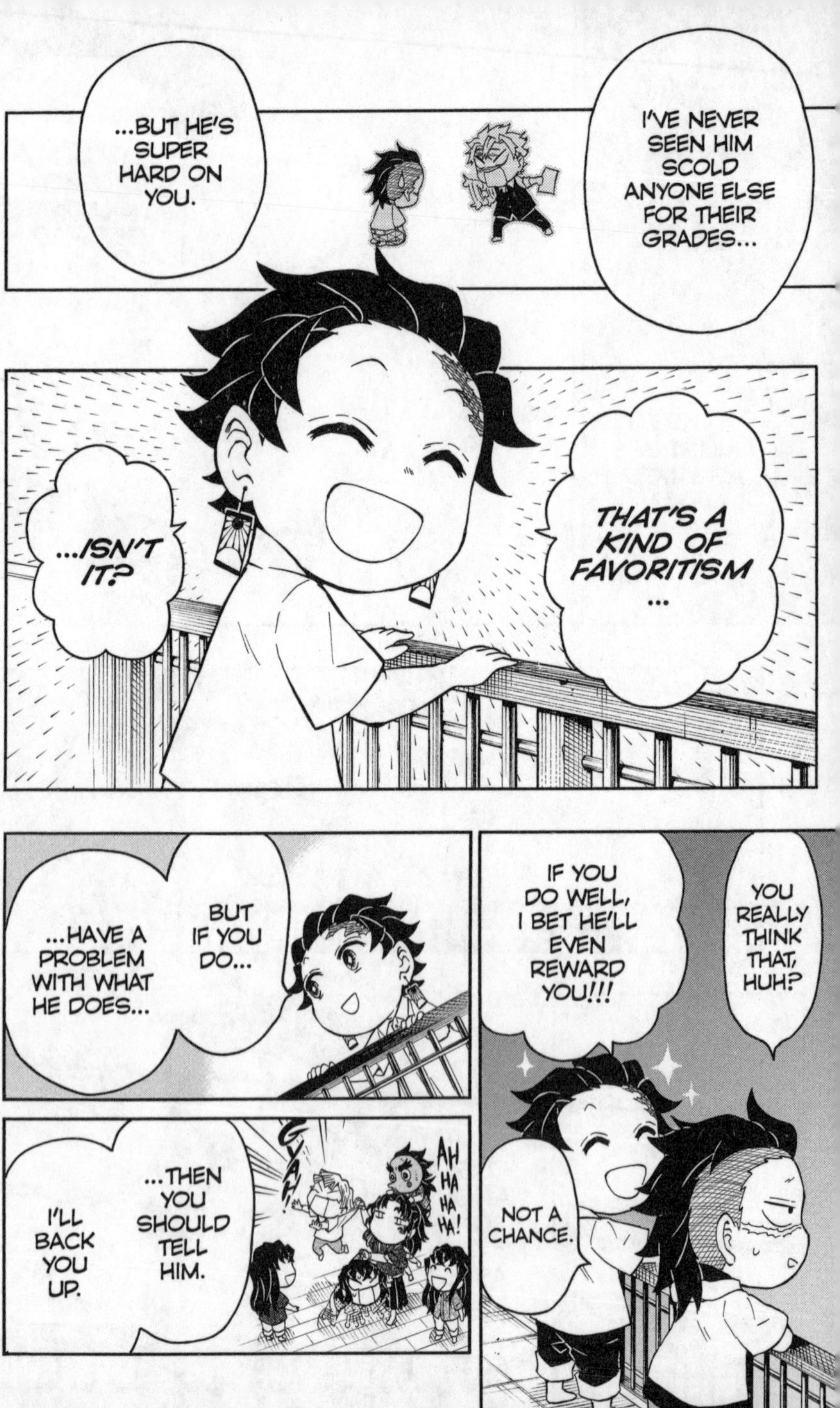
I'VE NEVER SEEN HIM SCOLD ANYONE ELSE FOR THEIR GRADES...
...BUT HE'S SUPER HARD ON YOU.
THAT'S A KIND OF FAVORITISM...
...ISN'T IT?
YOU REALLY THINK THAT, HUH?
IF YOU DO WELL, I BET HE'LL EVEN REWARD YOU!!!
NOT A CHANCE.
BUT IF YOU DO...
...HAVE A PROBLEM WITH WHAT HE DOES...
...THEN YOU SHOULD TELL HIM.
I'LL BACK YOU UP.
AH HA HA HA HA!
GYAH!

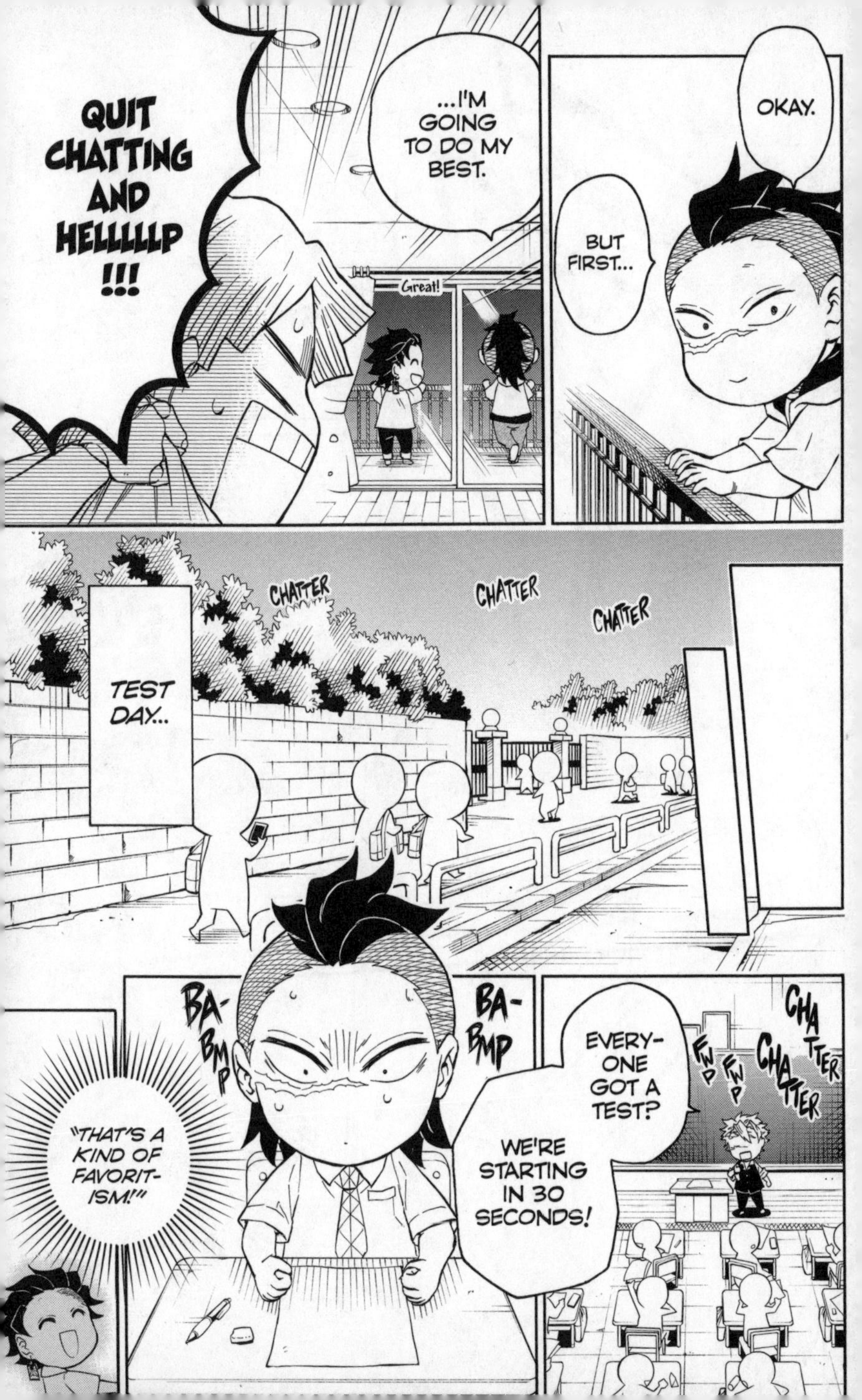
OKAY.
BUT FIRST...
...I'M GOING TO DO MY BEST.
Great!
QUIT CHATTING AND HELLLLLP!!!
CHATTER
CHATTER
CHATTER
TEST DAY...
CHATTER
CHATTER
FWP
FWP
EVERY-ONE GOT A TEST?
WE'RE STARTING IN 30 SECONDS!
BA-BMP
BA-BMP
"THAT'S A KIND OF FAVORIT-ISM!"

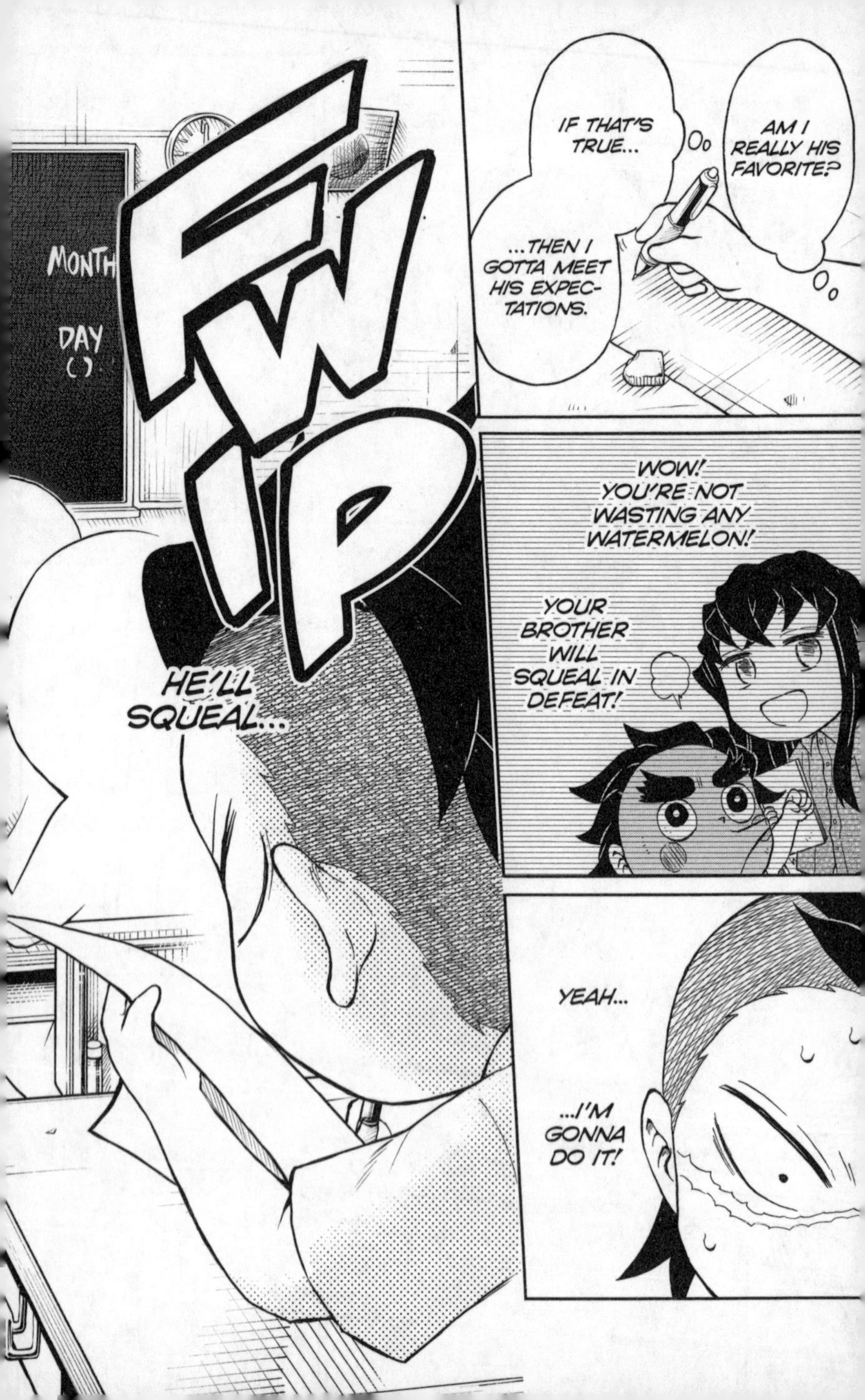
AM I REALLY HIS FAVORITE?
IF THAT'S TRUE...
...THEN I GOTTA MEET HIS EXPECTATIONS.
WOW! YOU'RE NOT WASTING ANY WATERMELON!
YOUR BROTHER WILL SQUEAL IN DEFEAT!
MONTH
DAY
( )
FWIP
HE'LL SQUEAL...
YEAH...
...I'M GONNA DO IT!

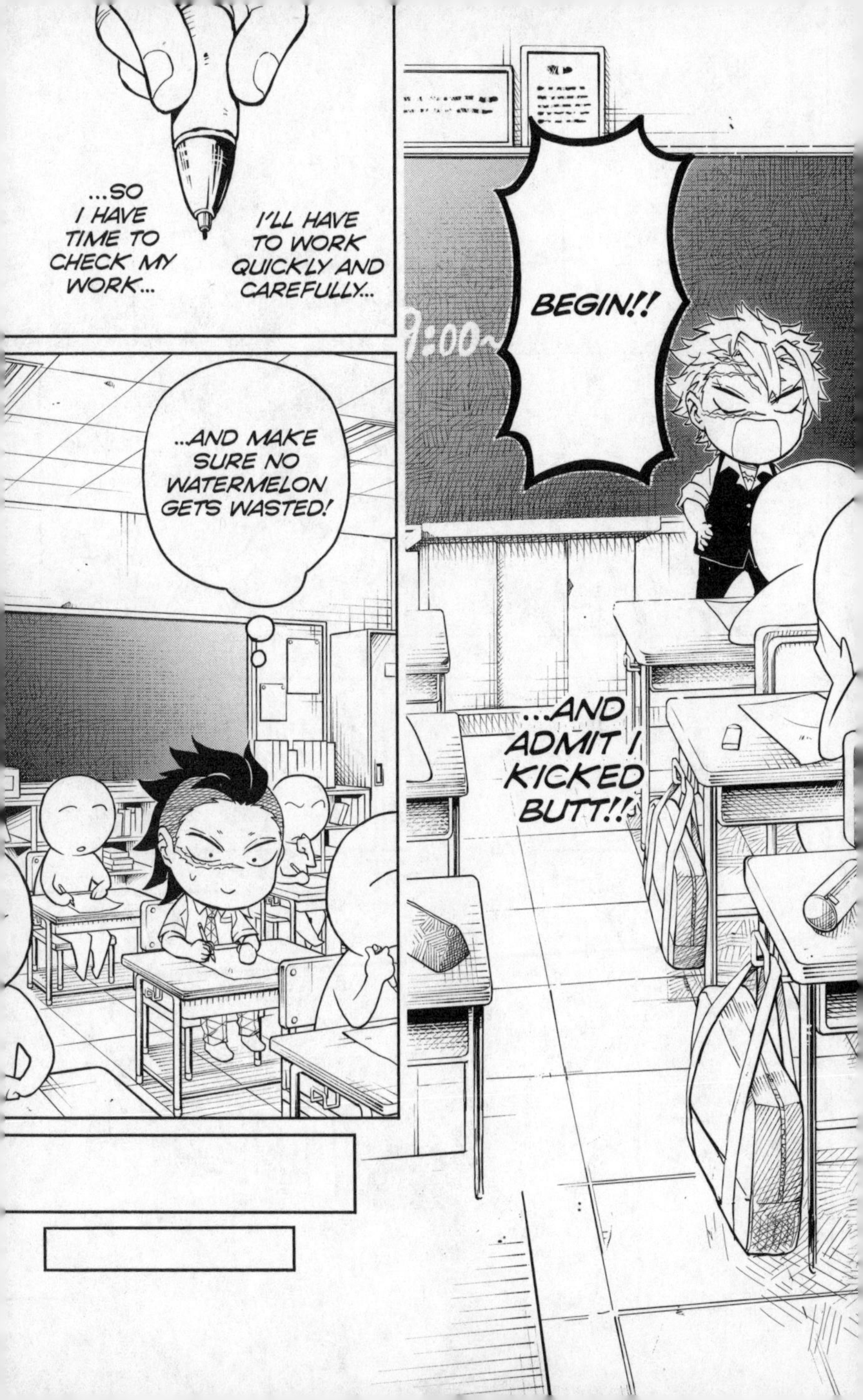
BEGIN!!
I'LL HAVE TO WORK QUICKLY AND CAREFULLY...
...SO I HAVE TIME TO CHECK MY WORK...
...AND MAKE SURE NO WATERMELON GETS WASTED!
...AND ADMIT I KICKED BUTT!!

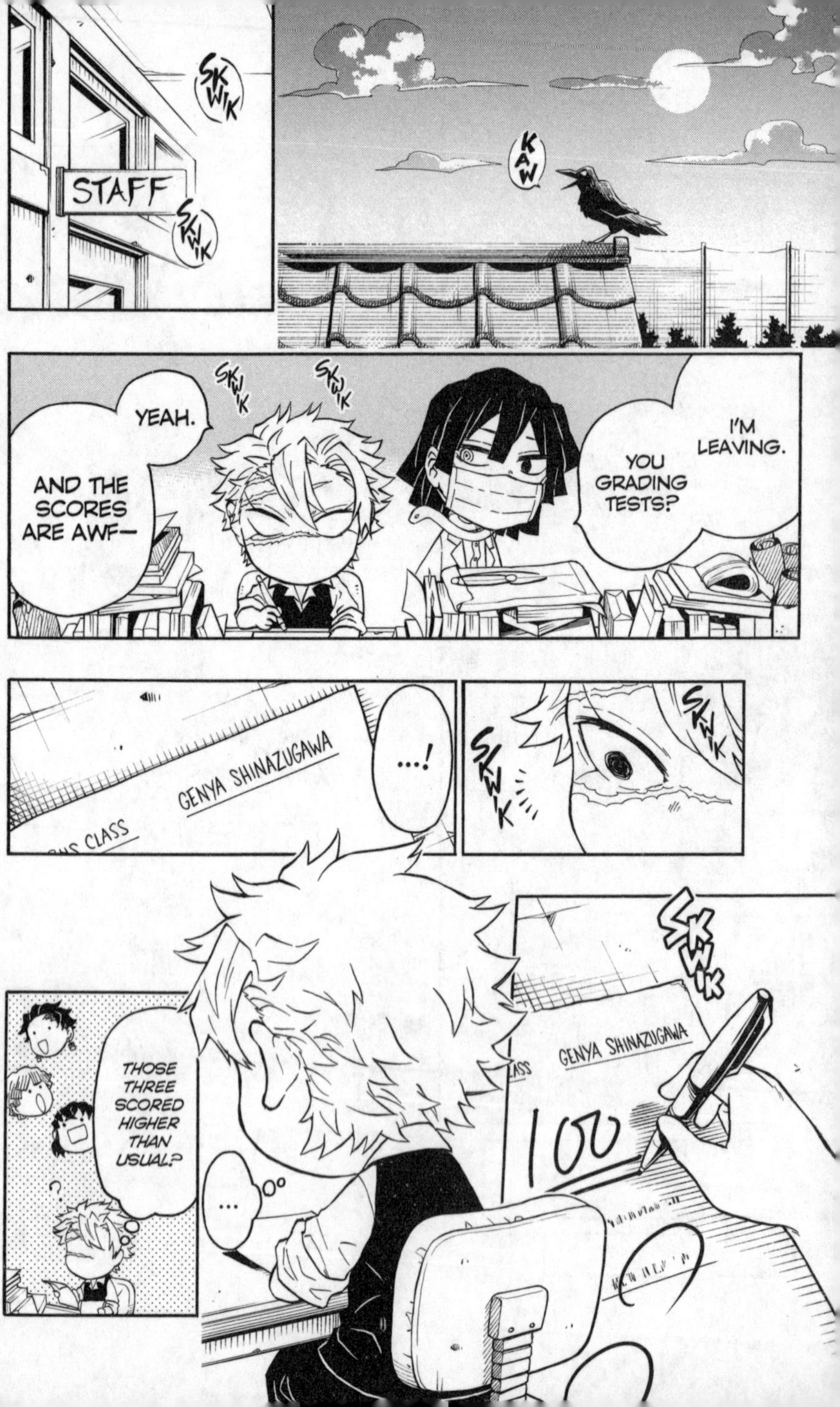
KAW
SKWIK
STAFF
SKWIK
I'M LEAVING.
YOU GRADING TESTS?
SKWIK
SKWIK
YEAH.
AND THE SCORES ARE AWF—
SKWIK
SKWIK
...!
GENYA SHINAZUGAWA
CLASS
SKWIK
GENYA SHINAZUGAWA
CLASS
100
...
THOSE THREE SCORED HIGHER THAN USUAL?

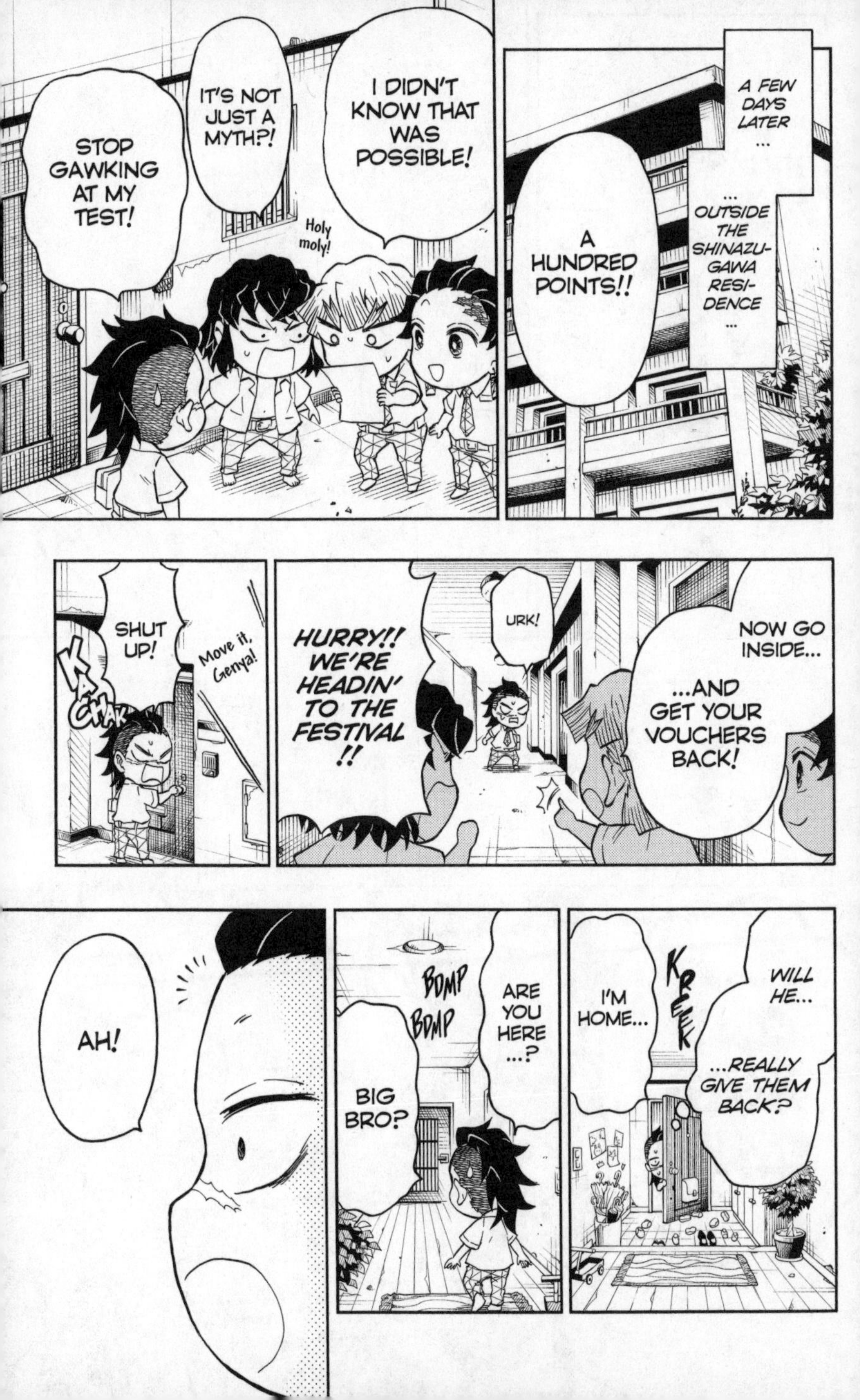
A FEW DAYS LATER...
...OUTSIDE THE SHINAZU-GAWA RESI-DENCE...
A HUNDRED POINTS!!
I DIDN'T KNOW THAT WAS POSSIBLE!
Holy moly!
IT'S NOT JUST A MYTH?!
STOP GAWKING AT MY TEST!
NOW GO INSIDE...
...AND GET YOUR VOUCHERS BACK!
URK!
HURRY!! WE'RE HEADIN' TO THE FESTIVAL!!
Move it, Genya!
SHUT UP!
KACHAK
WILL HE...
...REALLY GIVE THEM BACK?
KREEK
I'M HOME...
ARE YOU HERE...?
BDMP BDMP
BIG BRO?
AH!

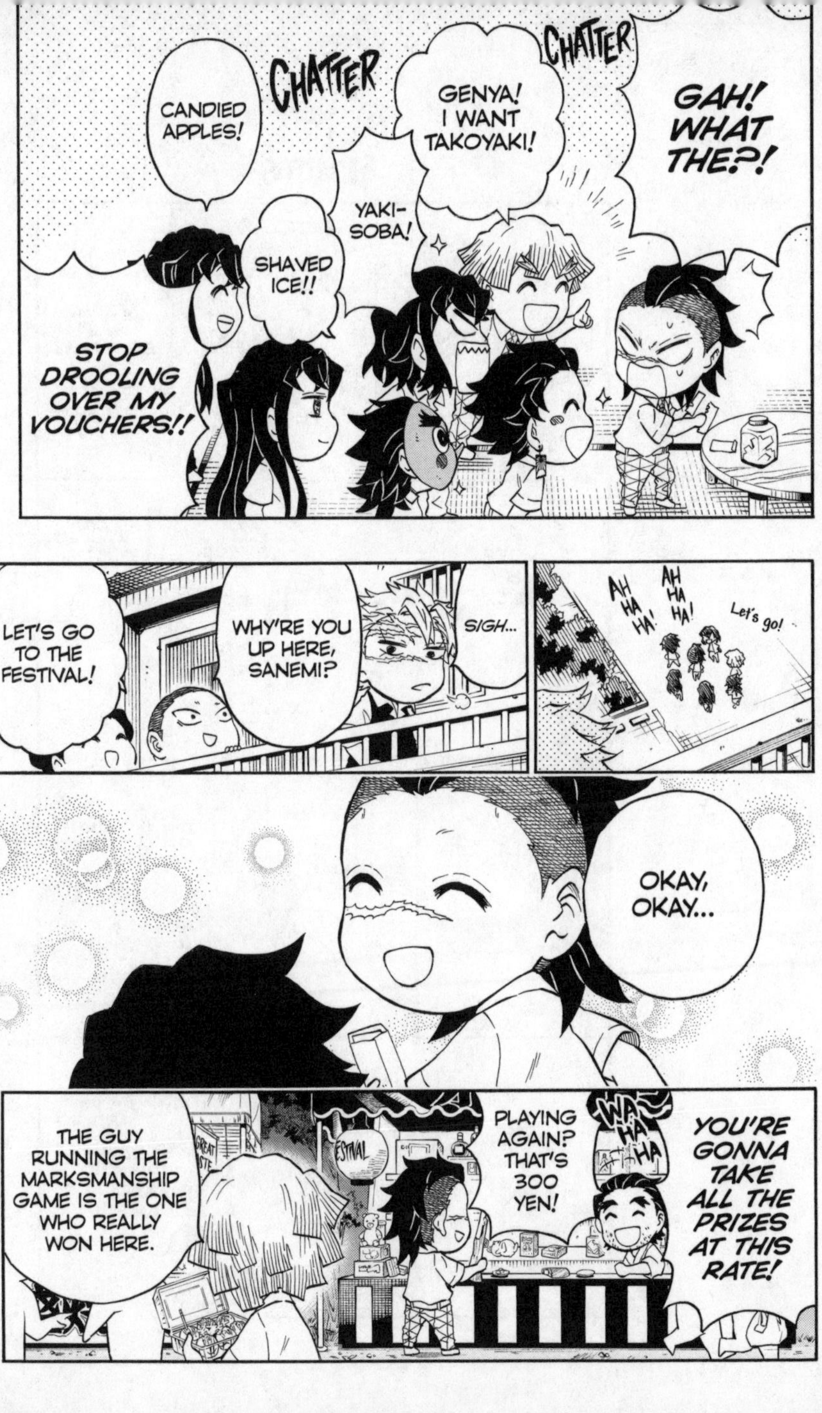
GAH! WHAT THE?!
CHATTER
GENYA! I WANT TAKOYAKI!
YAKI-SOBA!
CHATTER
CANDIED APPLES!
SHAVED ICE!!
STOP DROOLING OVER MY VOUCHERS!!
Let's go!
AH HA HA!
AH HA HA!
SIGH...
WHY'RE YOU UP HERE, SANEMI?
LET'S GO TO THE FESTIVAL!
OKAY, OKAY...
YOU'RE GONNA TAKE ALL THE PRIZES AT THIS RATE!
WA HA HA
PLAYING AGAIN? THAT'S 300 YEN!
FESTIVAL
THE GUY RUNNING THE MARKSMANSHIP GAME IS THE ONE WHO REALLY WON HERE.

TOKITOS

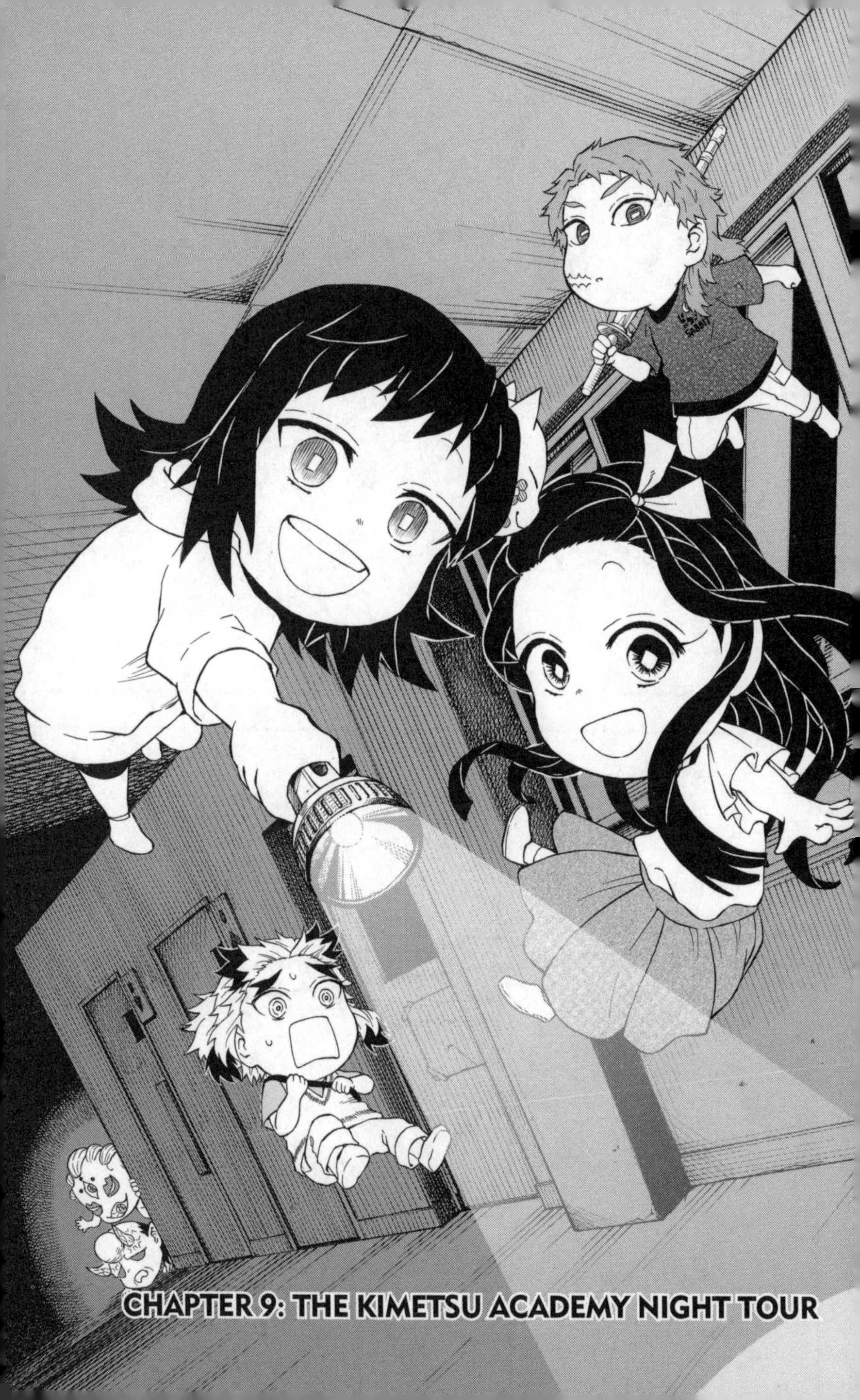

CHAPTER 9: THE KIMETSU ACADEMY NIGHT TOUR

IDEAS FOR THE SCHOOL'S SEVEN MYSTERIES?

...PUT OUT A CALL FOR IDEAS!

YEAH! THE SCHOOL PAPER...

Cool!

"ONCE WE HAVE SEVEN, WE'LL ANNOUNCE THE CHOSEN MYSTERIES."

SPOOKY STORIES, HUH?

"...SO WE'RE LOOKING FOR YOUR SPOOKY STORIES."

"LIKE OTHER SCHOOLS, KIMETSU ACADEMY SHOULD HAVE SEVEN MYSTERIOUS HAUNTINGS..."

IT SAYS, UM...

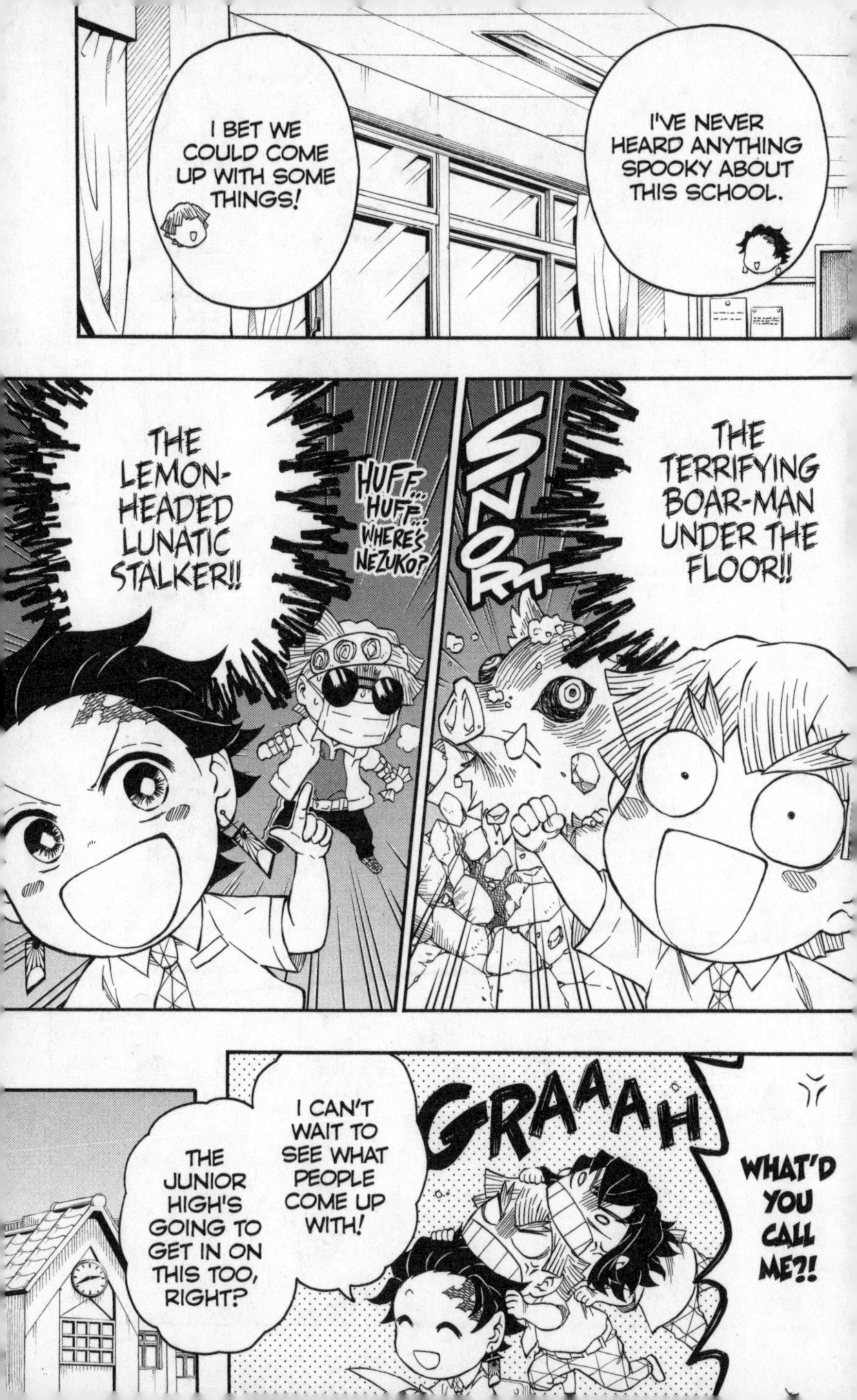
I'VE NEVER HEARD ANYTHING SPOOKY ABOUT THIS SCHOOL.
I BET WE COULD COME UP WITH SOME THINGS!
THE TERRIFYING BOAR-MAN UNDER THE FLOOR!!
SNORT
THE LEMON-HEADED LUNATIC STALKER!!
HUFF... HUFF... WHERE'S NEZUKO?
WHAT'D YOU CALL ME?!
GRAAAH
I CAN'T WAIT TO SEE WHAT PEOPLE COME UP WITH!
THE JUNIOR HIGH'S GOING TO GET IN ON THIS TOO, RIGHT?

THE JUNIOR HIGH...

TARO CLASS
SECOND-YEAR

LET'S VISIT THE SCHOOL AT NIGHT TO GET IDEAS!!

MAKOMO
TARO CLASS
JUNIOR HIGH, SECOND-YEAR

NEZUKO KAMADO
TARO CLASS
JUNIOR HIGH, SECOND-YEAR

IDEAS FOR WHAT?

...FOR A GHOST-HUNTING ADVENTURE!

SO WE'LL SNEAK INTO SCHOOL AT NIGHT...

DIDN'T YOU SEE THE SCHOOL PAPER?

WE NEED A GOOD STORY TO SUBMIT!

WHAT ARE YOU TALKING ABOUT?

THAT'S WHY WE'LL KEEP IT A SECRET!

THERE'S NO WAY THE TEACHERS OR OUR PARENTS WOULD LET US!

WAIT, WE CAN'T!

ADVENTURE...

YAY

HMM

BRING A FLASHLIGHT AND JUNK FOOD!

TELL YOUR PARENTS YOU'RE SLEEPING OVER AT MY HOUSE!

...

SABITO
TARO CLASS
JUNIOR HIGH,
SECOND-YEAR

COULD BE!

THAT'S WHY WE'LL NEED A BODY-GUARD!

WILL IT BE DANGER-OUS?

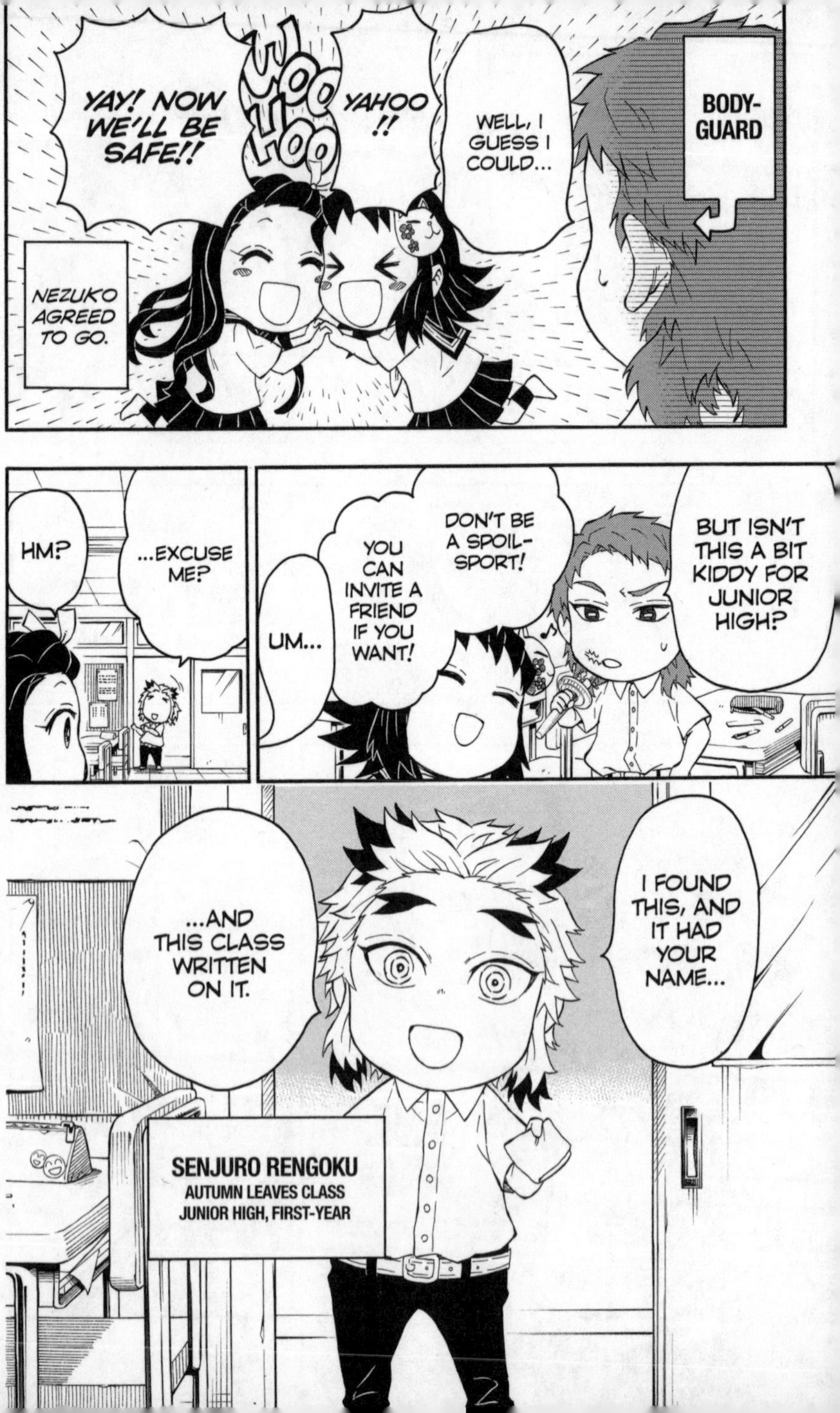
BODY-GUARD
WELL, I GUESS I COULD...
YAHOO!!
WOO HOO
YAY! NOW WE'LL BE SAFE!!
NEZUKO AGREED TO GO.
BUT ISN'T THIS A BIT KIDDY FOR JUNIOR HIGH?
DON'T BE A SPOIL-SPORT!
YOU CAN INVITE A FRIEND IF YOU WANT!
UM...
...EXCUSE ME?
HM?
I FOUND THIS, AND IT HAD YOUR NAME...
...AND THIS CLASS WRITTEN ON IT.
SENJURO RENGOKU
AUTUMN LEAVES CLASS
JUNIOR HIGH, FIRST-YEAR

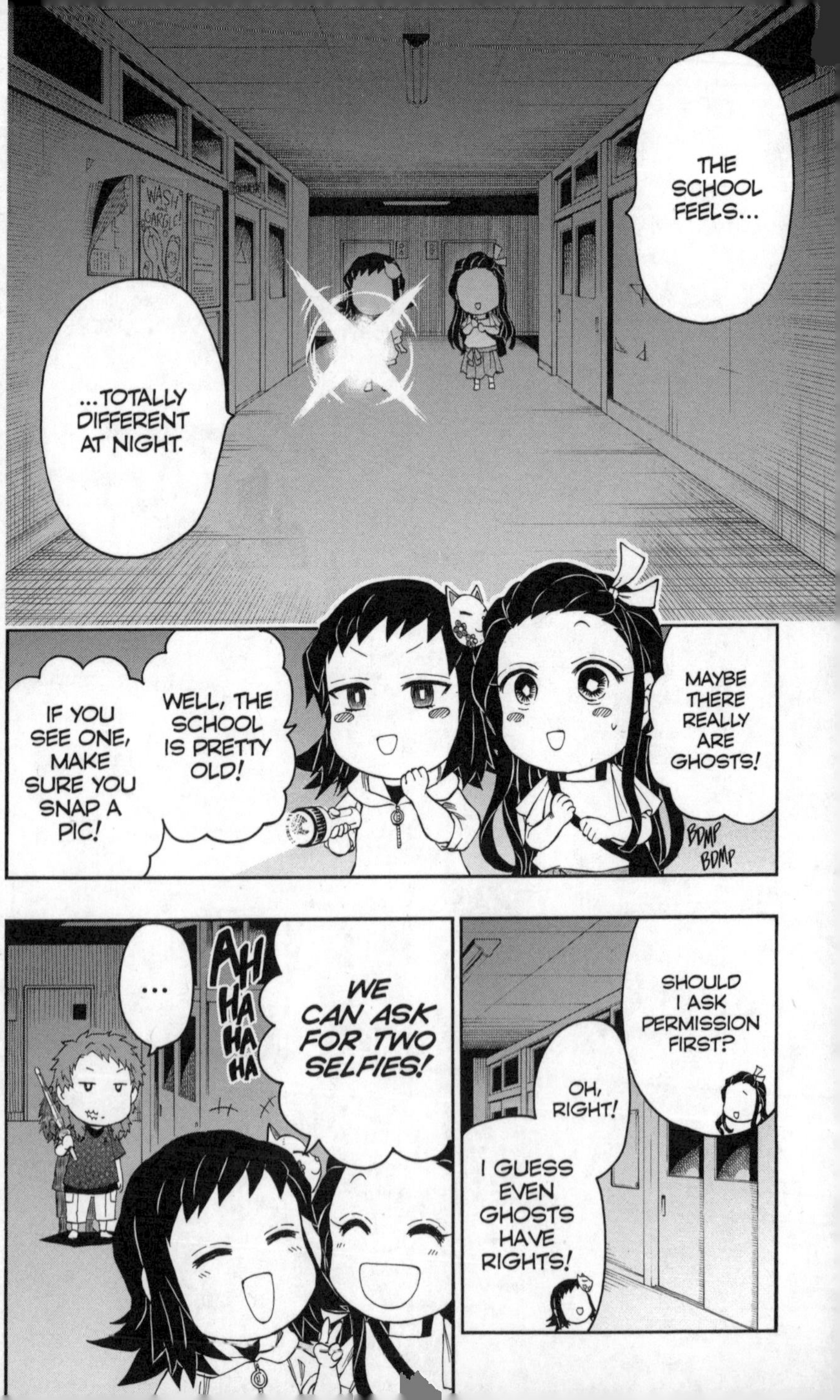
THE SCHOOL FEELS...
...TOTALLY DIFFERENT AT NIGHT.
MAYBE THERE REALLY ARE GHOSTS!
BDMP BDMP
WELL, THE SCHOOL IS PRETTY OLD!
IF YOU SEE ONE, MAKE SURE YOU SNAP A PIC!
SHOULD I ASK PERMISSION FIRST?
OH, RIGHT!
I GUESS EVEN GHOSTS HAVE RIGHTS!
WE CAN ASK FOR TWO SELFIES!
AHHAHAHAHA
...

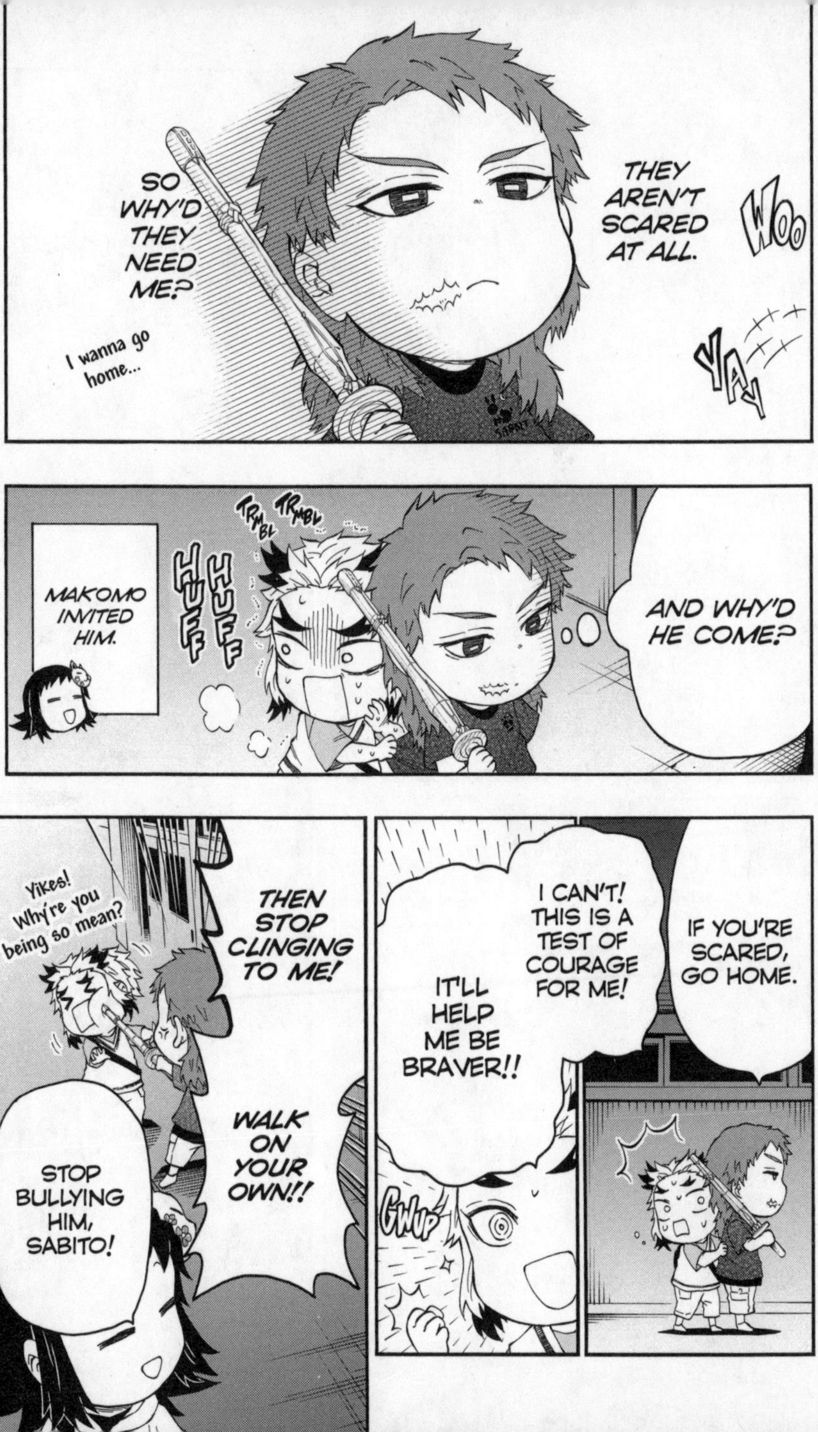
WOO
YAY
THEY AREN'T SCARED AT ALL.
SO WHY'D THEY NEED ME?
I wanna go home...
AND WHY'D HE COME?
TRMBL TRMBL
HUFF HUFF
MAKOMO INVITED HIM.
IF YOU'RE SCARED, GO HOME.
I CAN'T! THIS IS A TEST OF COURAGE FOR ME!
IT'LL HELP ME BE BRAVER!!
GWUP
THEN STOP CLINGING TO ME!
Yikes! Why're you being so mean?
WALK ON YOUR OWN!!
STOP BULLYING HIM, SABITO!

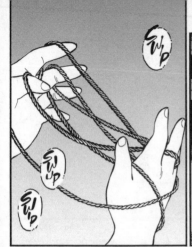

SO! WHERE SHOULD WE LOOK?

MAYBE THE SCIENCE ROOM?

!

SHH!

LOOK!

WHAT'S WRONG, SABITO?

SOME-ONE'S IN THE CLASS-ROOM!

WHAT ?!

TH-THEN IS THAT...

...A G-G-GHOST?

NO ONE ELSE SHOULD BE HERE THIS LATE!

AH!

WHERE?

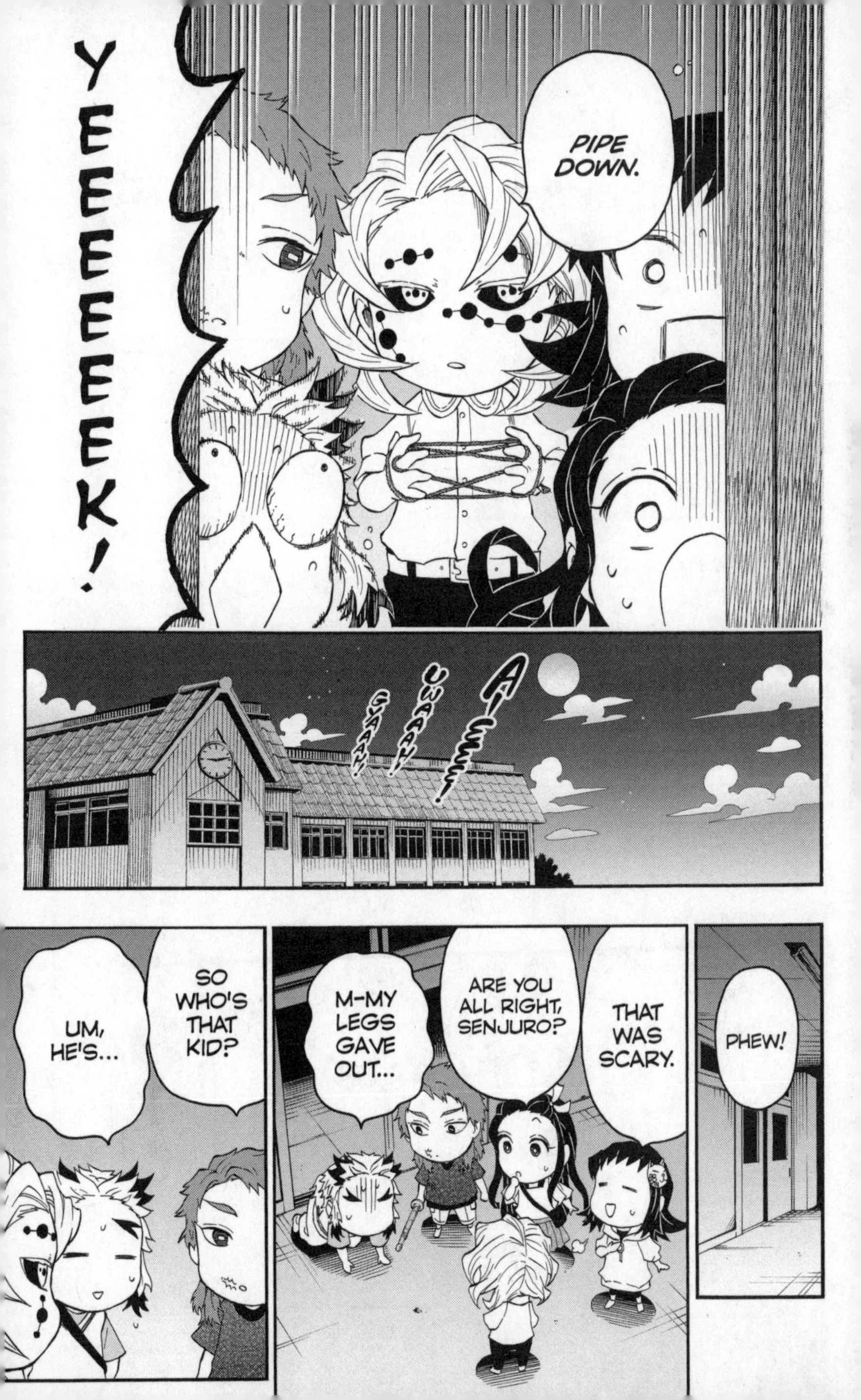
PIPE DOWN.
YEEEEEEK!
AIEEEE!
UWAAAAH!
GYAAAH!
PHEW!
THAT WAS SCARY.
ARE YOU ALL RIGHT, SENJURO?
M-MY LEGS GAVE OUT...
SO WHO'S THAT KID?
UM, HE'S...

...MY CLASSMATE *RUI AYAKI!*

RUI AYAKI
AUTUMN LEAVES CLASS
JUNIOR HIGH, FIRST-YEAR

WHAT'RE *YOU* DOING HERE?

I JUST DO THIS SOME- TIMES.

WHAT ARE YOU DOING HERE AT NIGHT?

I ENJOY PRACTICING CAT'S CRADLE...

BUT UNLIKE YOU, I DON'T MAKE A BUNCH OF NOISE.

DO WHAT?

...IN A NICE, QUIET, PEACEFUL ENVIRON- MENT!

HANG OUT AT SCHOOL AT NIGHT.

VEEN

SORRY. THEY'RE ALL IDIOTS.

...

CAN YOU MAKE TOKYO TOWER?!

YOU DON'T NEED TO BE SO GRUMPY.

OOH, *ATTITUDE* MUCH?

IF YOU WANT SPOOKS ...

...TRY THE HIGH SCHOOL.

NO IDEA.

CAN YOU S-SENSE SPIRITS?

SERI-OUSLY?

THERE'S A WEIRD FEELING IN THE AIR.

HUH? WHY?

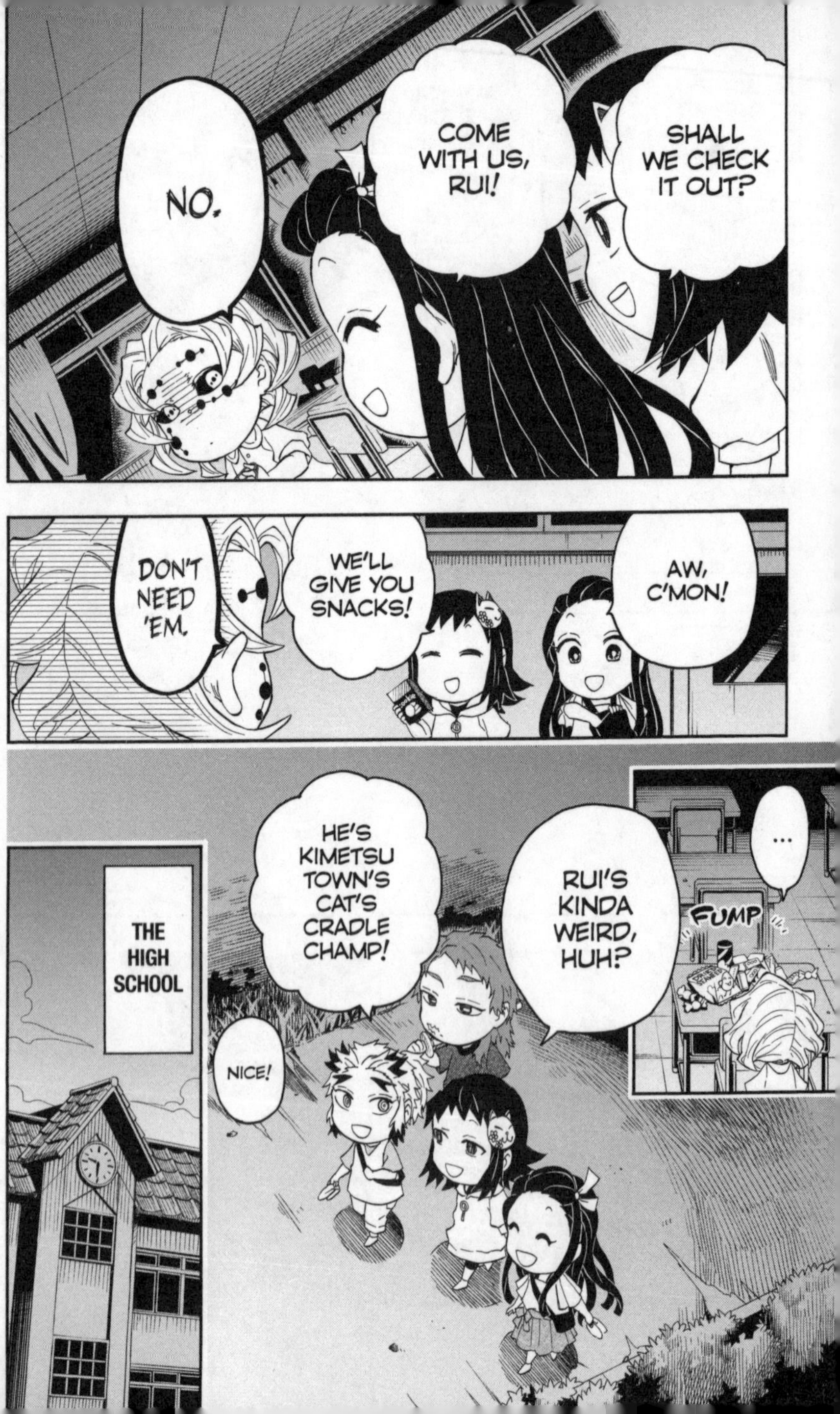
SHALL WE CHECK IT OUT?
COME WITH US, RUI!
NO.
AW, C'MON!
WE'LL GIVE YOU SNACKS!
DON'T NEED 'EM.
...
FUMP
RUI'S KINDA WEIRD, HUH?
HE'S KIMETSU TOWN'S CAT'S CRADLE CHAMP!
NICE!
THE HIGH SCHOOL

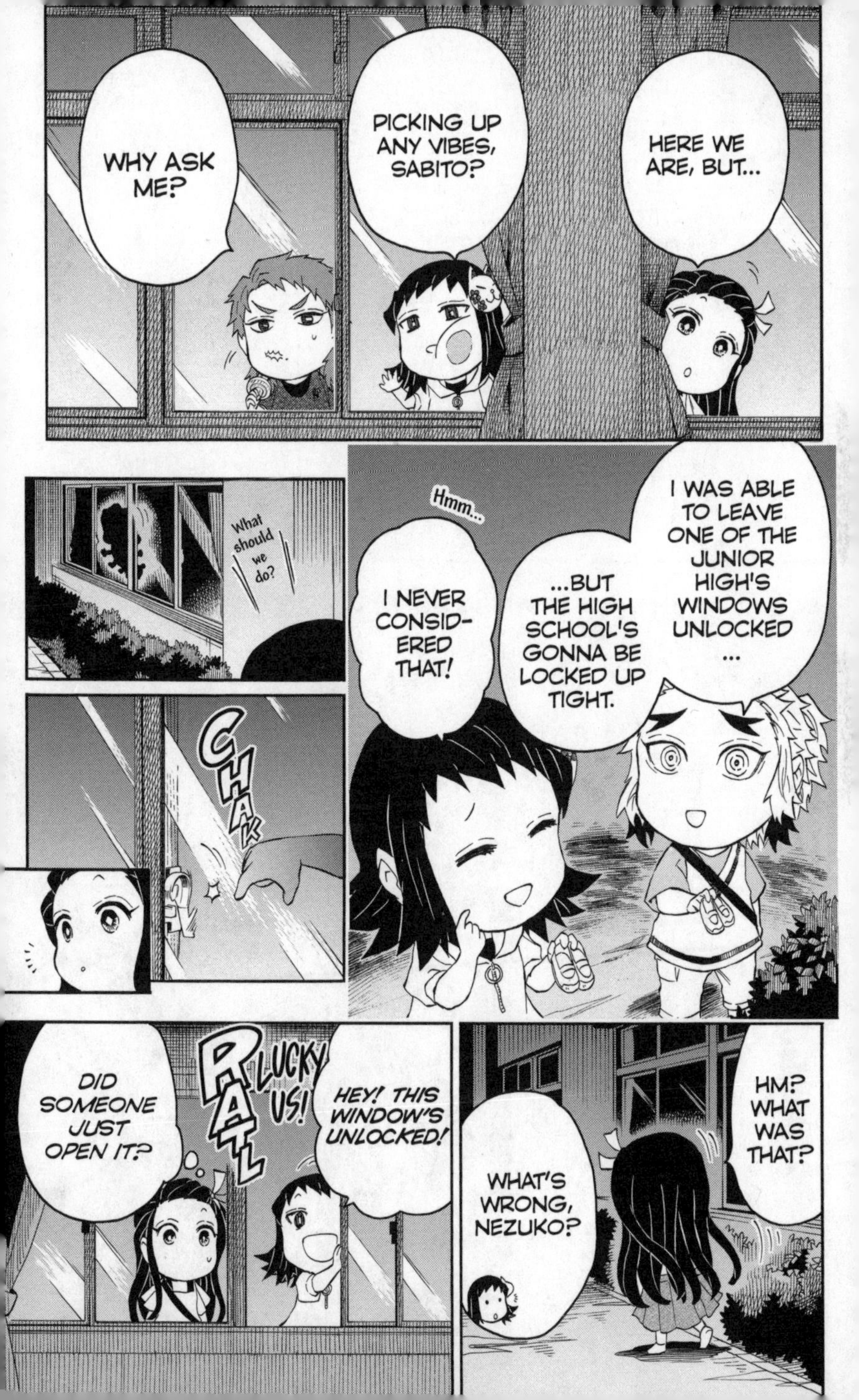
HERE WE ARE, BUT...
PICKING UP ANY VIBES, SABITO?
WHY ASK ME?
I WAS ABLE TO LEAVE ONE OF THE JUNIOR HIGH'S WINDOWS UNLOCKED...
...BUT THE HIGH SCHOOL'S GONNA BE LOCKED UP TIGHT.
Hmm...
I NEVER CONSID-ERED THAT!
What should we do?
CHAK
HM? WHAT WAS THAT?
WHAT'S WRONG, NEZUKO?
HEY! THIS WINDOW'S UNLOCKED!
LUCKY US!
RATTL
DID SOMEONE JUST OPEN IT?

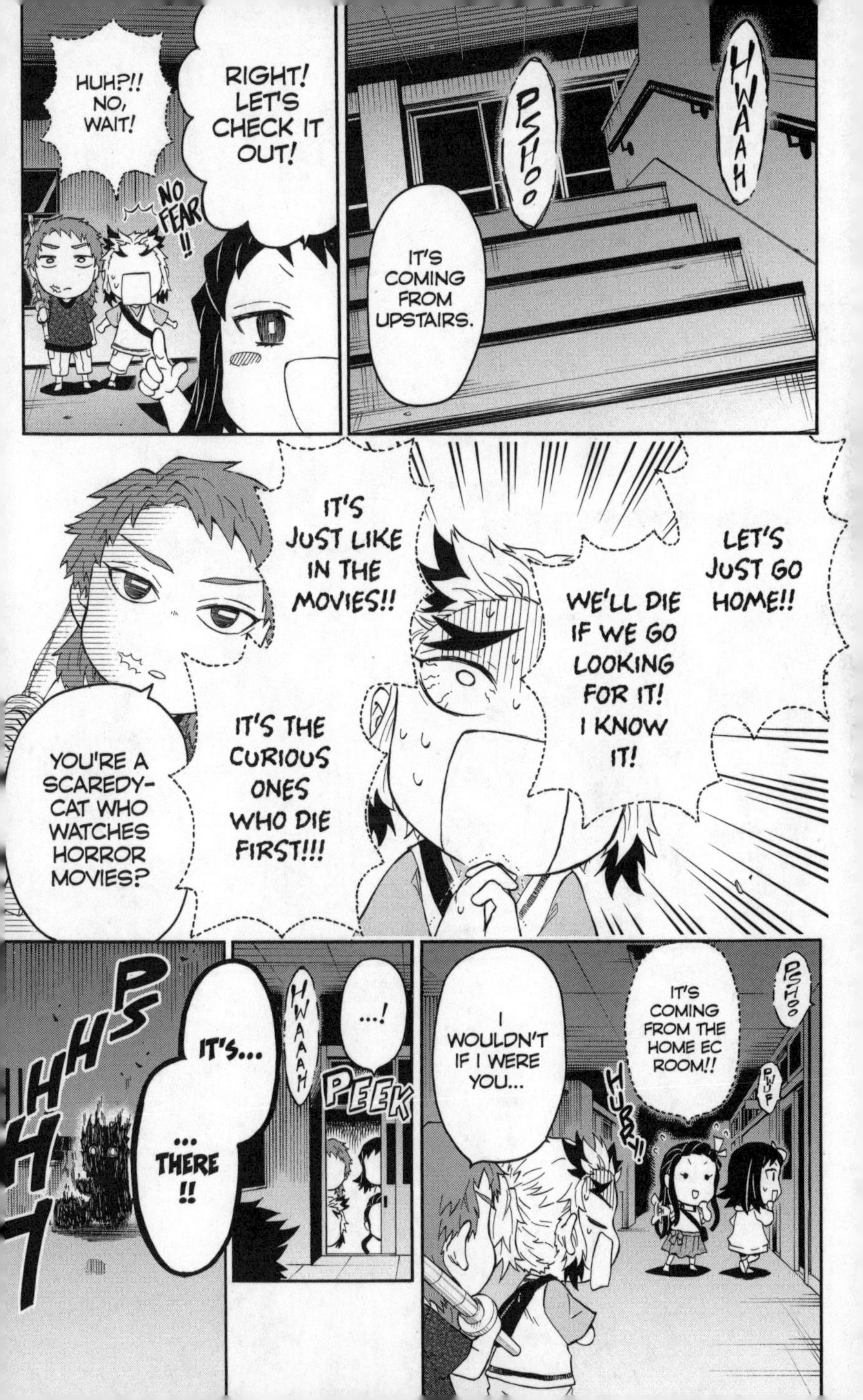
HWAAAH
PSHOO
IT'S COMING FROM UPSTAIRS.
RIGHT! LET'S CHECK IT OUT!
HUH?!! NO, WAIT!
NO FEAR!!
LET'S JUST GO HOME!!
WE'LL DIE IF WE GO LOOKING FOR IT! I KNOW IT!
IT'S JUST LIKE IN THE MOVIES!!
IT'S THE CURIOUS ONES WHO DIE FIRST!!!
YOU'RE A SCAREDY-CAT WHO WATCHES HORROR MOVIES?
PSHOO
IT'S COMING FROM THE HOME EC ROOM!!
PWUF
HURRY!!
I WOULDN'T IF I WERE YOU...
...!
HWAAAH
PEEK
IT'S...
...THERE!!
PSHHHH

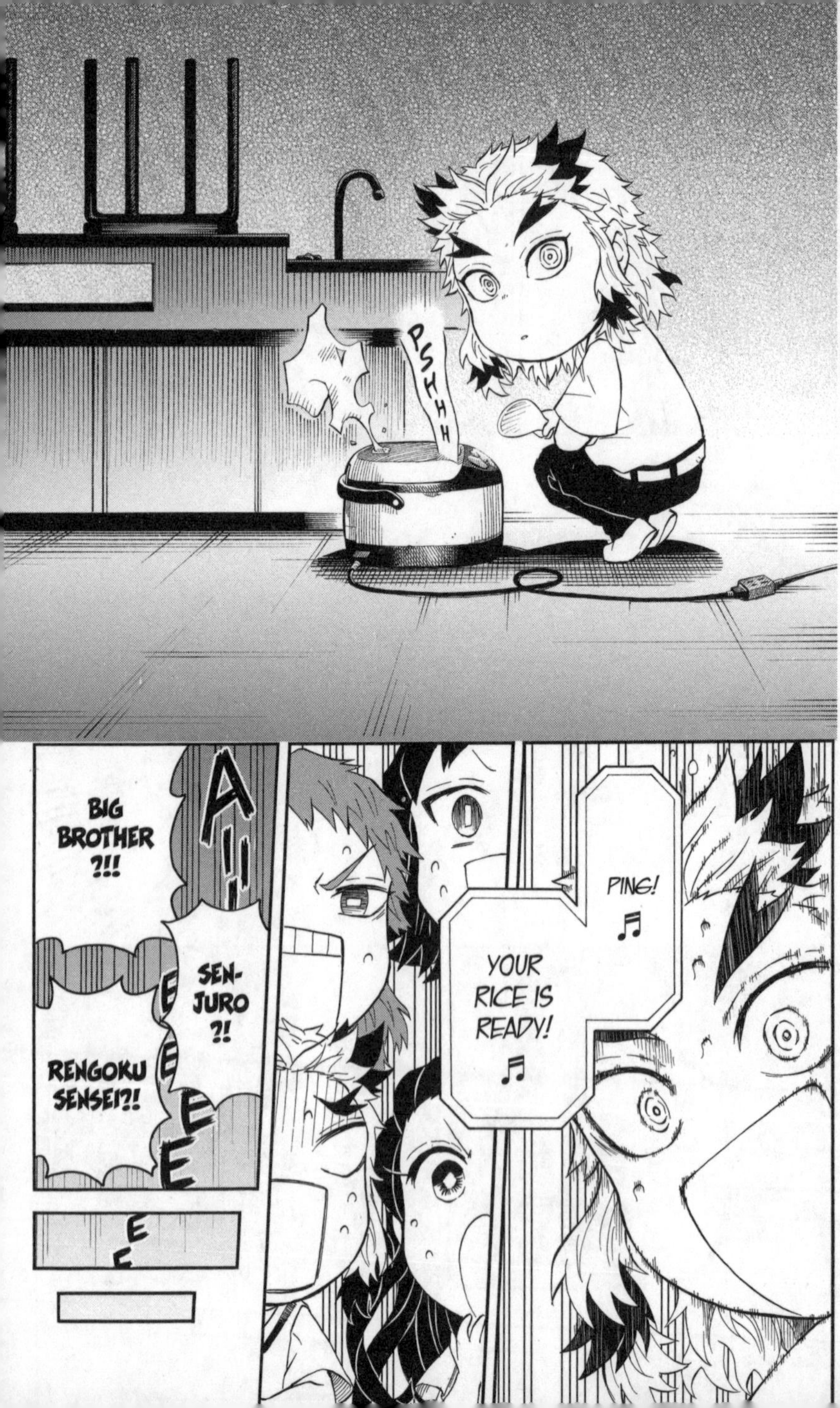
PSHHH
PING! ♬
YOUR RICE IS READY! ♬
AIIEEEEEEE
SEN-JURO?!
BIG BROTHER?!!
RENGOKU SENSEI?!
EE

OH DEAR...

KYOJURO RENGOKU
HISTORY TEACHER
(SENJURO'S OLDER BROTHER)

FWOO

YOU'RE HERE TOO, BIG BRO...

IS HE GONNA LECTURE US?!

WHAT ARE YOU DOING HERE AT THIS HOUR?!

...who reaps rice in the home ec room!

The steamy specter..

CAN I TAKE A PIC FOR THE SCHOOL PAPER?

PLEASE DON'T, YOUNG MAN!

YEP!! I'VE GOT THE MUNCHIES!

HERE FOR A LATE-NIGHT SNACK?

BUT WHY SNACK AT SCHOOL?

BASICALLY.

YOU'RE ALL TESTING YOUR COURAGE?!

ANYWAY, LEMME GUESS!

OH...

OKAY SORRY

YOU ALL NEED TO HEAD HOME!!

WHILE THAT SOUNDS FUN, I CAN'T ALLOW IT!

NEZUKO...

PSST

...AND TAKE THEM WITH YOU!!

BUT YOU CAN WAIT UNTIL I FINISH A FEW RICE BALLS...

UM... OKAY, SURE.

...LOOK.

PAT

PAT

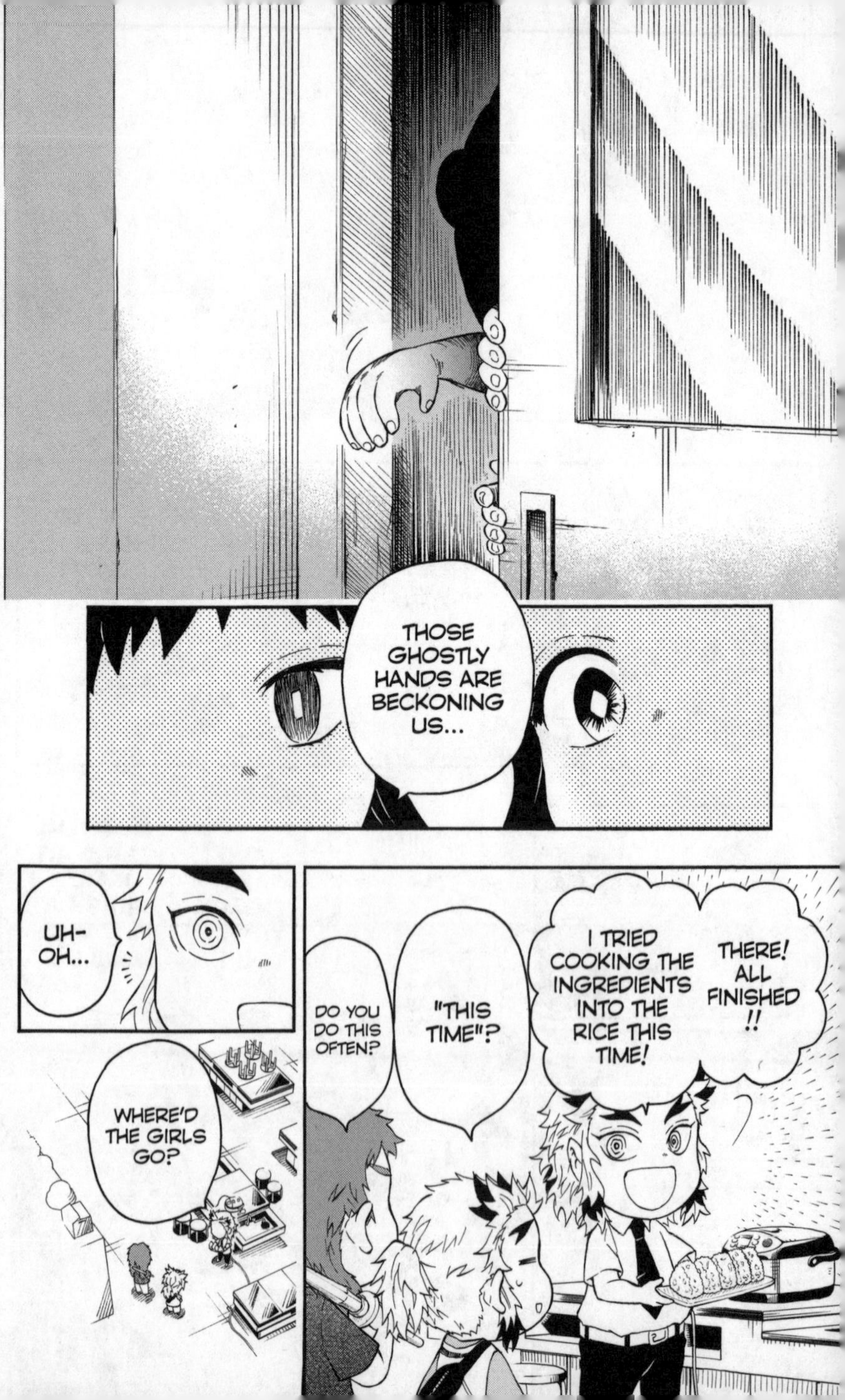
THOSE GHOSTLY HANDS ARE BECKONING US...
THERE! ALL FINISHED !!
I TRIED COOKING THE INGREDIENTS INTO THE RICE THIS TIME!
"THIS TIME"?
DO YOU DO THIS OFTEN?
UH-OH...
WHERE'D THE GIRLS GO?

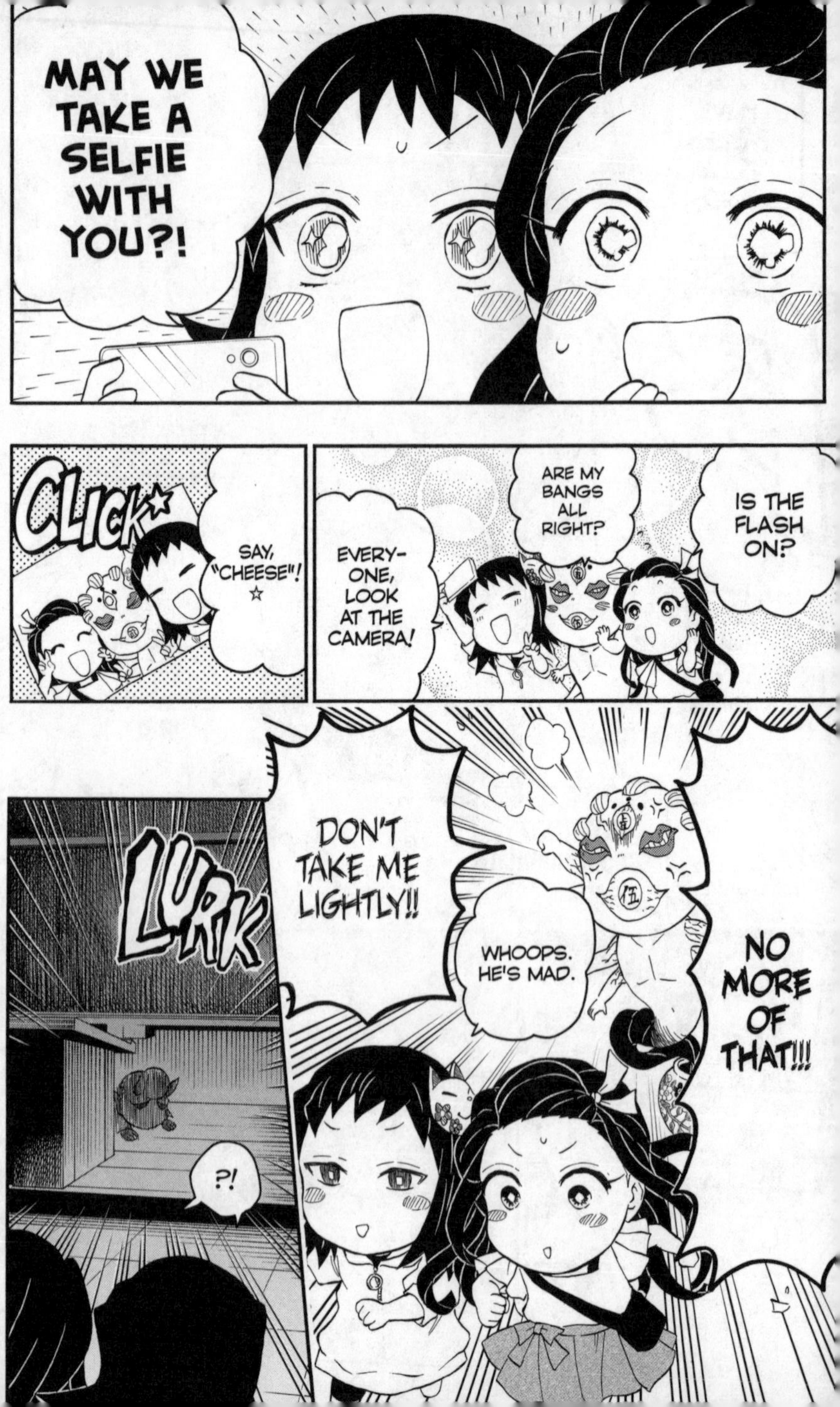
MAY WE TAKE A SELFIE WITH YOU?!
IS THE FLASH ON?
ARE MY BANGS ALL RIGHT?
EVERY-ONE, LOOK AT THE CAMERA!
SAY, "CHEESE"! ☆
CLICK☆
NO MORE OF THAT!!!
DON'T TAKE ME LIGHTLY!!
WHOOPS. HE'S MAD.
LURK
?!

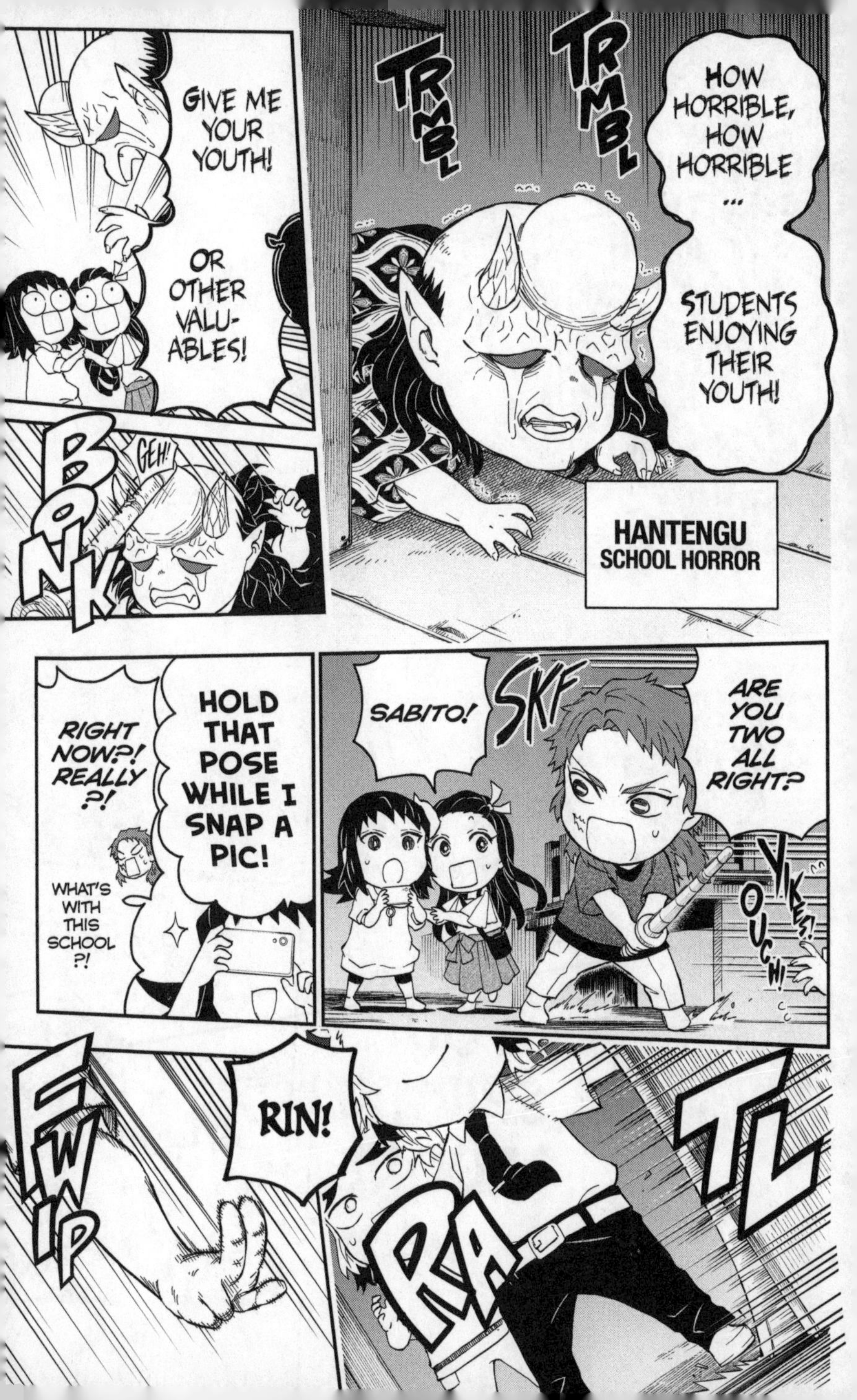
TRMBL
TRMBL
HOW HORRIBLE, HOW HORRIBLE...
STUDENTS ENJOYING THEIR YOUTH!
HANTENGU SCHOOL HORROR
GIVE ME YOUR YOUTH!
OR OTHER VALU-ABLES!
GEH!
BONK
SKF
ARE YOU TWO ALL RIGHT?
SABITO!
YIKES!
OUCH!
HOLD THAT POSE WHILE I SNAP A PIC!
RIGHT NOW?! REALLY?!
WHAT'S WITH THIS SCHOOL?!
RATL
RIN!
FWIP

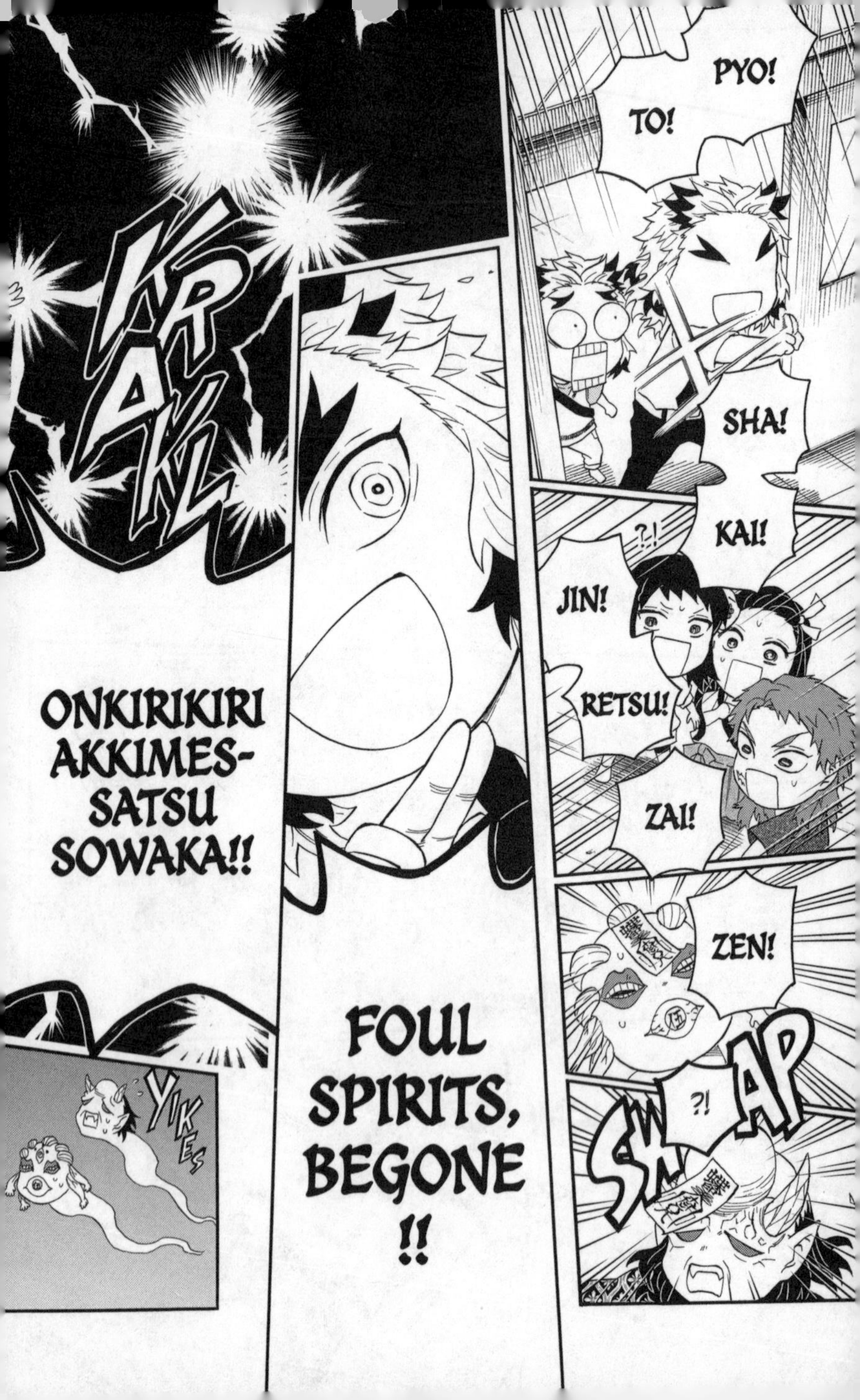

PYO!
TO!
SHA!
KAI!
?!
JIN!
RETSU!
ZAI!
ZEN!
?!
SNAP
FOUL SPIRITS, BEGONE !!
ONKIRIKIRI AKKIMES-SATSU SOWAKA!!
YIKES

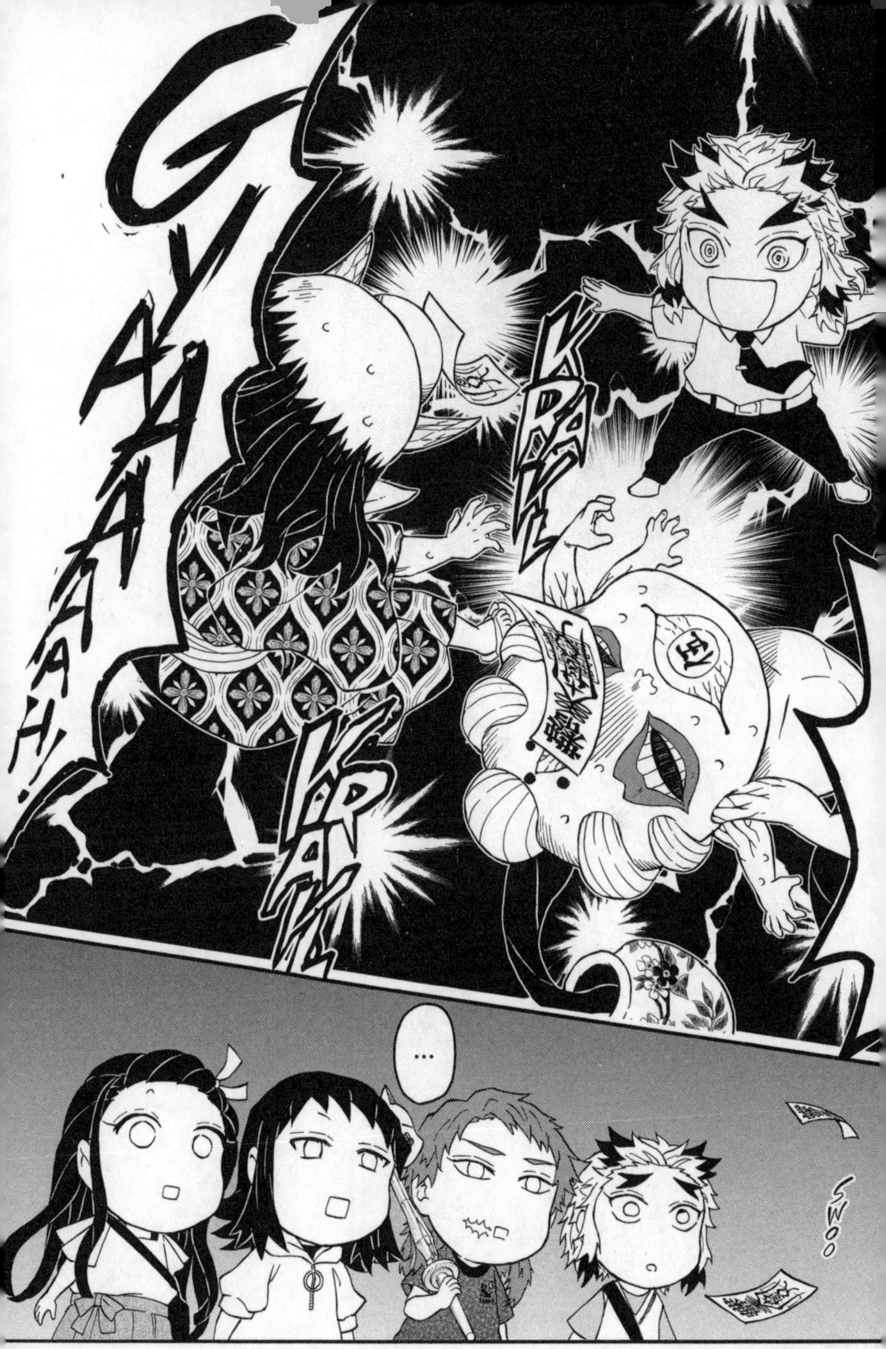
GYAAAHAHAH!!
VRAAA
VRAAA
...
SWOO

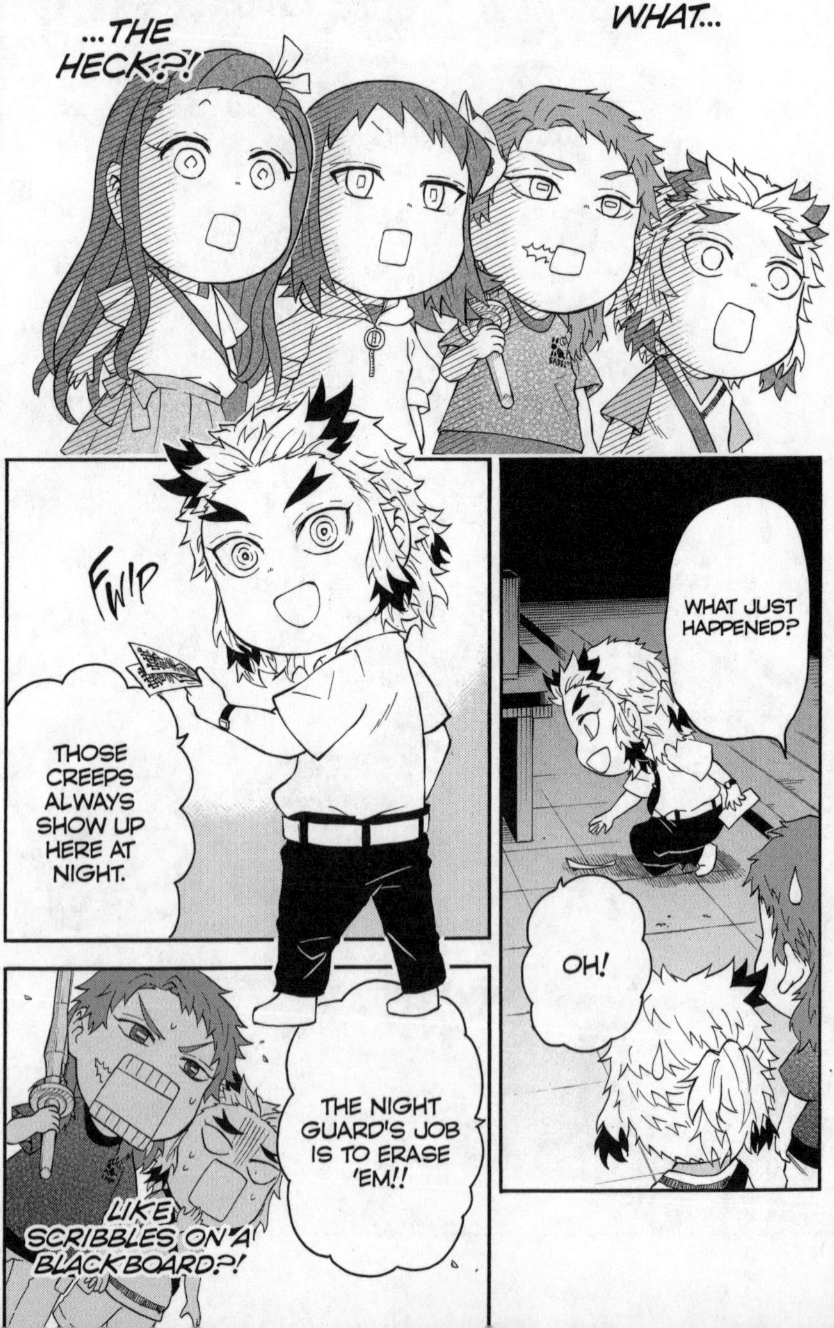
WHAT...
...THE HECK?!
WHAT JUST HAPPENED?
OH!
FWIP
THOSE CREEPS ALWAYS SHOW UP HERE AT NIGHT.
THE NIGHT GUARD'S JOB IS TO ERASE 'EM!!
LIKE SCRIBBLES ON A BLACKBOARD?!

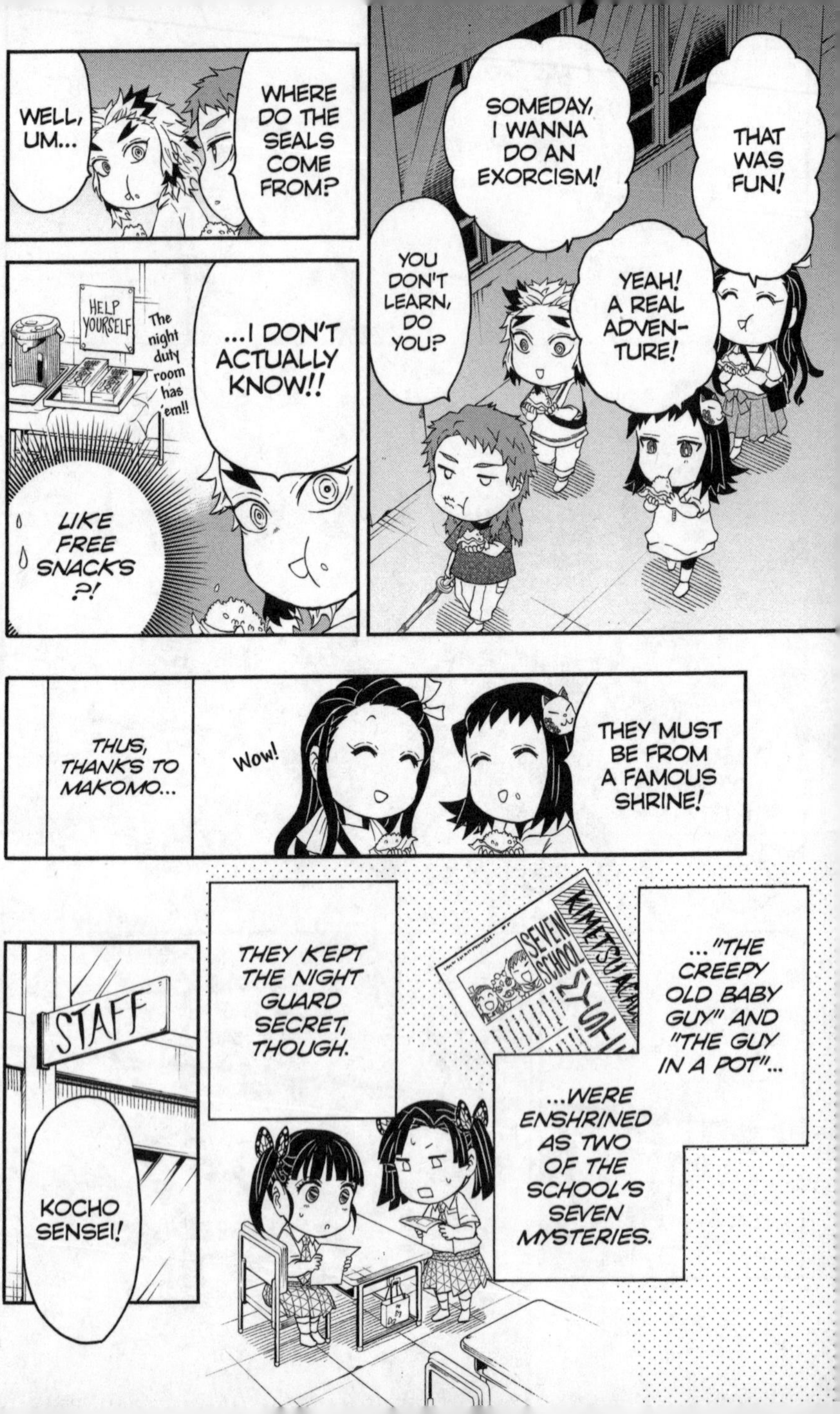
THAT WAS FUN!
SOMEDAY, I WANNA DO AN EXORCISM!
YEAH! A REAL ADVEN-TURE!
YOU DON'T LEARN, DO YOU?
WHERE DO THE SEALS COME FROM?
WELL, UM...
...I DON'T ACTUALLY KNOW!!
HELP YOURSELF
The night duty room has 'em!!
LIKE FREE SNACKS ?!
THEY MUST BE FROM A FAMOUS SHRINE!
Wow!
THUS, THANKS TO MAKOMO...
..."THE CREEPY OLD BABY GUY" AND "THE GUY IN A POT"...
...WERE ENSHRINED AS TWO OF THE SCHOOL'S SEVEN MYSTERIES.
THEY KEPT THE NIGHT GUARD SECRET, THOUGH.
STAFF
KOCHO SENSEI!

ARE YOU USING THE COPY MACHINE?

YES?

YES, I AM.

KANAE KOCHO
BIOLOGY TEACHER

...

NO, BUT...

DO YOU NEED TO USE IT?

IT BEATS WRITING THEM BY HAND!

TEE HEE!

Right?

??

THE SOURCE OF THE SEALS WAS CLOSE AT HAND.

GWOOOO

...WHAT ARE YOU COPYING?

OH, THAT?

LIFE IN TARO CLASS

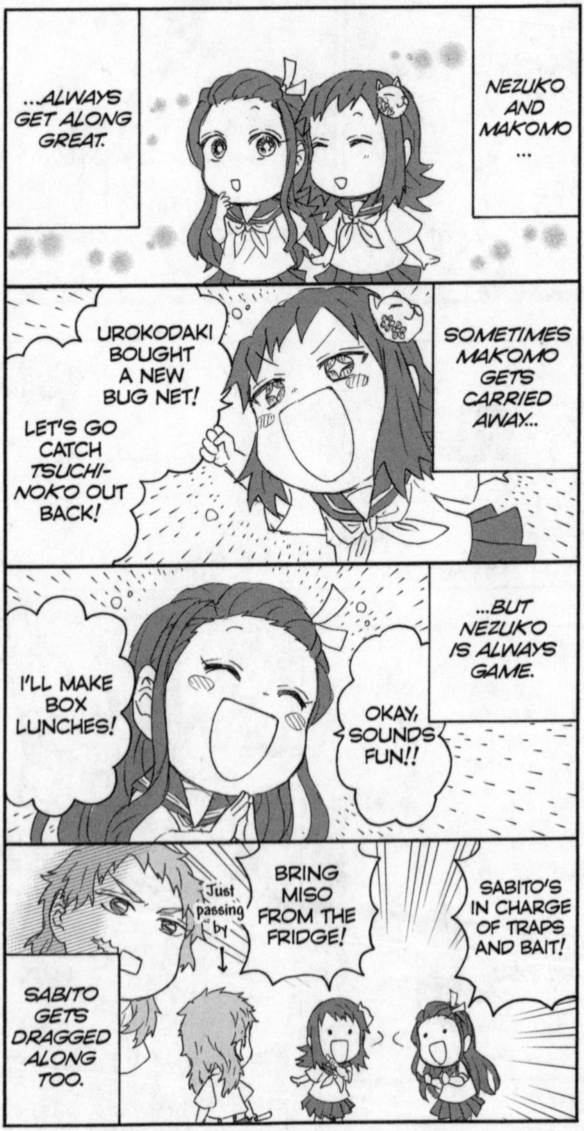
NEZUKO AND MAKOMO ...
...ALWAYS GET ALONG GREAT.
SOMETIMES MAKOMO GETS CARRIED AWAY...
UROKODAKI BOUGHT A NEW BUG NET!
LET'S GO CATCH TSUCHI-NOKO OUT BACK!
...BUT NEZUKO IS ALWAYS GAME.
OKAY, SOUNDS FUN!!
I'LL MAKE BOX LUNCHES!
SABITO'S IN CHARGE OF TRAPS AND BAIT!
BRING MISO FROM THE FRIDGE!
Just passing by
SABITO GETS DRAGGED ALONG TOO.

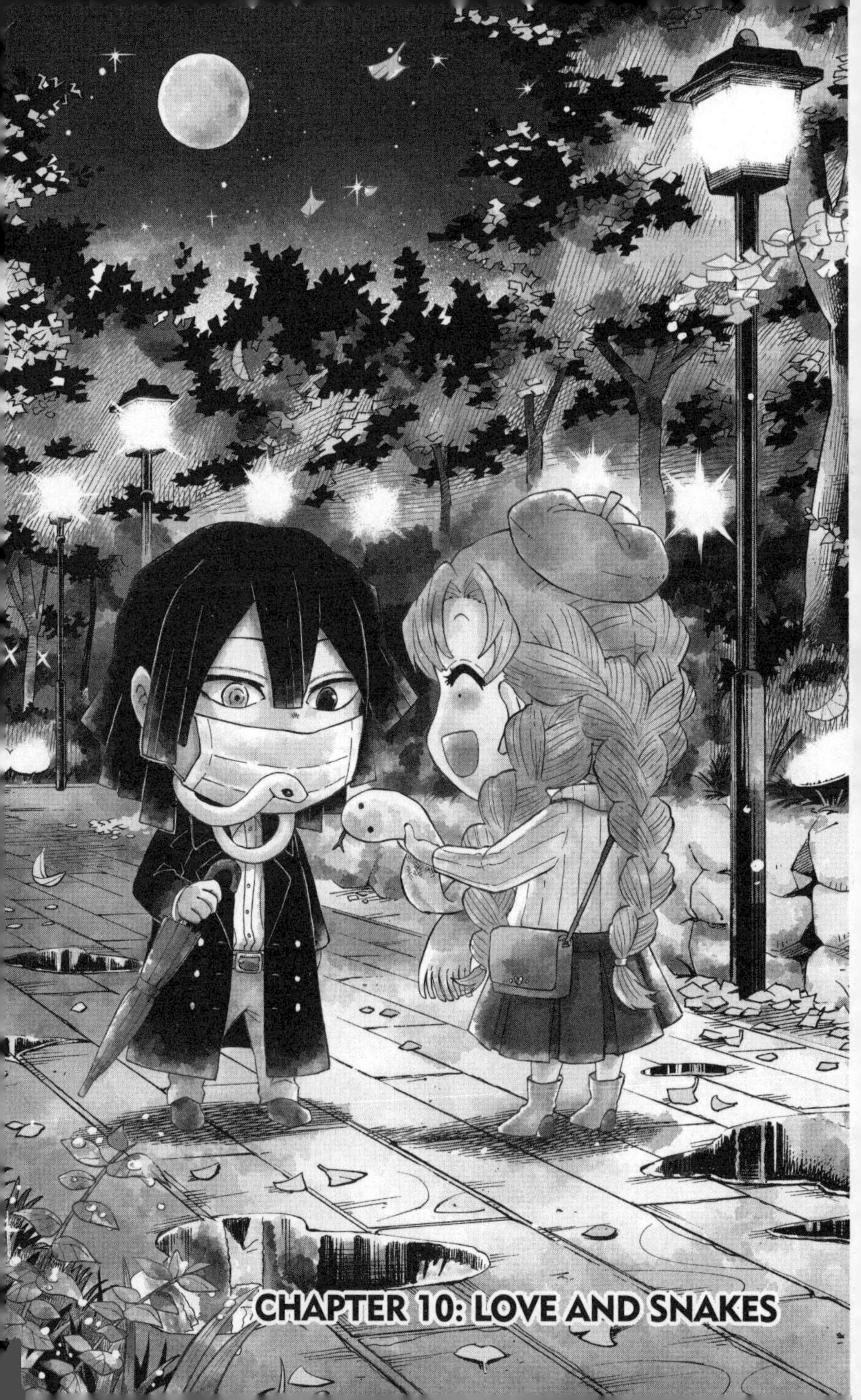

CHAPTER 10: LOVE AND SNAKES

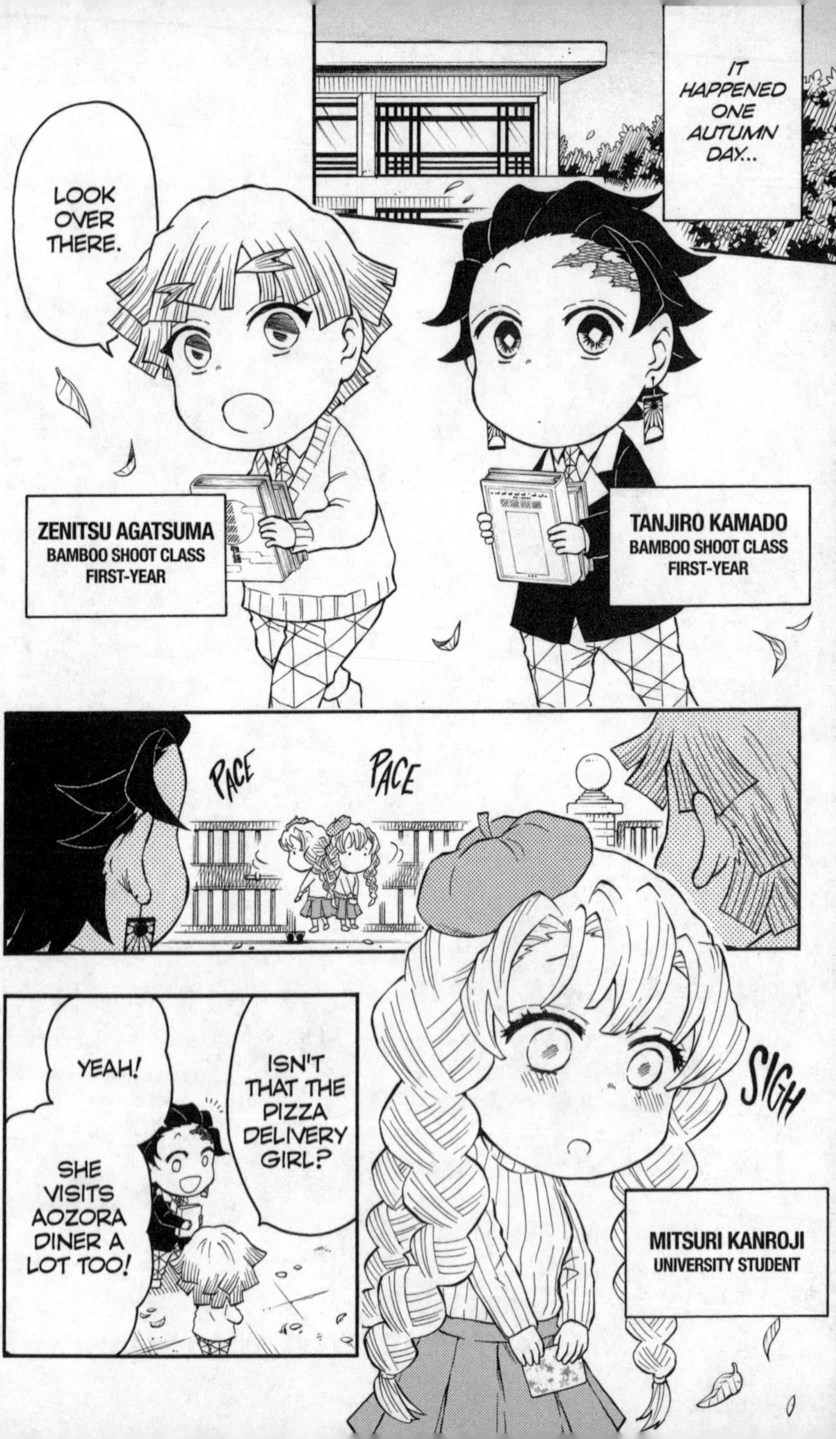
IT HAPPENED ONE AUTUMN DAY...
LOOK OVER THERE.
TANJIRO KAMADO
BAMBOO SHOOT CLASS
FIRST-YEAR
ZENITSU AGATSUMA
BAMBOO SHOOT CLASS
FIRST-YEAR
PACE
PACE
SIGH
MITSURI KANROJI
UNIVERSITY STUDENT
ISN'T THAT THE PIZZA DELIVERY GIRL?
YEAH!
SHE VISITS AOZORA DINER A LOT TOO!

AFTER ALL...

HM?

I BET SHE'LL DUMP HIM!

...THAT GUY AND KANROJI?

HE'LL PROBABLY FROTH AT THE MOUTH AND COLLAPSE!

Mask

WOMAN WOMAN

...HE'S BASICALLY ALLERGIC TO WOMEN!

HIS HEART POUNDS AND HE SWEATS BUCKETS!

Ward against women? Kaburamaru (snake)

...

ANYWAY, UM...

WELL, IT'S NOT OUR DECISION.

SO MAYBE IT'D BE BEST IF WE DIDN'T DELIVER THIS.

OBANAI IGURO
CHEMISTRY TEACHER

...THIS LETTER IS FOR YOU.

Keep that away from me!

HISSS

CHOMP

HWIP

THANK YOU FOR DELIVERING IT.

GRIP

GOOD.

?!!

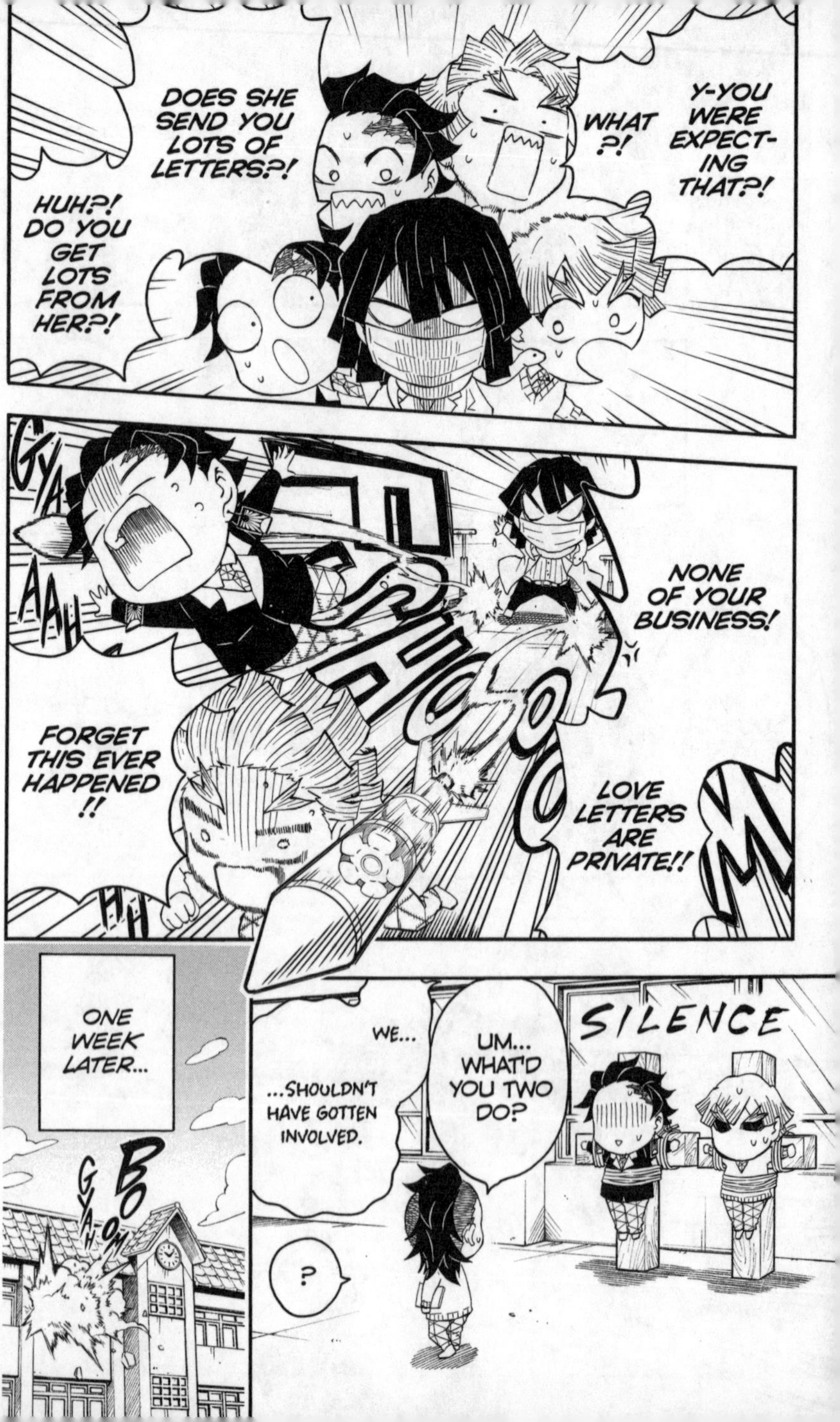
Y-YOU WERE EXPECTING THAT?!
WHAT?!
DOES SHE SEND YOU LOTS OF LETTERS?!
HUH?! DO YOU GET LOTS FROM HER?!
NONE OF YOUR BUSINESS!
LOVE LETTERS ARE PRIVATE!!
FORGET THIS EVER HAPPENED!!
SILENCE
UM... WHAT'D YOU TWO DO?
WE...
...SHOULDN'T HAVE GOTTEN INVOLVED.
?
ONE WEEK LATER...
BOOM
GYAH

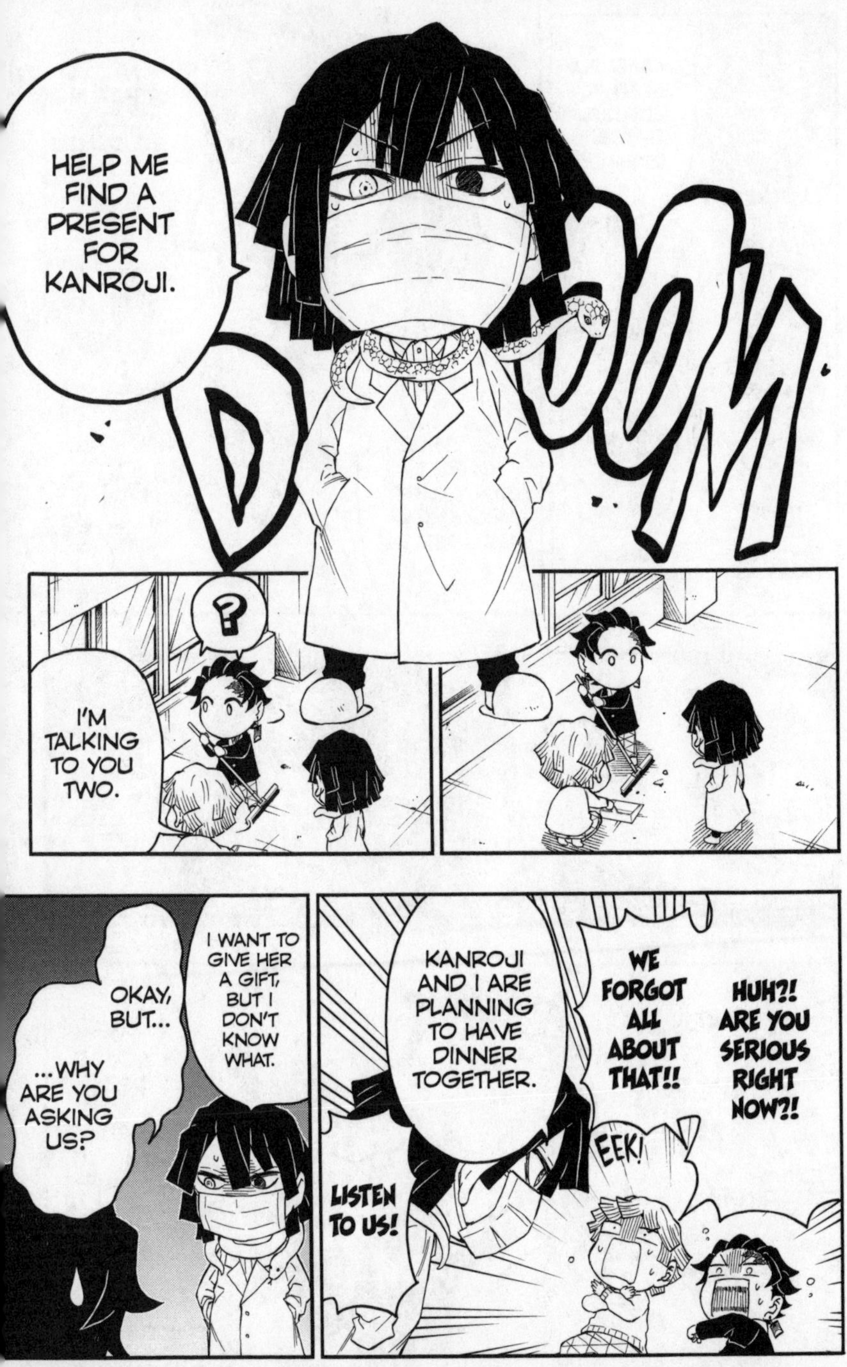
HELP ME FIND A PRESENT FOR KANROJI.
DOOOM
?
I'M TALKING TO YOU TWO.
KANROJI AND I ARE PLANNING TO HAVE DINNER TOGETHER.
HUH?! ARE YOU SERIOUS RIGHT NOW?!
WE FORGOT ALL ABOUT THAT!!
EEK!
LISTEN TO US!
I WANT TO GIVE HER A GIFT, BUT I DON'T KNOW WHAT.
OKAY, BUT...
...WHY ARE YOU ASKING US?

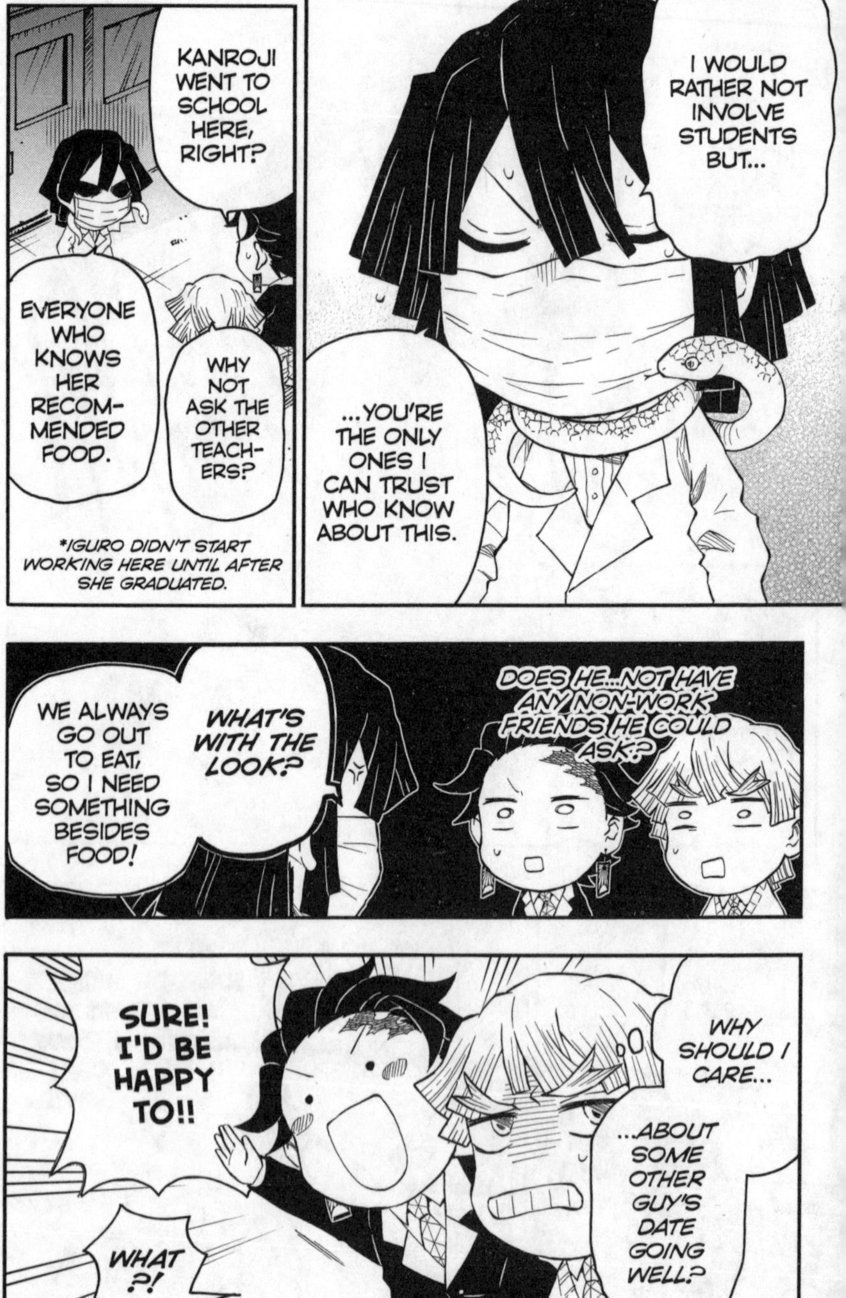
I WOULD RATHER NOT INVOLVE STUDENTS BUT...
...YOU'RE THE ONLY ONES I CAN TRUST WHO KNOW ABOUT THIS.
KANROJI WENT TO SCHOOL HERE, RIGHT?
WHY NOT ASK THE OTHER TEACHERS?
EVERYONE WHO KNOWS HER RECOMMENDED FOOD.
*IGURO DIDN'T START WORKING HERE UNTIL AFTER SHE GRADUATED.
DOES HE...NOT HAVE ANY NON-WORK FRIENDS HE COULD ASK?
WHAT'S WITH THE LOOK?
WE ALWAYS GO OUT TO EAT, SO I NEED SOMETHING BESIDES FOOD!
WHY SHOULD I CARE...
...ABOUT SOME OTHER GUY'S DATE GOING WELL?
SURE! I'D BE HAPPY TO!!
WHAT ?!

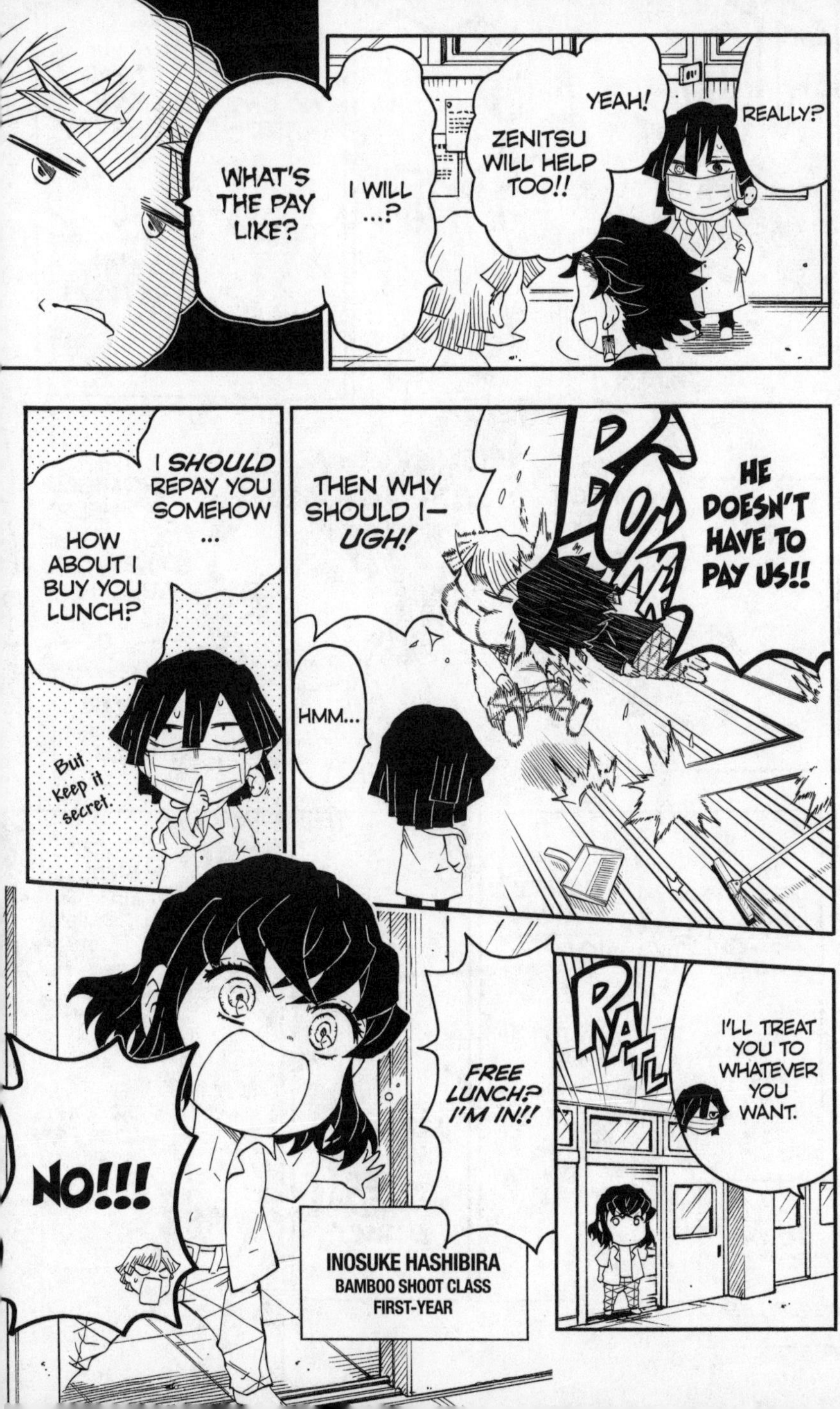
REALLY?
YEAH!
ZENITSU WILL HELP TOO!!
I WILL ...?
WHAT'S THE PAY LIKE?
HE DOESN'T HAVE TO PAY US!!
BONK
THEN WHY SHOULD I— *UGH!*
HMM...
I *SHOULD* REPAY YOU SOMEHOW ...
HOW ABOUT I BUY YOU LUNCH?
But keep it secret.
I'LL TREAT YOU TO WHATEVER YOU WANT.
RATL
FREE LUNCH? I'M IN!!
NO!!!
INOSUKE HASHIBIRA
BAMBOO SHOOT CLASS
FIRST-YEAR

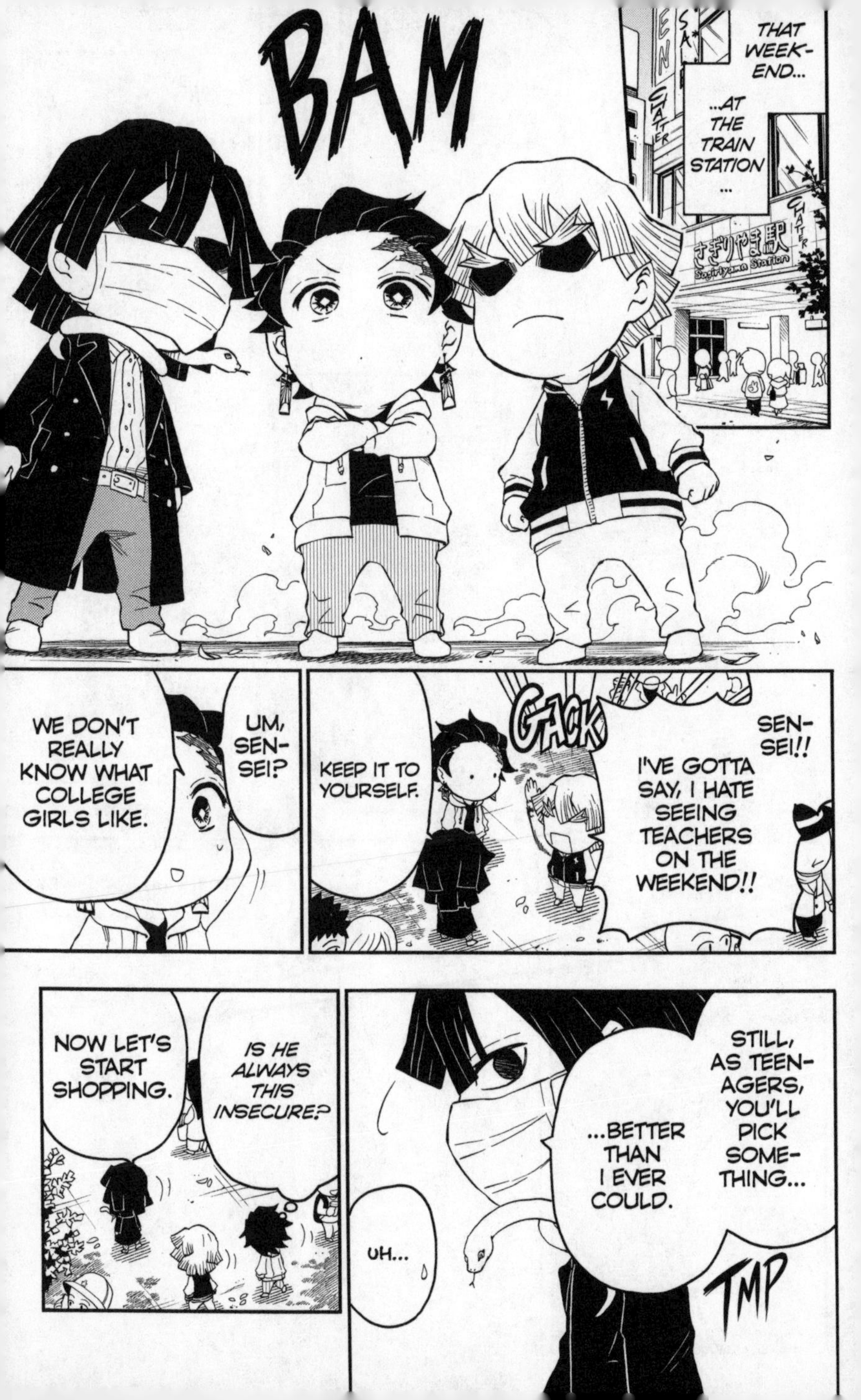

THAT WEEK-END...
...AT THE TRAIN STATION...
CHATTER
CHATTER
さぎりやま駅
Sagiriyama Station
BAM
SEN-SEI!!
I'VE GOTTA SAY, I HATE SEEING TEACHERS ON THE WEEKEND!!
GACK
KEEP IT TO YOURSELF.
UM, SEN-SEI?
WE DON'T REALLY KNOW WHAT COLLEGE GIRLS LIKE.
STILL, AS TEEN-AGERS, YOU'LL PICK SOME-THING...
...BETTER THAN I EVER COULD.
UH...
TMP
IS HE ALWAYS THIS INSECURE?
NOW LET'S START SHOPPING.

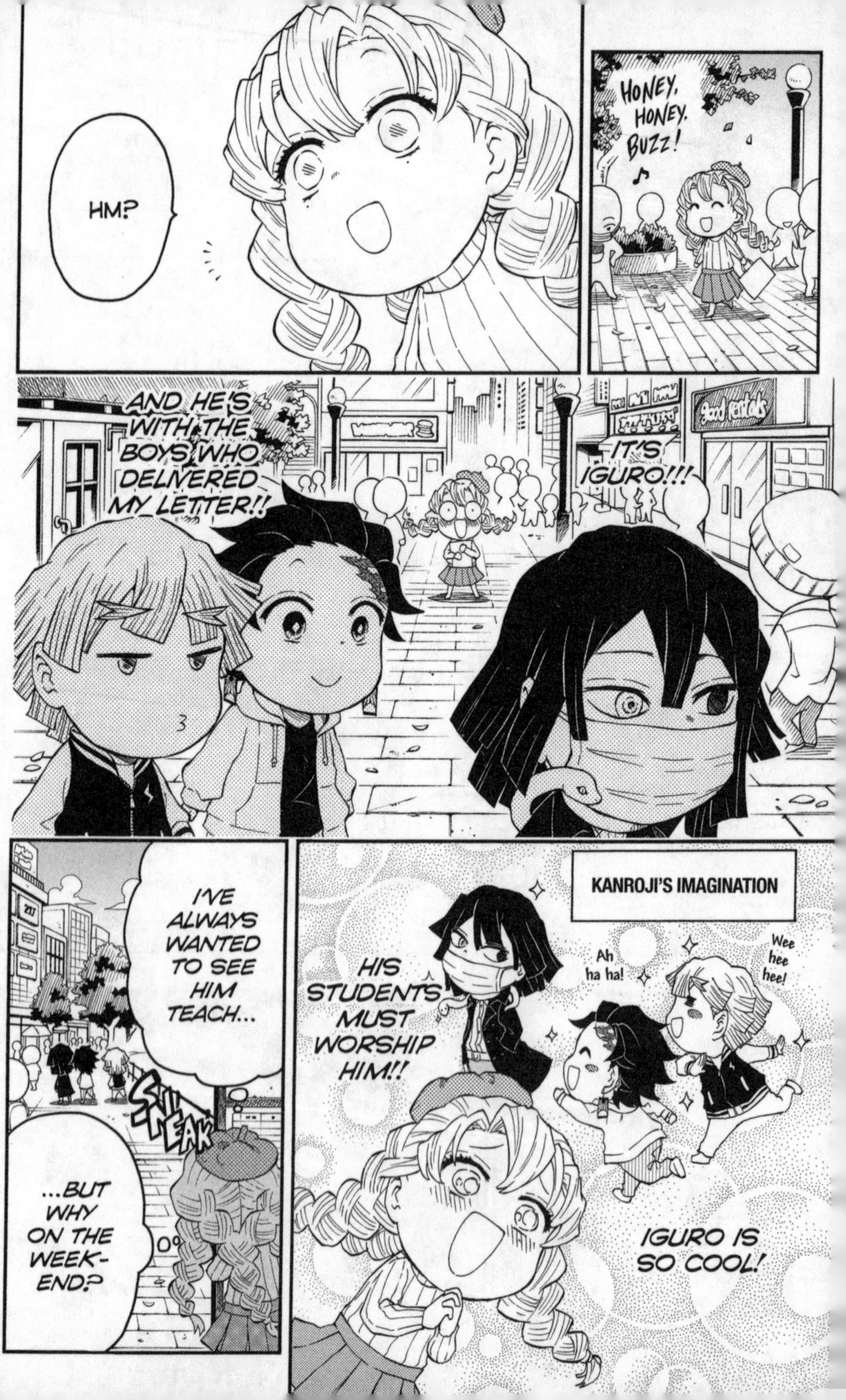
HONEY, HONEY, BUZZ! ♪
HM?
IT'S IGURO!!!
AND HE'S WITH THE BOYS WHO DELIVERED MY LETTER!!
KANROJI'S IMAGINATION
Wee hee hee!
Ah ha ha!
HIS STUDENTS MUST WORSHIP HIM!!
IGURO IS SO COOL!
I'VE ALWAYS WANTED TO SEE HIM TEACH...
SNEAK
...BUT WHY ON THE WEEK-END?

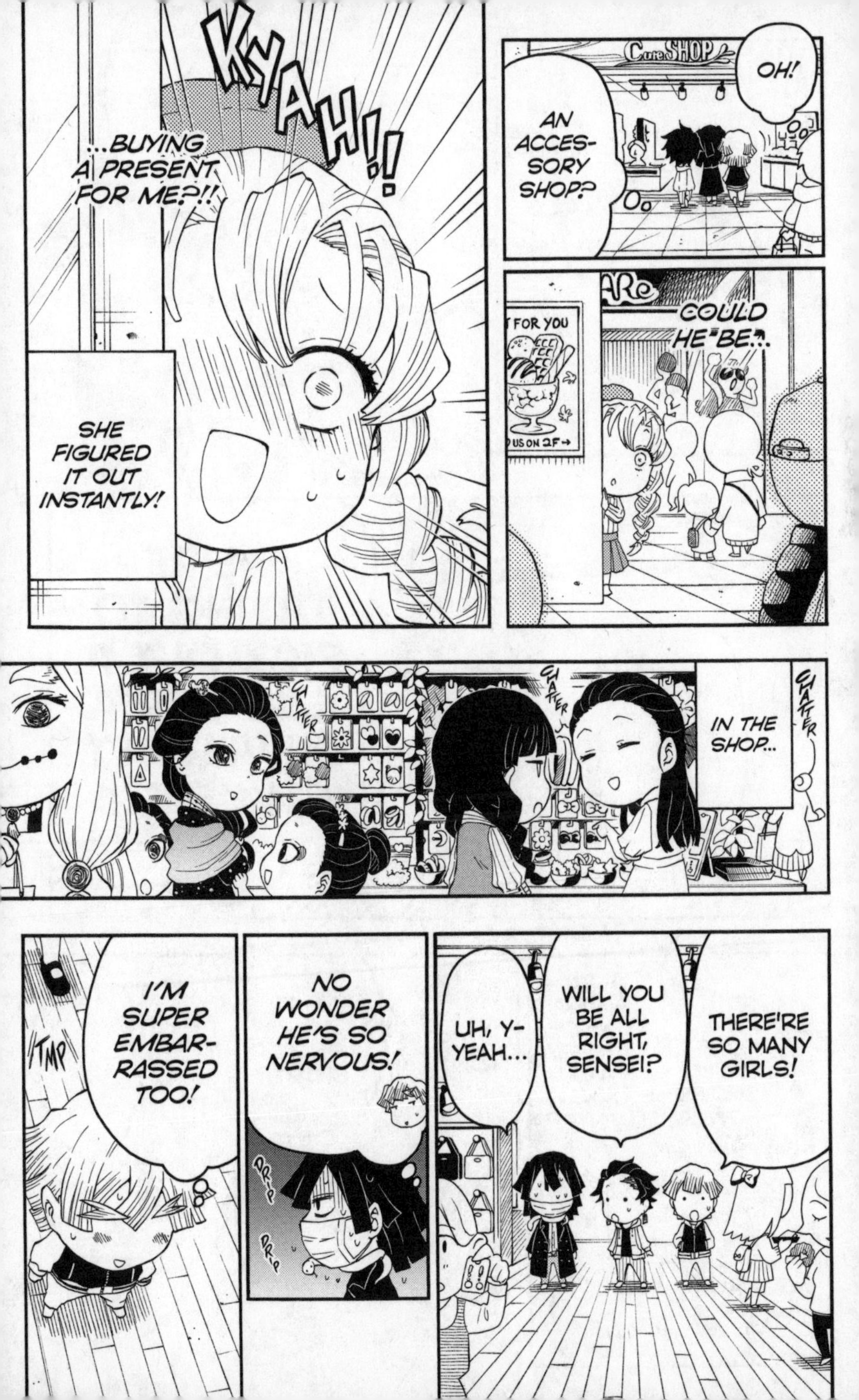
Cute SHOP
OH!
AN ACCES-SORY SHOP?
COULD HE BE...
FOR YOU
US ON 2F →
KYAH!!
...BUYING A PRESENT FOR ME?!!
SHE FIGURED IT OUT INSTANTLY!
CHATTER
IN THE SHOP...
CHATTER
CHATTER
THERE'RE SO MANY GIRLS!
WILL YOU BE ALL RIGHT, SENSEI?
UH, Y-YEAH...
NO WONDER HE'S SO NERVOUS!
DRIP
DRIP
I'M SUPER EMBAR-RASSED TOO!
TMP

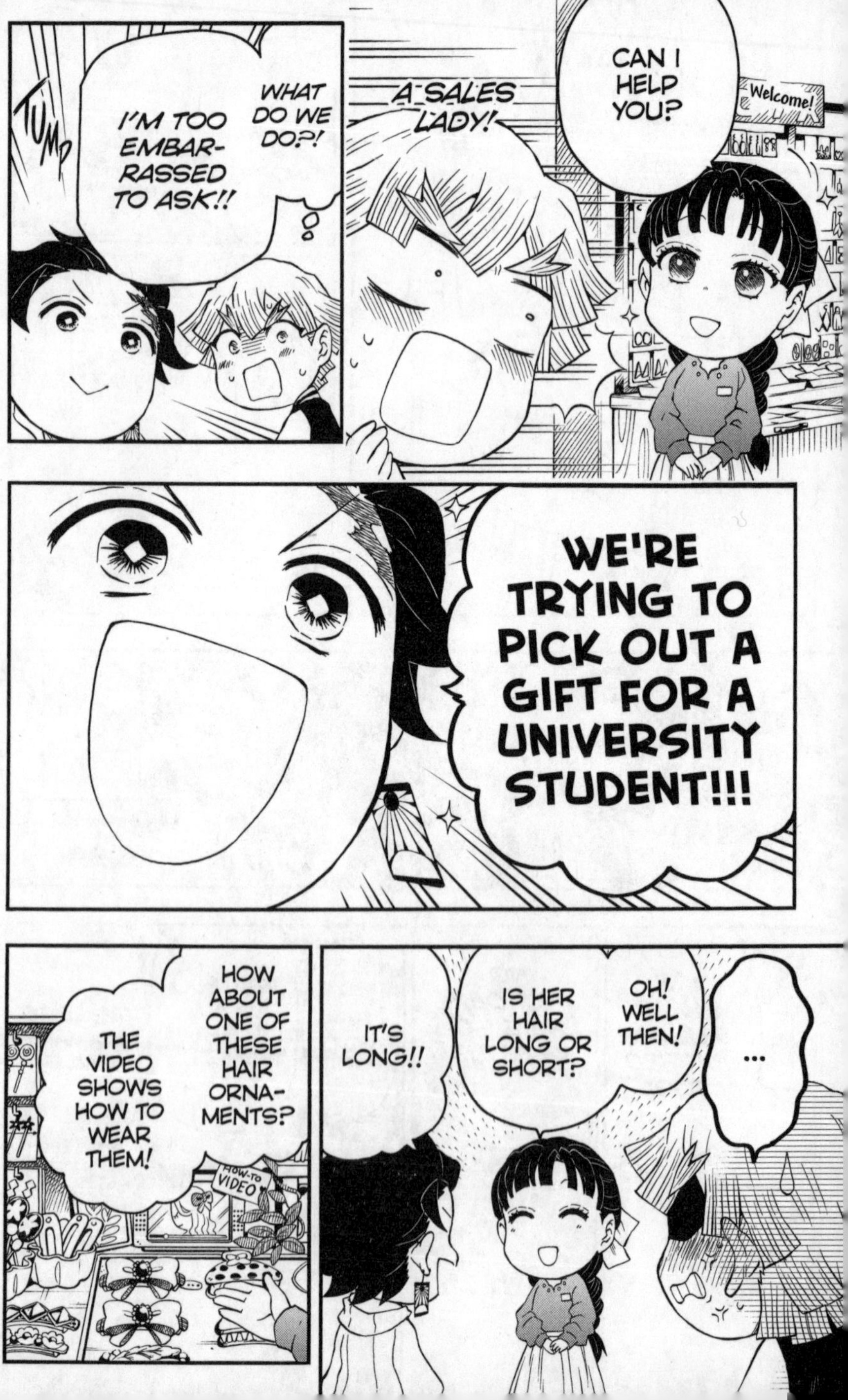
CAN I HELP YOU?
Welcome!
A SALES LADY!
WHAT DO WE DO?!
I'M TOO EMBARRASSED TO ASK!!
TUMP
WE'RE TRYING TO PICK OUT A GIFT FOR A UNIVERSITY STUDENT!!!
...
OH! WELL THEN!
IS HER HAIR LONG OR SHORT?
IT'S LONG!!
HOW ABOUT ONE OF THESE HAIR ORNAMENTS?
THE VIDEO SHOWS HOW TO WEAR THEM!
HOW-TO VIDEO

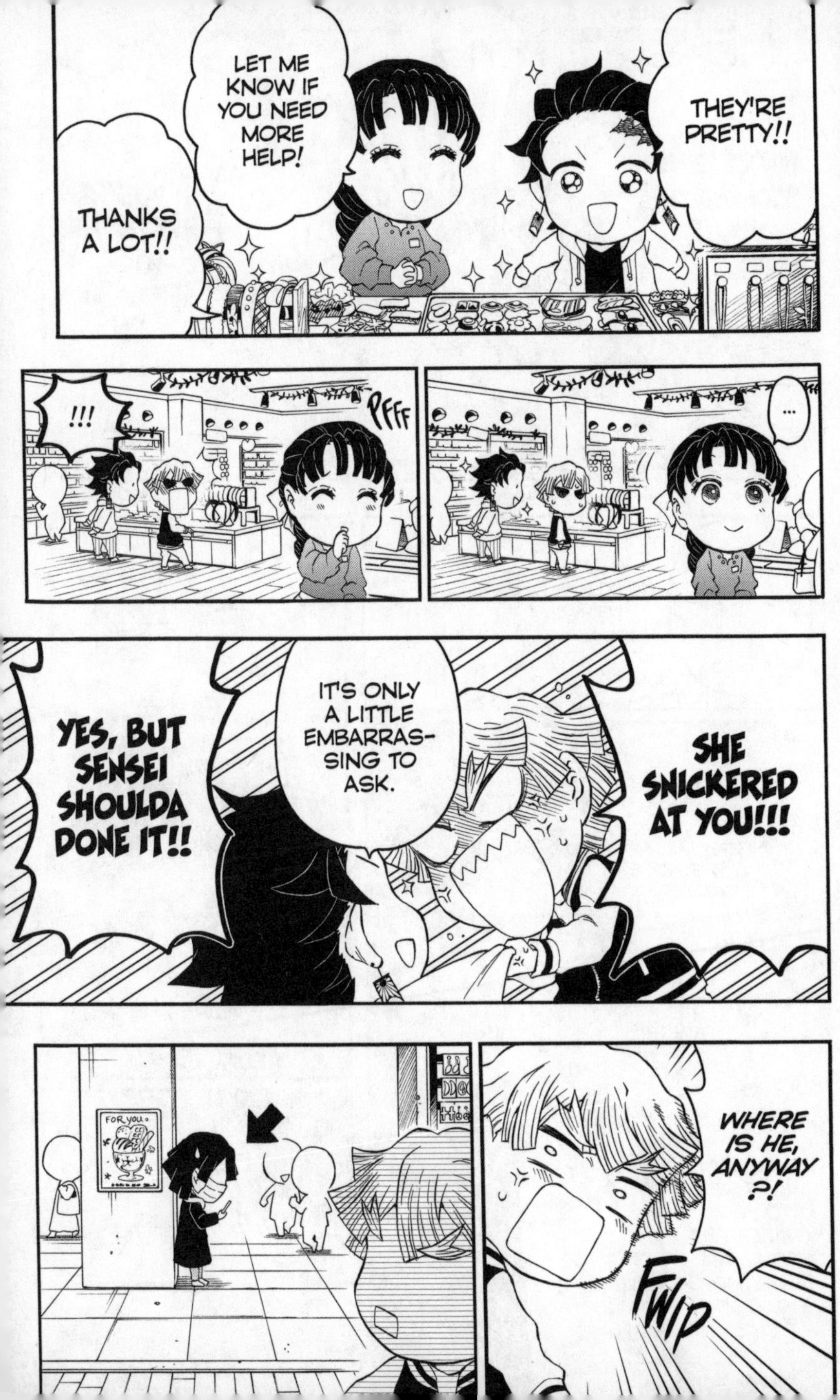
THEY'RE PRETTY!!
LET ME KNOW IF YOU NEED MORE HELP!
THANKS A LOT!!
...
PFFF
!!!
SHE SNICKERED AT YOU!!!
IT'S ONLY A LITTLE EMBARRAS-SING TO ASK.
YES, BUT SENSEI SHOULDA DONE IT!!
WHERE IS HE, ANYWAY?!
FWIP
FOR YOU.

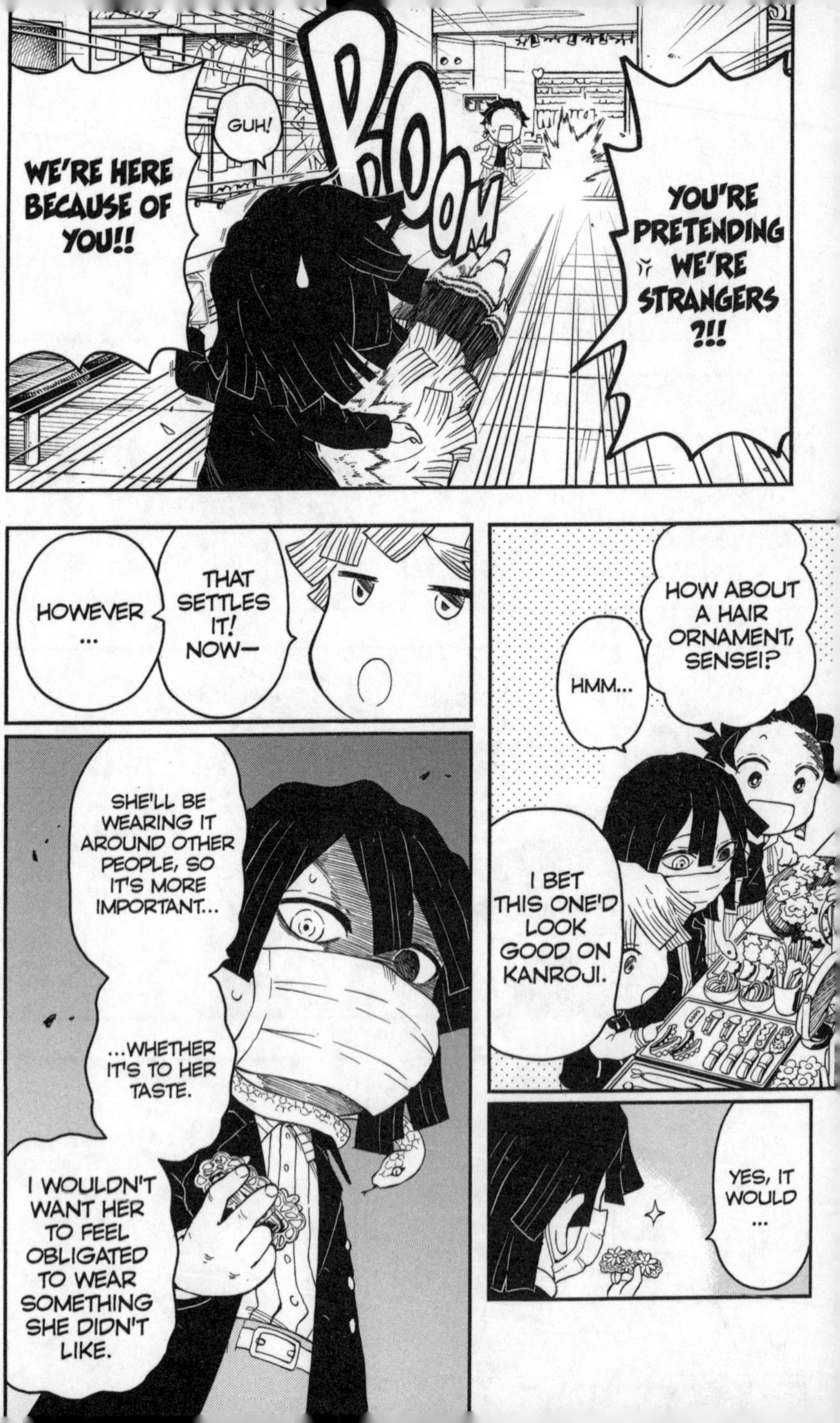
YOU'RE PRETENDING WE'RE STRANGERS ?!!
GUH!
WE'RE HERE BECAUSE OF YOU!!
HOW ABOUT A HAIR ORNAMENT, SENSEI?
HMM...
I BET THIS ONE'D LOOK GOOD ON KANROJI.
YES, IT WOULD ...
THAT SETTLES IT! NOW—
HOWEVER ...
SHE'LL BE WEARING IT AROUND OTHER PEOPLE, SO IT'S MORE IMPORTANT...
...WHETHER IT'S TO HER TASTE.
I WOULDN'T WANT HER TO FEEL OBLIGATED TO WEAR SOMETHING SHE DIDN'T LIKE.

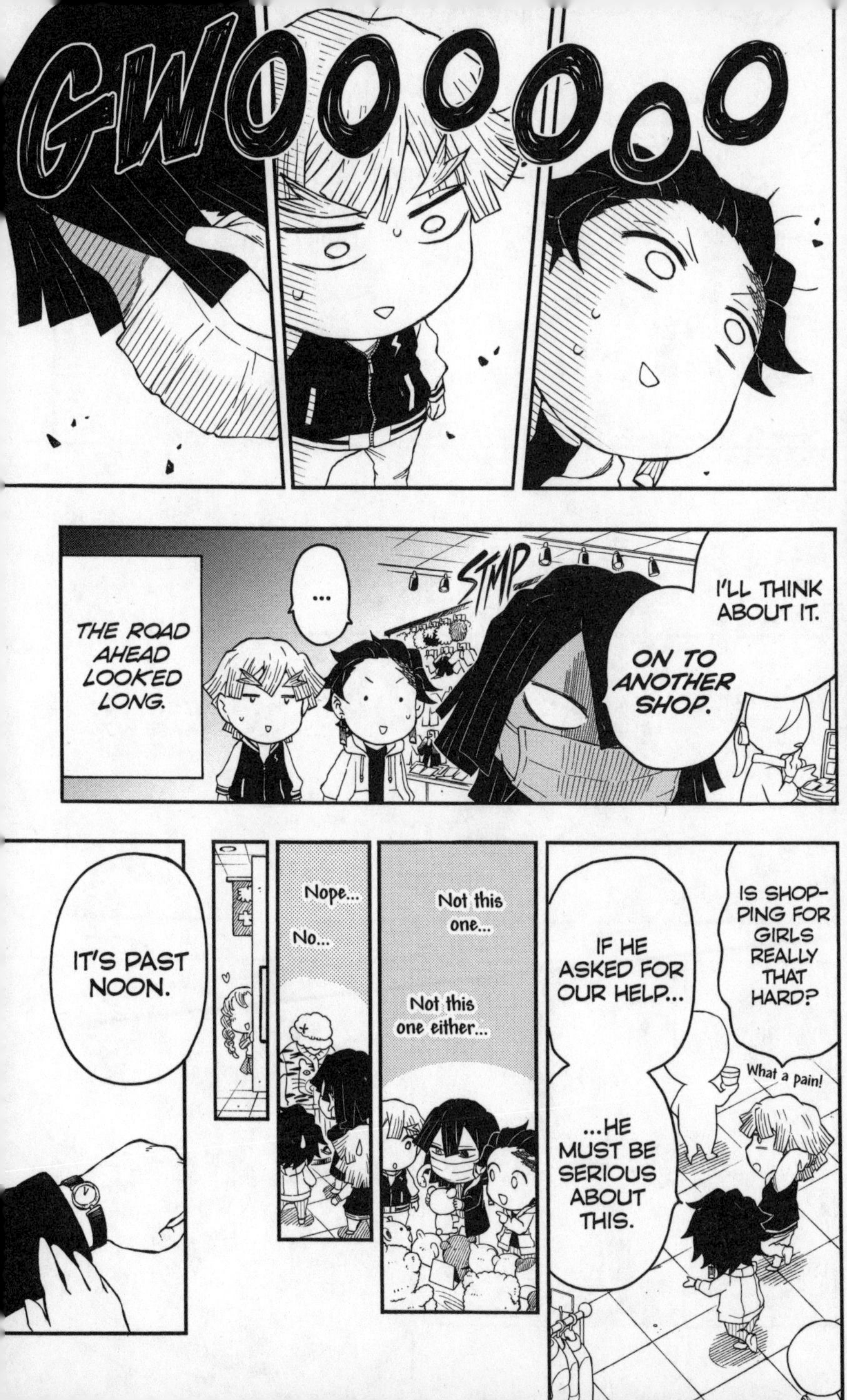
GWOOOOOOO
I'LL THINK ABOUT IT.
ON TO ANOTHER SHOP.
STMP
...
THE ROAD AHEAD LOOKED LONG.
IS SHOP-PING FOR GIRLS REALLY THAT HARD?
What a pain!
IF HE ASKED FOR OUR HELP...
...HE MUST BE SERIOUS ABOUT THIS.
Not this one...
Not this one either...
Nope...
No...
IT'S PAST NOON.

WE HAVEN'T MADE ANY PROGRESS ALL MORNING!

ARE YOU EVEN TRYING ?!

SHALL WE BREAK FOR LUNCH?

I'LL DECIDE THIS AFTERNOON.

Welcome!

HONESTLY, I PREFER FINER DINING...

DOES THIS PLACE WORK FOR YOU?

YEAH! THE MENU'S GOT VARIETY!

WHOA

LET'S DIG IN!!

MNCH NOM MNCH NOM

HERE YOU GO!

HAMBURGER STEAK, GRILLED EEL, AND FRIED CHICKEN!

...!!

NO WAY! IT'S HIDEOUS!

YEAH!! MY BOO BOUGHT THIS BAG FOR ME!!

REALLY, HEBIKO?!

GUY'S GOT NO FASHION SENSE! WA HA HA!

BWA HA HA

DON'T WORRY.

UM, IGURO SENSEI?

HM?

I'M FINE.

KANROJI ISN'T LIKE THAT.

DO THEY HAVE TO BE...

...SO LOUD?

HE EVEN SAID HE SPENT ALL DAY PICKING IT OUT!!

EW! CREEPY!!

TITTER TITTER GIGGLE GIGGLE GUFFAW

...

Thanks for coming in!

FAMILY RESTAURANT

WELL, IF YOU'RE SURE...

NO, NOT AT ALL!!!

HM...

BUT... AM I CREEPY TOO?

...some eats!

I love me...

WHAT KANROJI LIKES IS OBVIOUS...

...SO I SHOULD GET HER SOMETHING SWEET.

NO...

YOU'RE DOING FINE!!

...I'M OVER-THINKING THINGS.

GLASSES

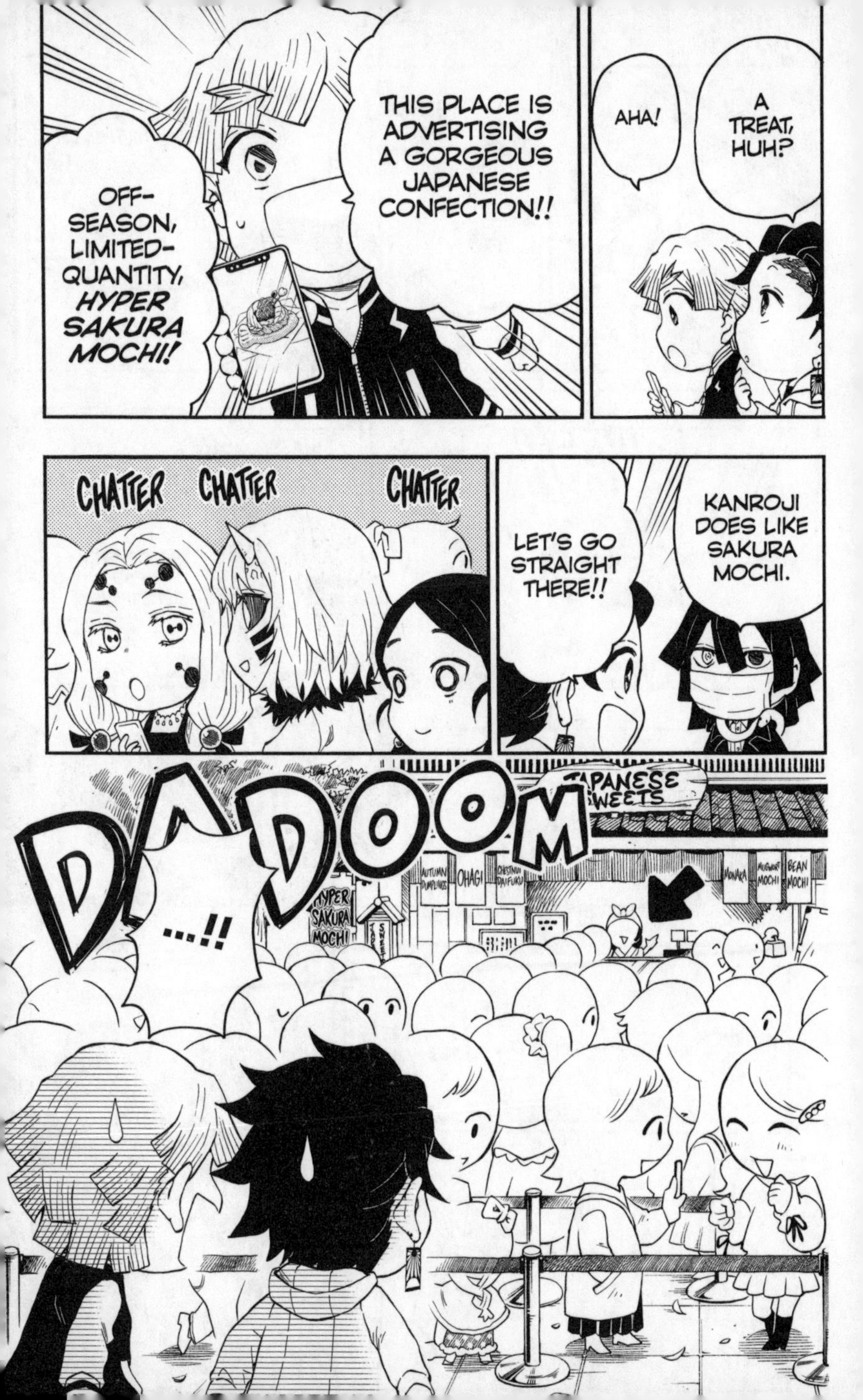
A TREAT, HUH?
AHA!
THIS PLACE IS ADVERTISING A GORGEOUS JAPANESE CONFECTION!!
OFF-SEASON, LIMITED-QUANTITY, HYPER SAKURA MOCHI!
KANROJI DOES LIKE SAKURA MOCHI.
LET'S GO STRAIGHT THERE!!
CHATTER
CHATTER
CHATTER
JAPANESE SWEETS
BEAN MOCHI
MUGWORT MOCHI
MONAKA
CHESTNUT DAIFUKU
OHAGI
AUTUMN DUMPLINGS
HYPER SAKURA MOCHI
DADOOM
...!!

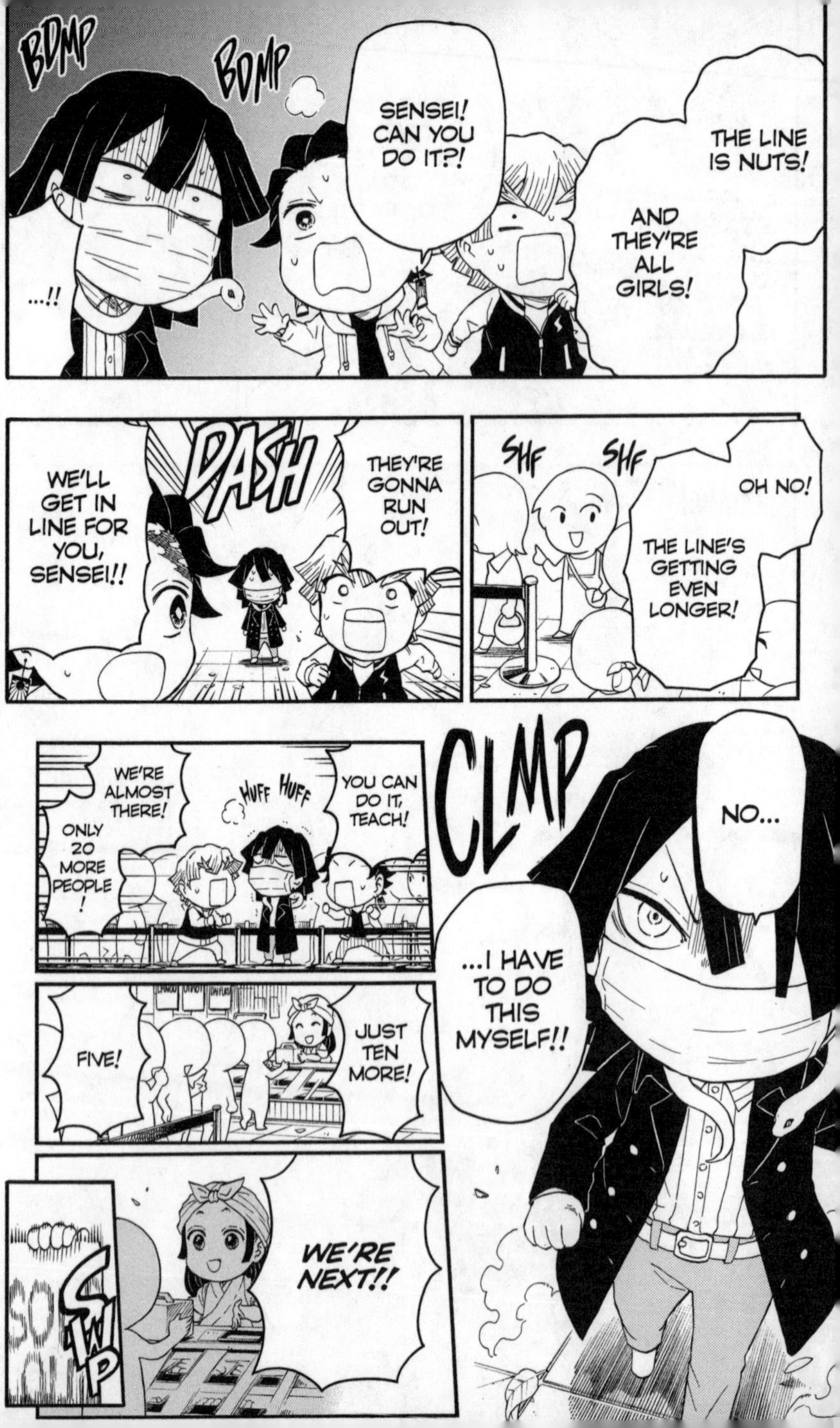
THE LINE IS NUTS!
AND THEY'RE ALL GIRLS!
SENSEI! CAN YOU DO IT?!
BDMP
BDMP
...!!
SHF SHF
OH NO!
THE LINE'S GETTING EVEN LONGER!
THEY'RE GONNA RUN OUT!
DASH
WE'LL GET IN LINE FOR YOU, SENSEI!!
CLMP
NO...
...I HAVE TO DO THIS MYSELF!!
YOU CAN DO IT, TEACH!
HUFF HUFF
WE'RE ALMOST THERE!
ONLY 20 MORE PEOPLE!
JUST TEN MORE!
FIVE!
WE'RE NEXT!!
SWP

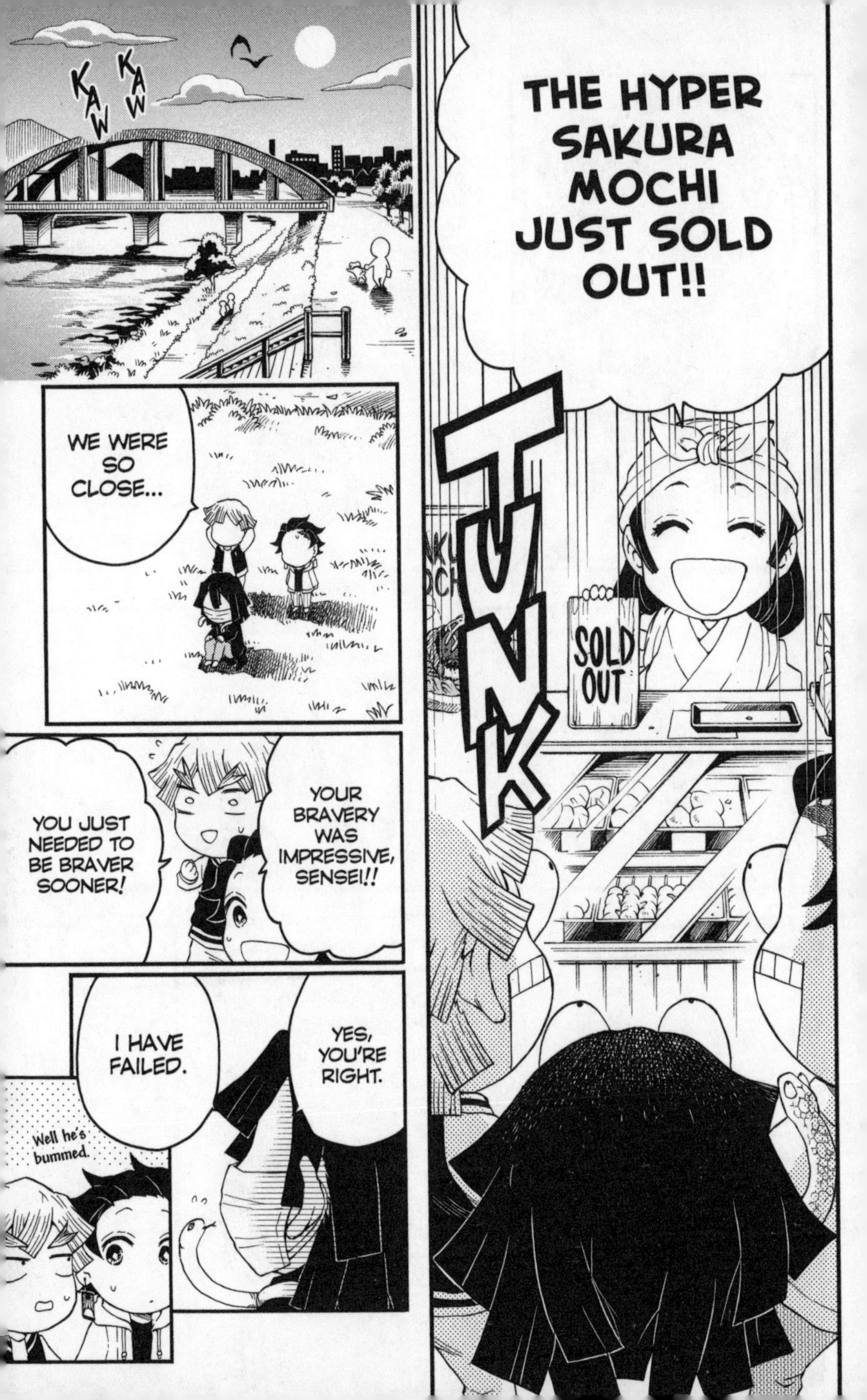
THE HYPER SAKURA MOCHI JUST SOLD OUT!!
TUNK
SOLD OUT
KAW KAW
WE WERE SO CLOSE...
YOUR BRAVERY WAS IMPRESSIVE, SENSEI!!
YOU JUST NEEDED TO BE BRAVER SOONER!
YES, YOU'RE RIGHT.
I HAVE FAILED.
Well he's bummed.

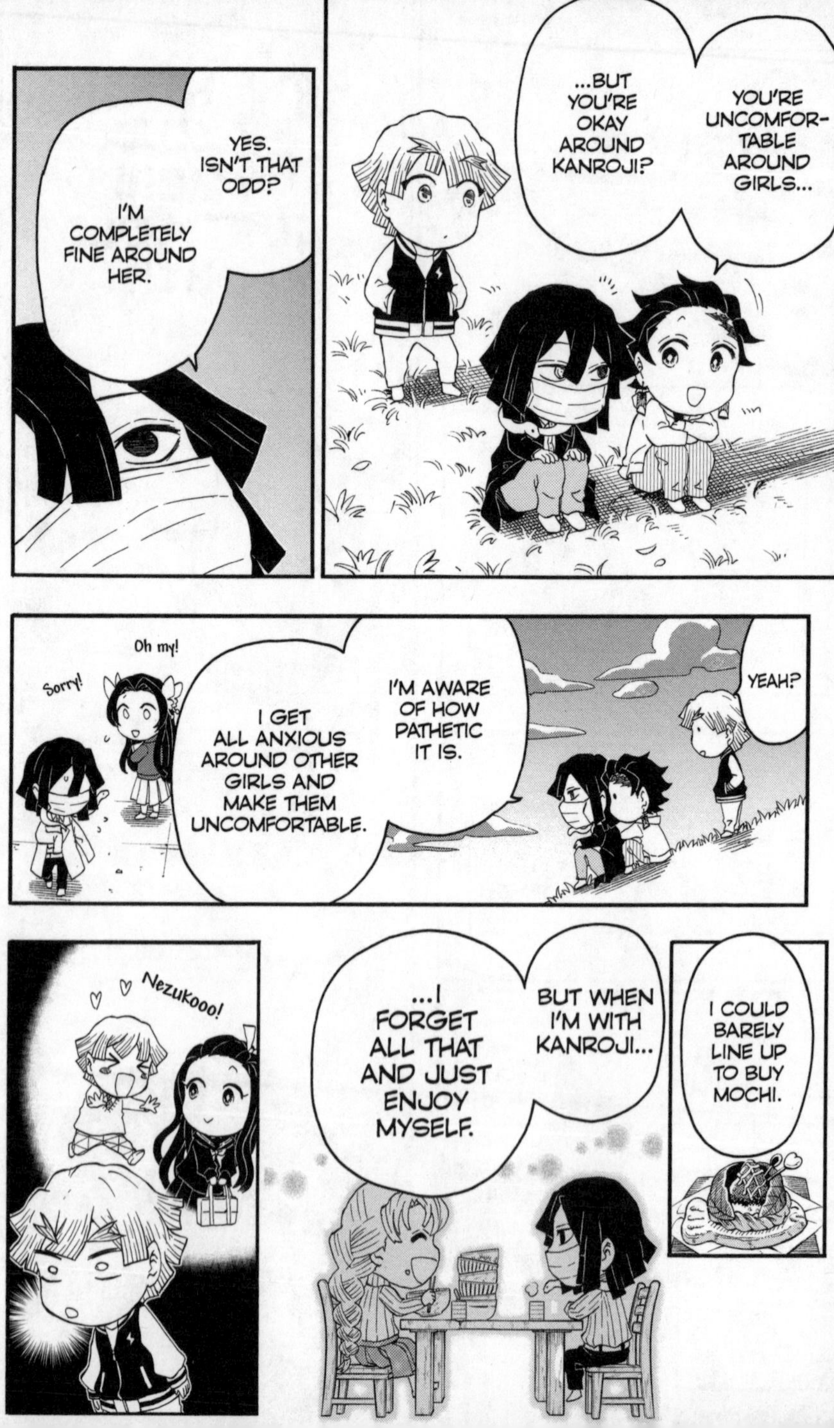
YOU'RE UNCOMFORTABLE AROUND GIRLS...
...BUT YOU'RE OKAY AROUND KANROJI?
YES. ISN'T THAT ODD?
I'M COMPLETELY FINE AROUND HER.
YEAH?
I'M AWARE OF HOW PATHETIC IT IS.
I GET ALL ANXIOUS AROUND OTHER GIRLS AND MAKE THEM UNCOMFORTABLE.
Oh my!
Sorry!
I COULD BARELY LINE UP TO BUY MOCHI.
BUT WHEN I'M WITH KANROJI...
...I FORGET ALL THAT AND JUST ENJOY MYSELF.
Nezukooo!

SHE GAVE ME A BIRTHDAY PRESENT THE OTHER DAY.

SNAKE SCARF

...SO I WANTED TO DO THE SAME FOR HER...

SHE GIVES ME SO MUCH...

SORRY FOR BOTHERING YOU TWO WITH THIS.

HUH?!

SWIP

OH WELL. LET'S GO HOME.

IT WAS JUST SOMETHING I WANTED TO DO.

"THANKS SO MUCH, ZENITSU!"

"IT WAS TASTY!"

BUT WHAT ABOUT A PRESENT?!

THIS ISN'T A SPECIAL OCCASION.

I'LL GET HER SOMETHING SOME OTHER TIME.

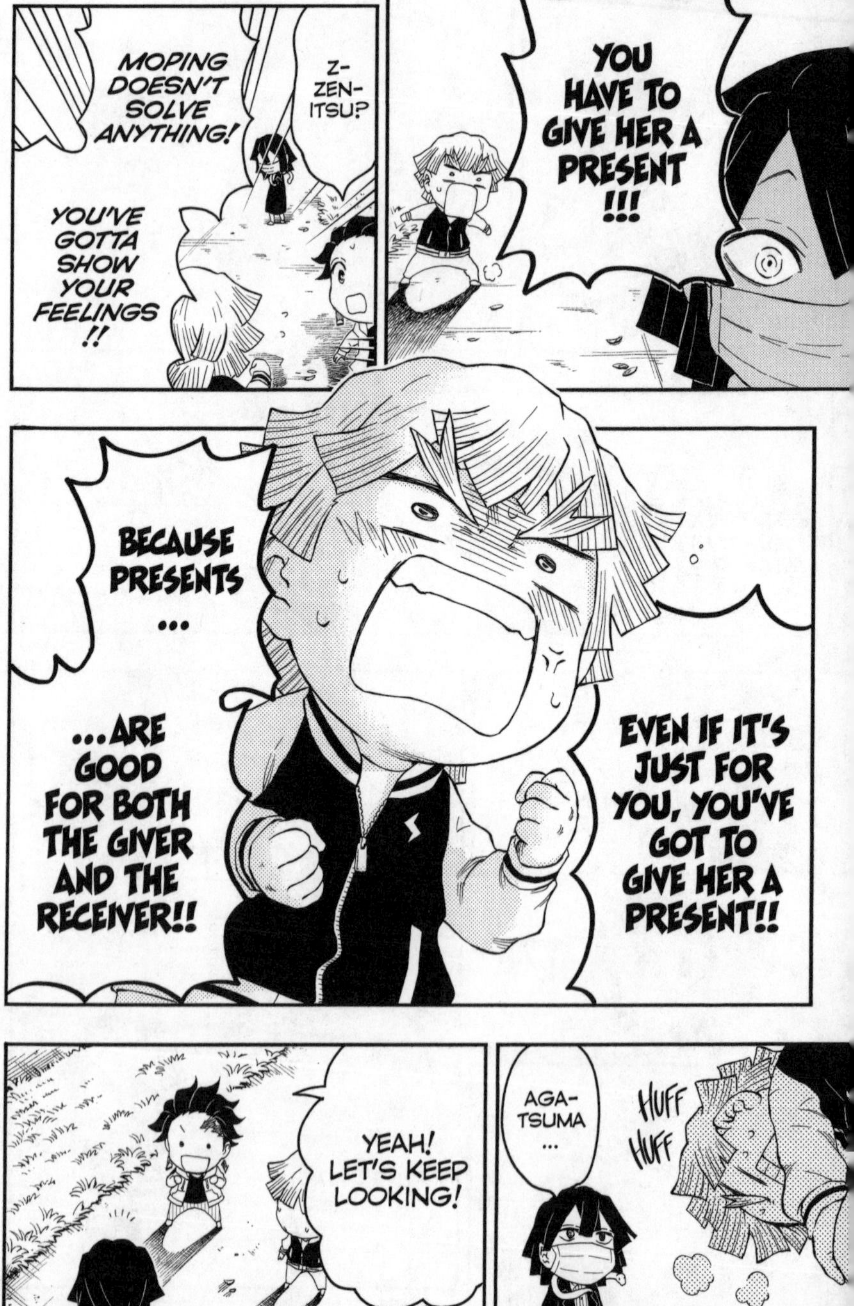
YOU HAVE TO GIVE HER A PRESENT !!!
Z-ZEN-ITSU?
MOPING DOESN'T SOLVE ANYTHING!
YOU'VE GOTTA SHOW YOUR FEELINGS !!
EVEN IF IT'S JUST FOR YOU, YOU'VE GOT TO GIVE HER A PRESENT!!
BECAUSE PRESENTS ...
...ARE GOOD FOR BOTH THE GIVER AND THE RECEIVER!!
HUFF HUFF
AGA-TSUMA ...
YEAH! LET'S KEEP LOOKING!

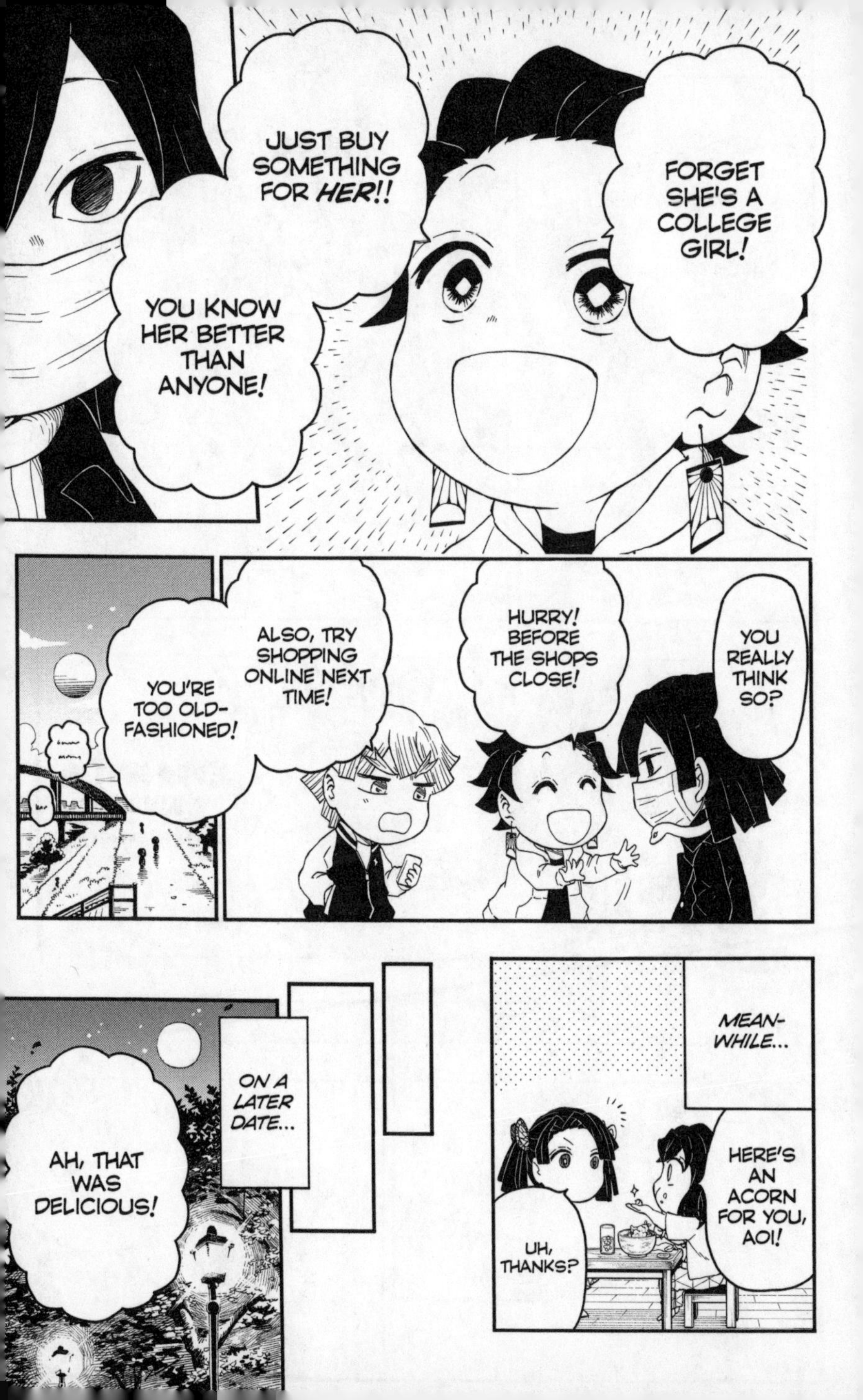
FORGET SHE'S A COLLEGE GIRL!
JUST BUY SOMETHING FOR HER!!
YOU KNOW HER BETTER THAN ANYONE!
YOU REALLY THINK SO?
HURRY! BEFORE THE SHOPS CLOSE!
ALSO, TRY SHOPPING ONLINE NEXT TIME!
YOU'RE TOO OLD-FASHIONED!
MEAN-WHILE...
HERE'S AN ACORN FOR YOU, AOI!
UH, THANKS?
ON A LATER DATE...
AH, THAT WAS DELICIOUS!

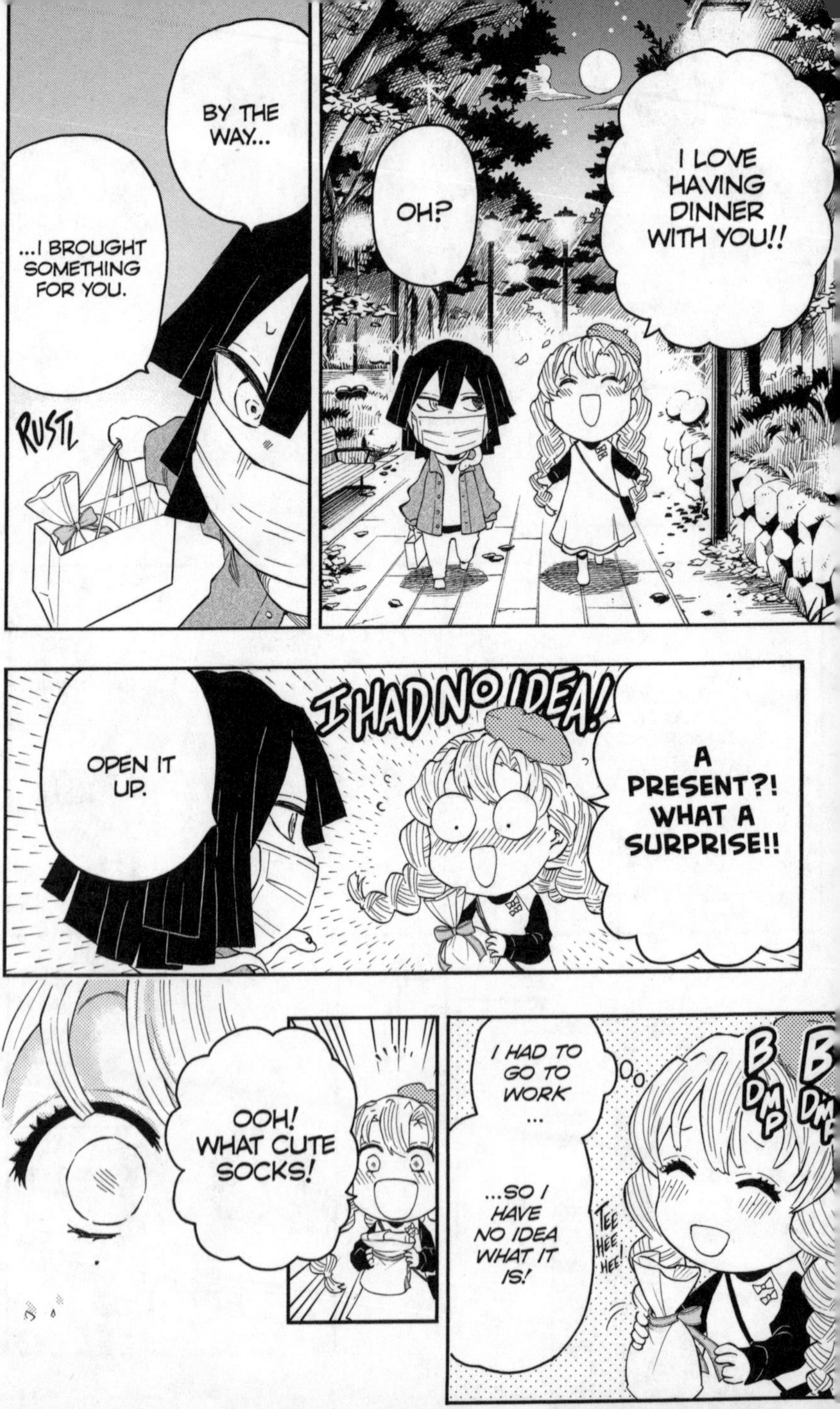
I LOVE HAVING DINNER WITH YOU!!
OH?
BY THE WAY...
...I BROUGHT SOMETHING FOR YOU.
RUSTL
A PRESENT?! WHAT A SURPRISE!!
I HAD NO IDEA!
OPEN IT UP.
BDMP BDMP
I HAD TO GO TO WORK ...
...SO I HAVE NO IDEA WHAT IT IS!
TEE HEE HEE!
OOH! WHAT CUTE SOCKS!

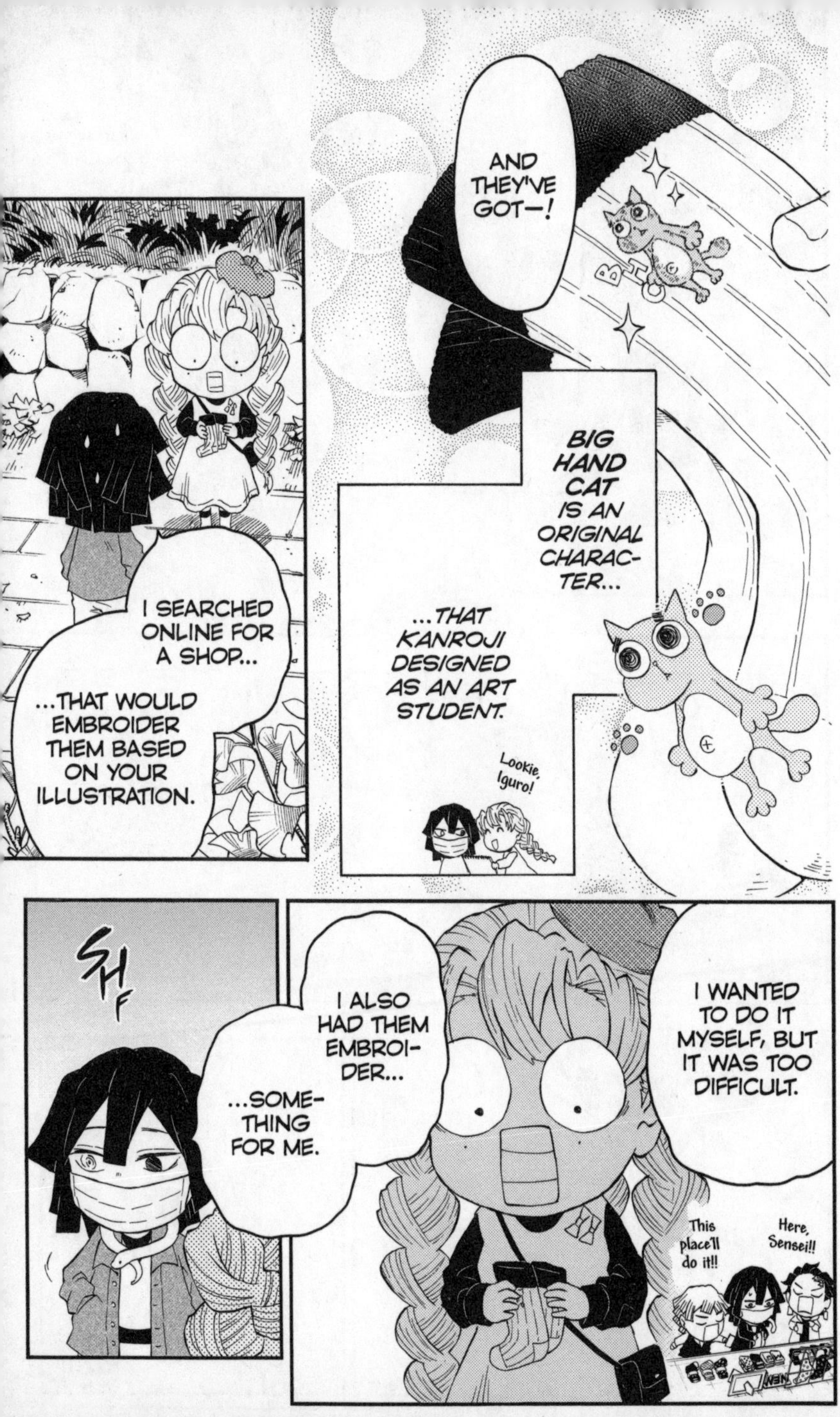
AND THEY'VE GOT—!
BIG HAND CAT IS AN ORIGINAL CHARACTER...
...THAT KANROJI DESIGNED AS AN ART STUDENT.
Lookie, Iguro!
I SEARCHED ONLINE FOR A SHOP...
...THAT WOULD EMBROIDER THEM BASED ON YOUR ILLUSTRATION.
I WANTED TO DO IT MYSELF, BUT IT WAS TOO DIFFICULT.
Here, Sensei!!
This place'll do it!!
I ALSO HAD THEM EMBROIDER...
...SOMETHING FOR ME.
SHF

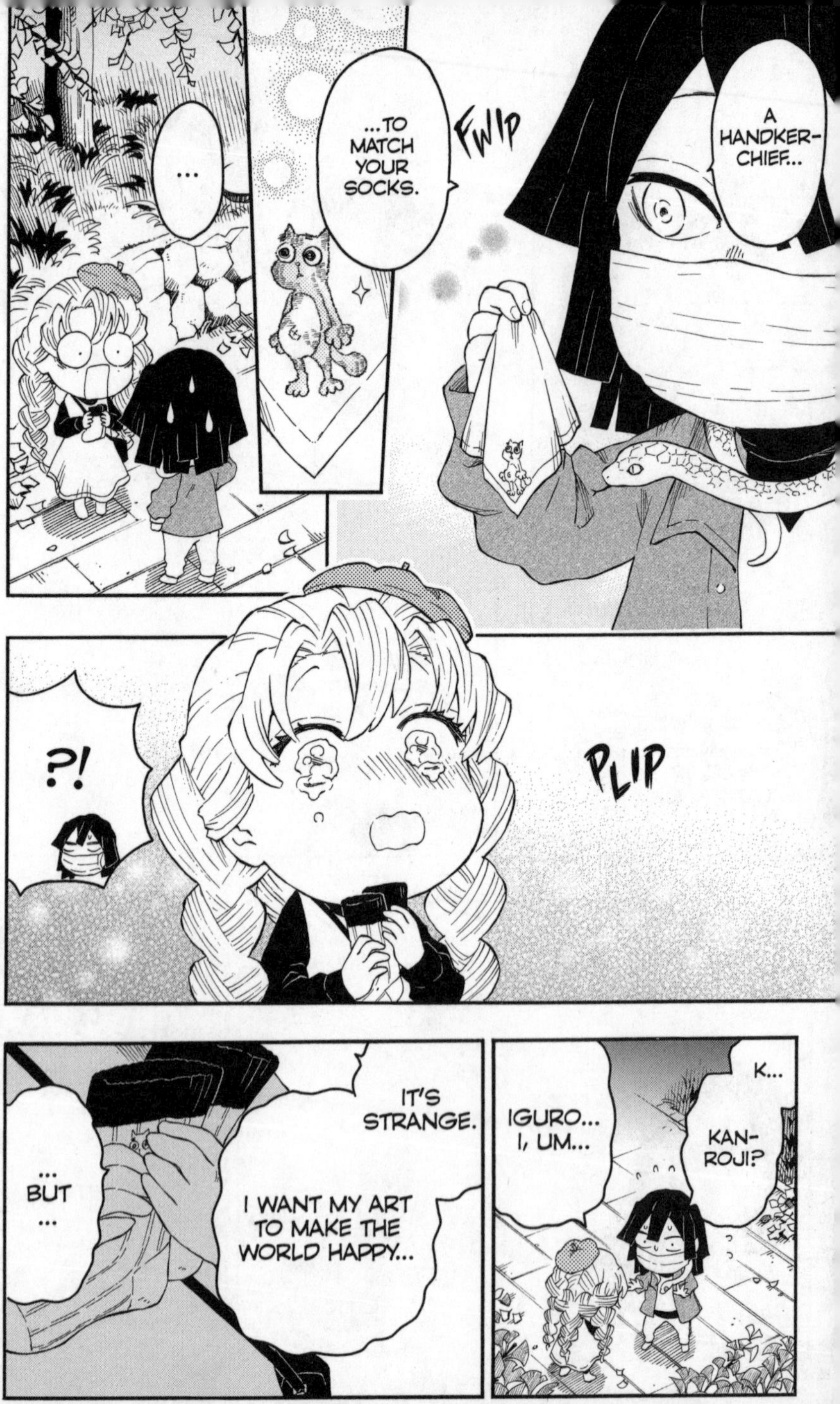
A HANDKER-CHIEF...
FWIP
...TO MATCH YOUR SOCKS.
...
PLIP
?!
K...
KAN-ROJI?
IGURO... I, UM...
IT'S STRANGE.
I WANT MY ART TO MAKE THE WORLD HAPPY...
...BUT...

...RIGHT NOW...

...IT'S MAKING ME THE HAPPIEST OF ALL!

OH...

THAT'S GOOD.

...WOULD GO ON TO BE MUCH KINDER TO TANJIRO AND ZENITSU.

IGURO...

I'M GLAD.

...A CROW CARRYING A LOVE LETTER...

...THEY CAN'T HELP BUT SMILE.

BUT NOW WHEN THEY SEE...

JUST KIDDING!

NO NAPPING IN CLASS!

CHAPTER 10 DELETED SCENES
USELESS TEACHERS

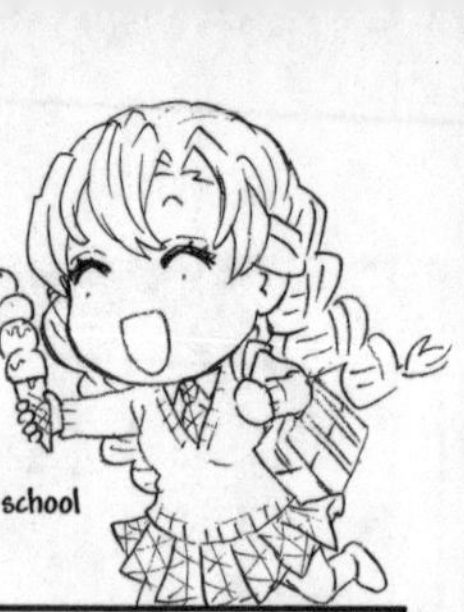
Kanroji in high school

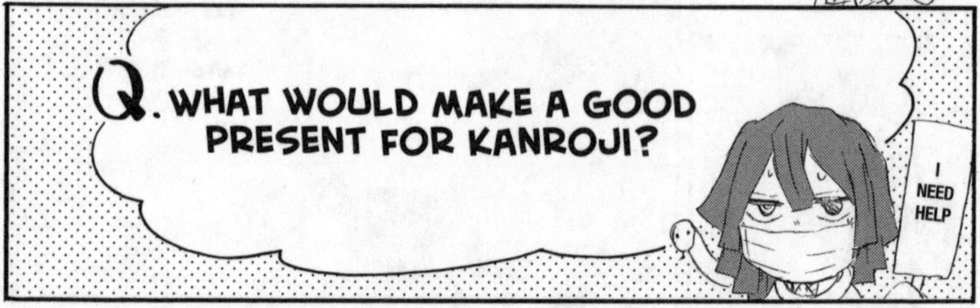
Q. WHAT WOULD MAKE A GOOD PRESENT FOR KANROJI?
I NEED HELP

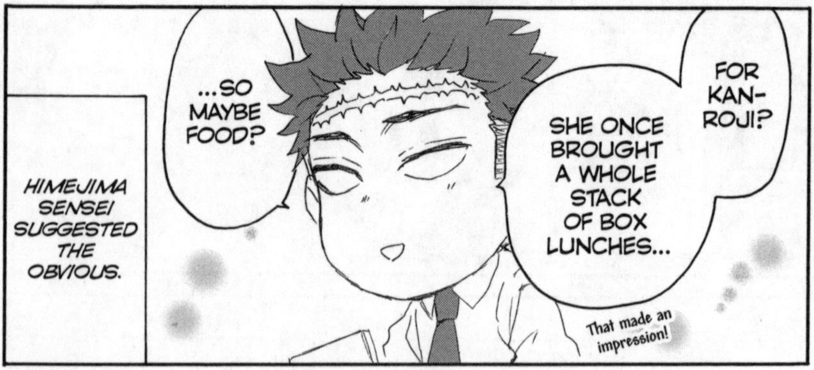
FOR KAN-ROJI?
SHE ONCE BROUGHT A WHOLE STACK OF BOX LUNCHES...
That made an impression!
...SO MAYBE FOOD?
HIMEJIMA SENSEI SUGGESTED THE OBVIOUS.

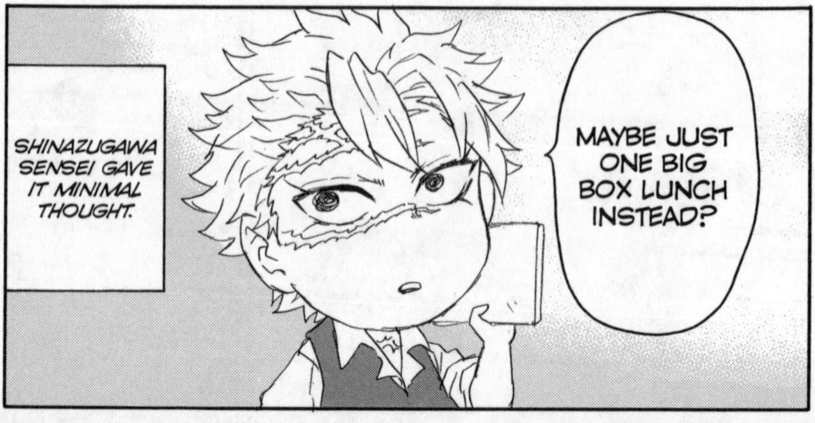
MAYBE JUST ONE BIG BOX LUNCH INSTEAD?
SHINAZUGAWA SENSEI GAVE IT MINIMAL THOUGHT.

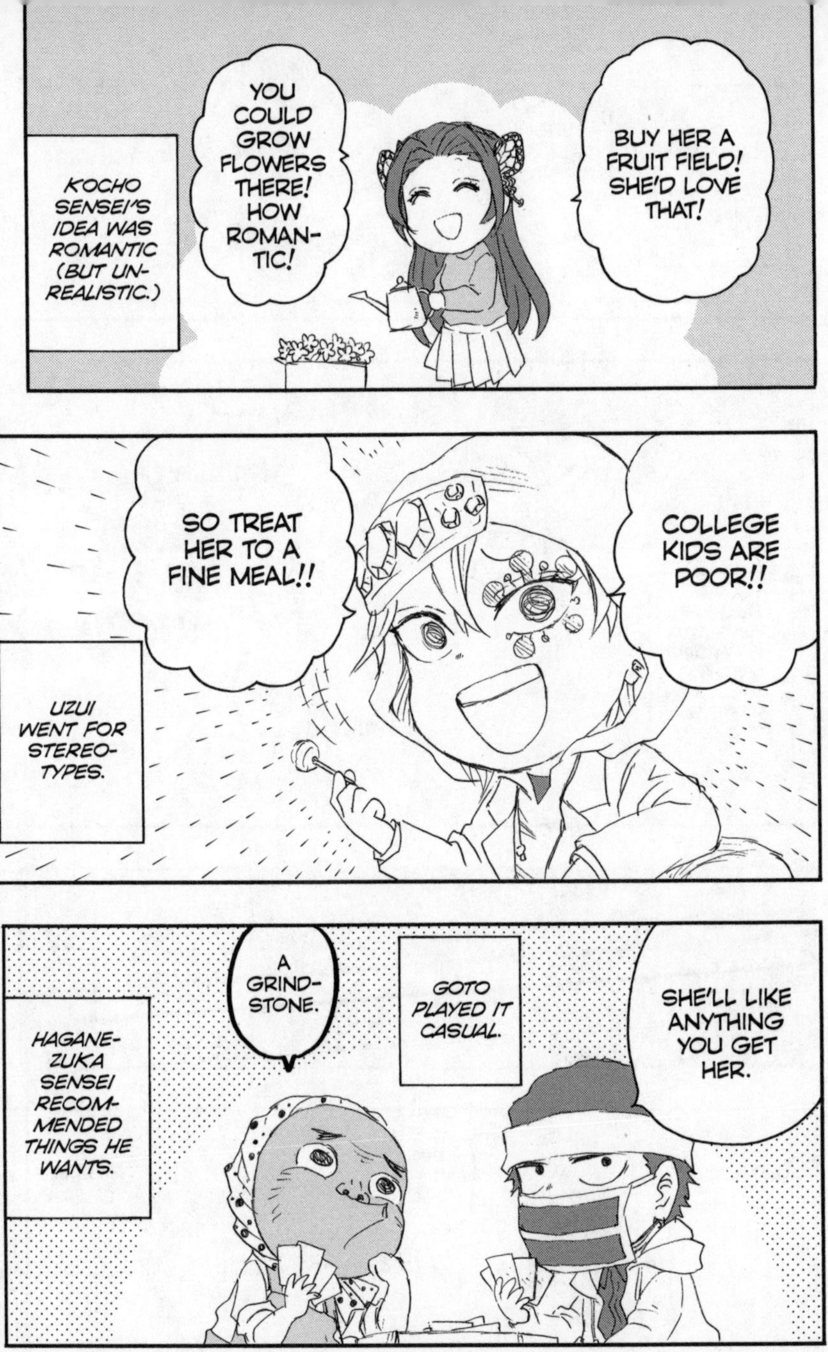
BUY HER A FRUIT FIELD! SHE'D LOVE THAT!
YOU COULD GROW FLOWERS THERE! HOW ROMANTIC!
KOCHO SENSEI'S IDEA WAS ROMANTIC (BUT UNREALISTIC.)
COLLEGE KIDS ARE POOR!!
SO TREAT HER TO A FINE MEAL!!
UZUI WENT FOR STEREOTYPES.
SHE'LL LIKE ANYTHING YOU GET HER.
GOTO PLAYED IT CASUAL.
A GRINDSTONE.
HAGANEZUKA SENSEI RECOMMENDED THINGS HE WANTS.

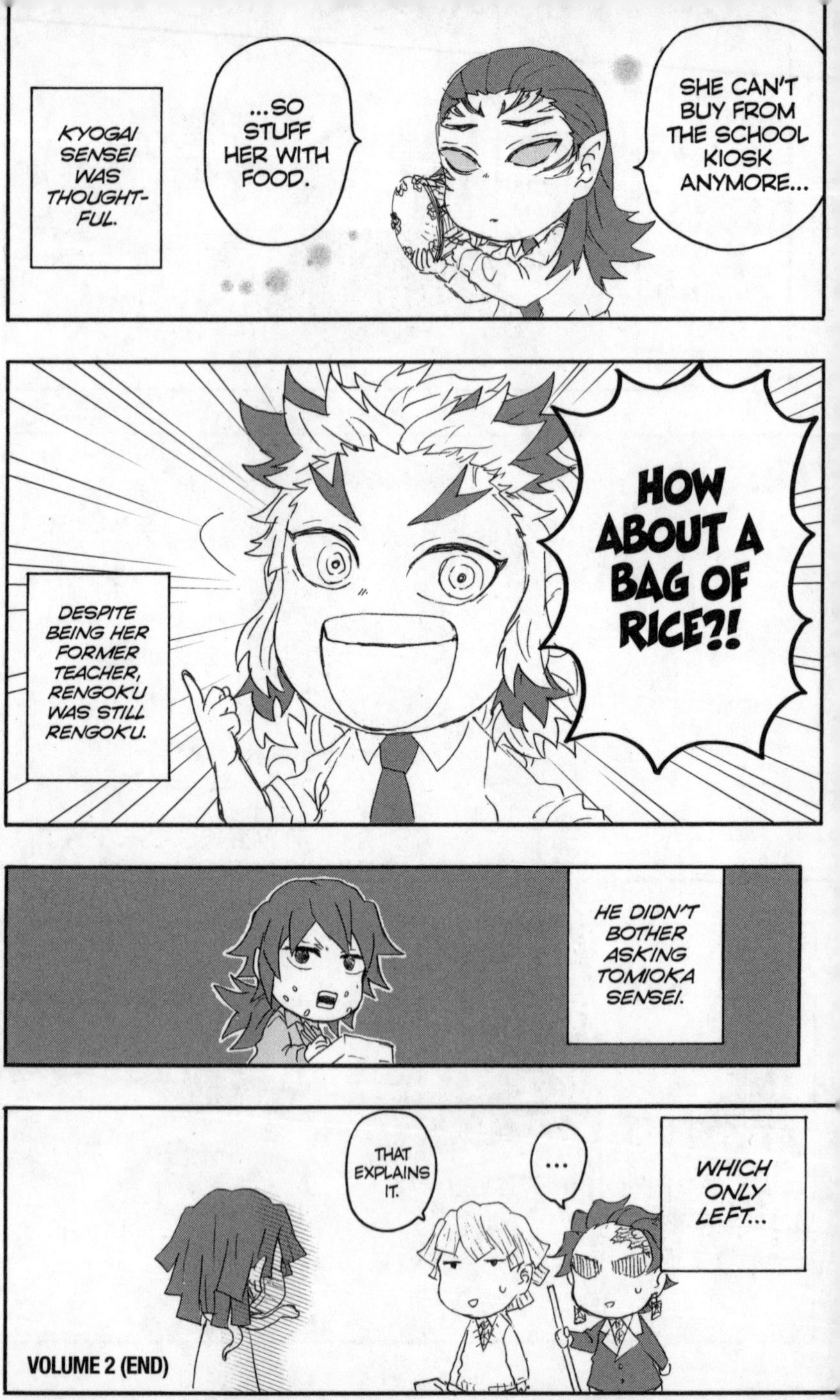
SHE CAN'T BUY FROM THE SCHOOL KIOSK ANYMORE...
...SO STUFF HER WITH FOOD.
KYOGAI SENSEI WAS THOUGHT-FUL.
HOW ABOUT A BAG OF RICE?!
DESPITE BEING HER FORMER TEACHER, RENGOKU WAS STILL RENGOKU.
HE DIDN'T BOTHER ASKING TOMIOKA SENSEI.
WHICH ONLY LEFT...
...
THAT EXPLAINS IT.
VOLUME 2 (END)

THIS IS TAMIO ENMU.

TANJIRO ALWAYS CATCHES HIM MISBEHAVING ON THE TRAIN.*

*SEE VOL. 1, CHAPTER 1.

HE'S A TRAIN GEEK WITH A CRIMINAL HABIT.

*EYES: LOWER ONE

BONUS CHAPTER: KUMOTORI STATION, 7:30 A.M.

...

TMP
TMP
TMP
TMP

TMP
TMP

FOMP

GWOOOOOOO

YOU MAKE ME SOUND LIKE A FLASHER!

WELL, AREN'T YOU?

YES, I AM.

HOW RUDE!

SO I CAN NAB YOU WHEN YOU MOON PEOPLE!

WHY DID YOU SIT NEXT TO ME?

175

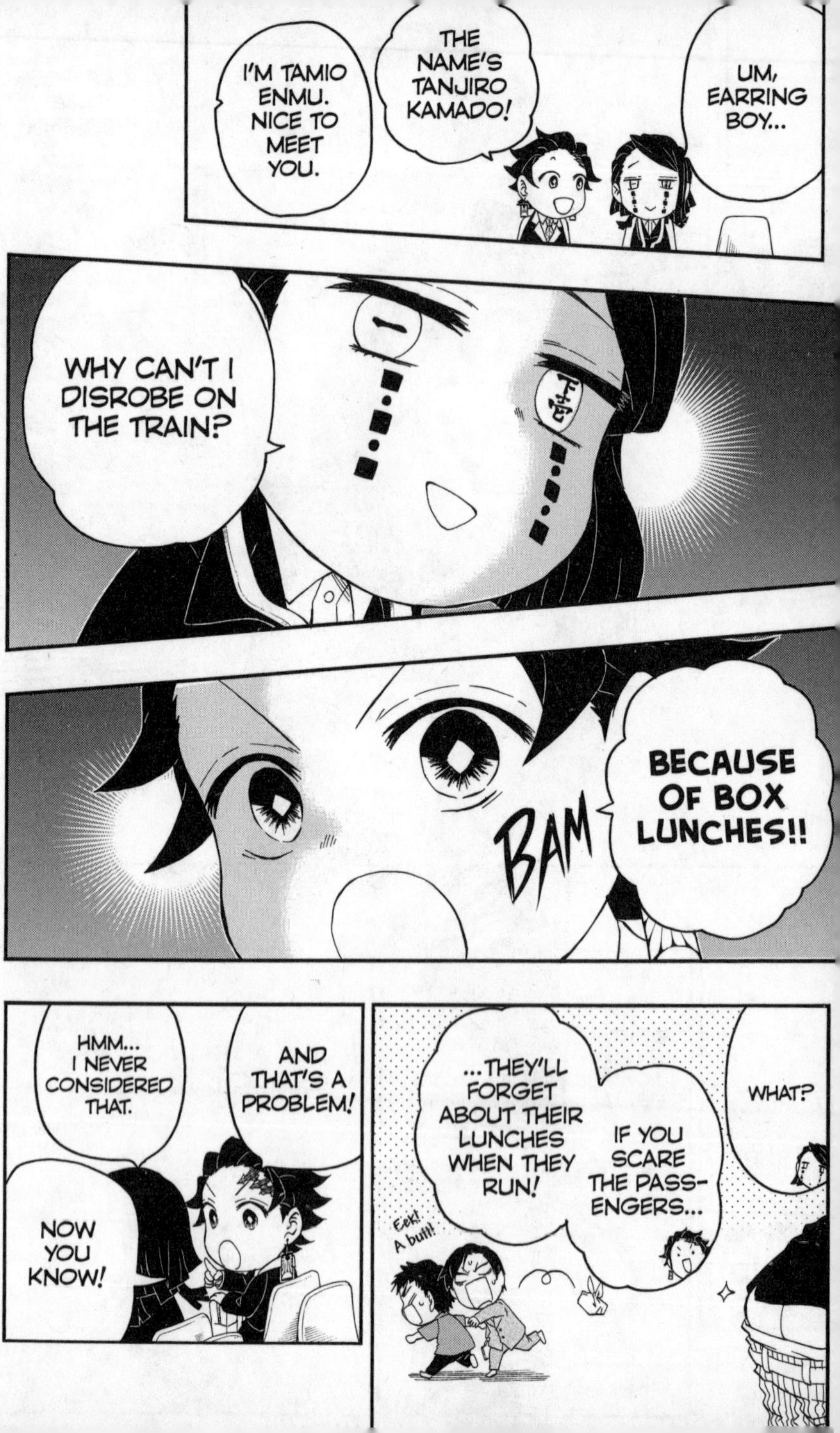
UM, EARRING BOY...
THE NAME'S TANJIRO KAMADO!
I'M TAMIO ENMU. NICE TO MEET YOU.
WHY CAN'T I DISROBE ON THE TRAIN?
BAM
BECAUSE OF BOX LUNCHES!!
WHAT?
IF YOU SCARE THE PASSENGERS...
...THEY'LL FORGET ABOUT THEIR LUNCHES WHEN THEY RUN!
Eek! A bull!
AND THAT'S A PROBLEM!
HMM... I NEVER CONSIDERED THAT.
NOW YOU KNOW!

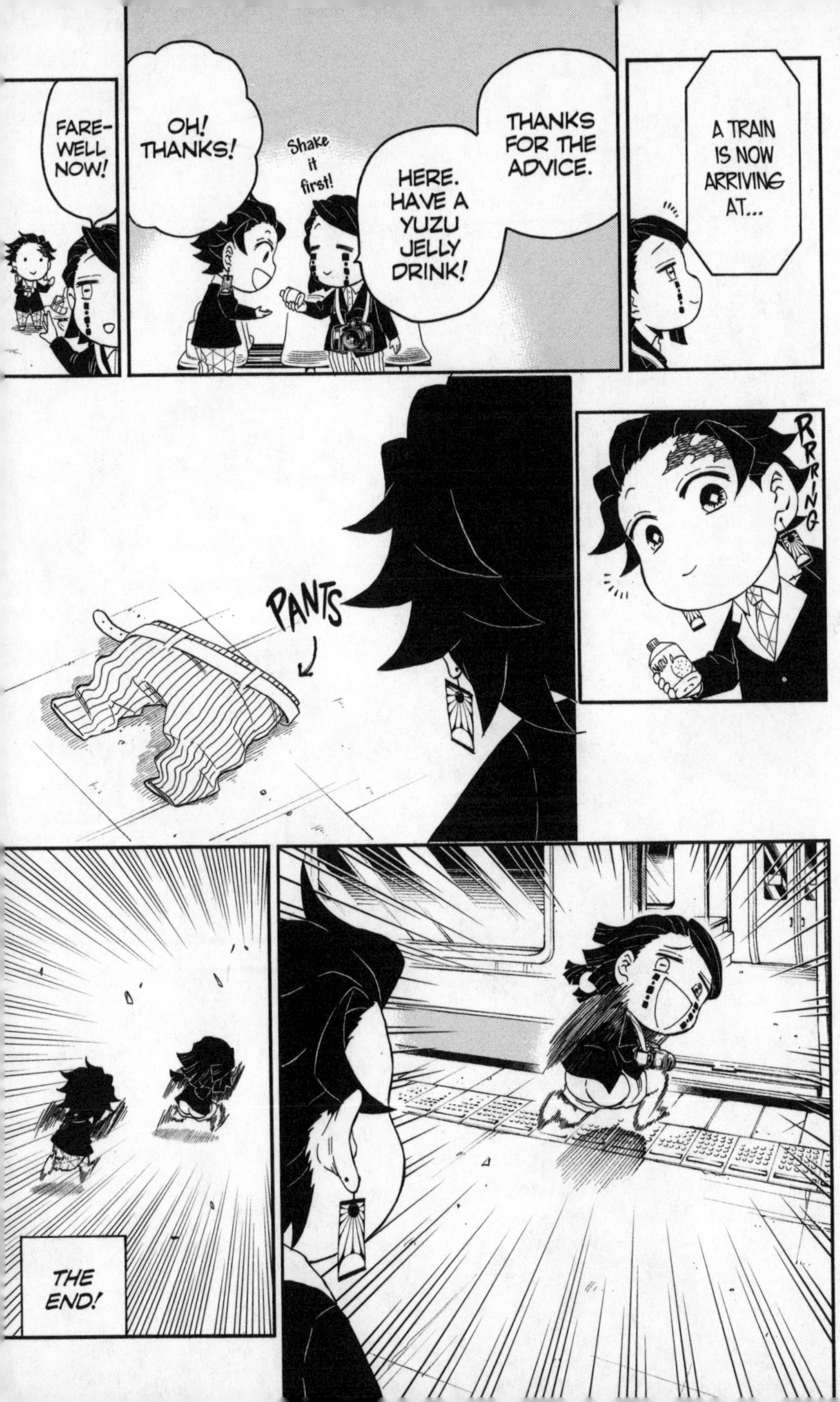
A TRAIN IS NOW ARRIVING AT...
THANKS FOR THE ADVICE.
HERE. HAVE A YUZU JELLY DRINK!
Shake it first!
OH! THANKS!
FARE-WELL NOW!
RRRING
PANTS
THE END!

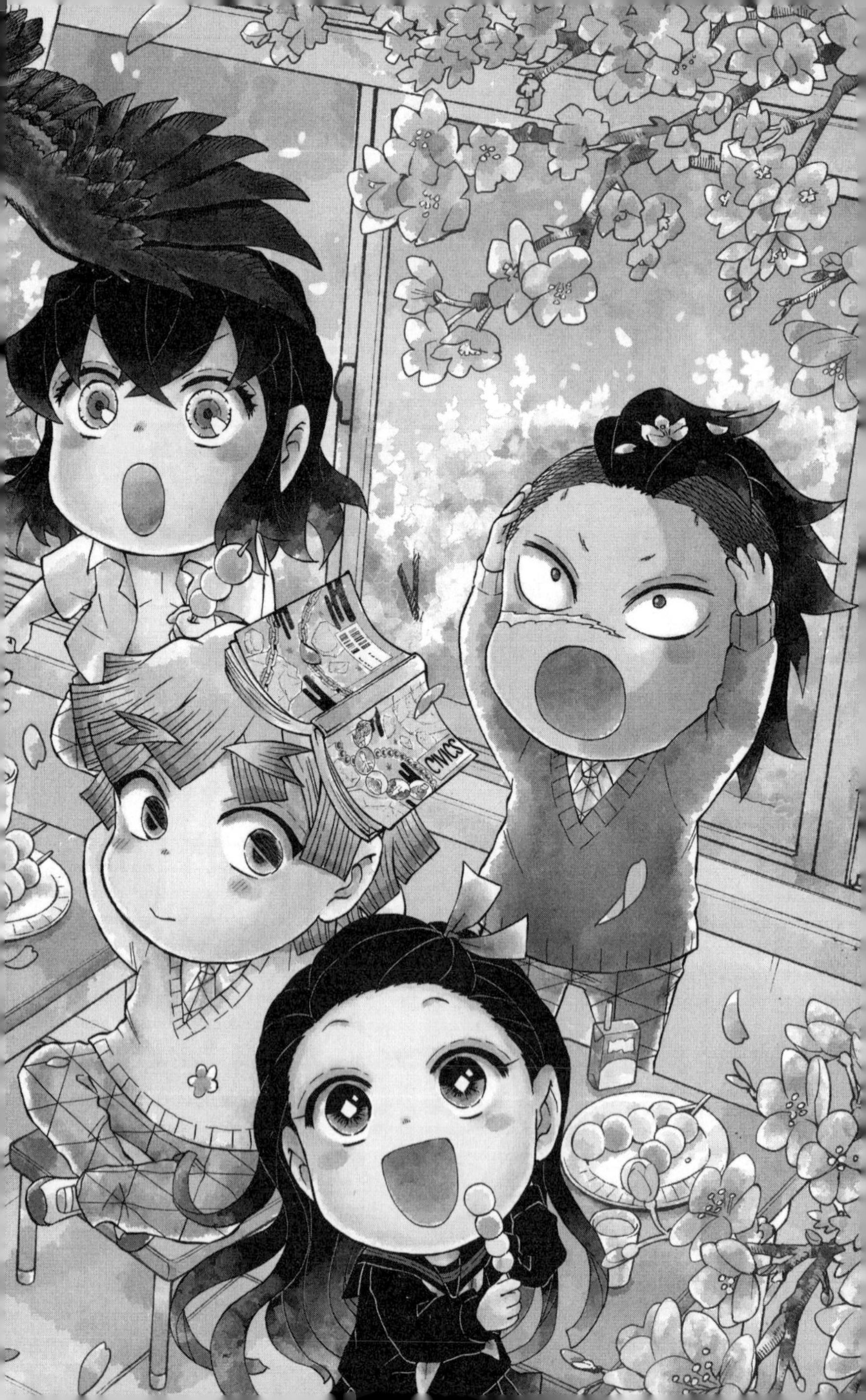
CIVICS

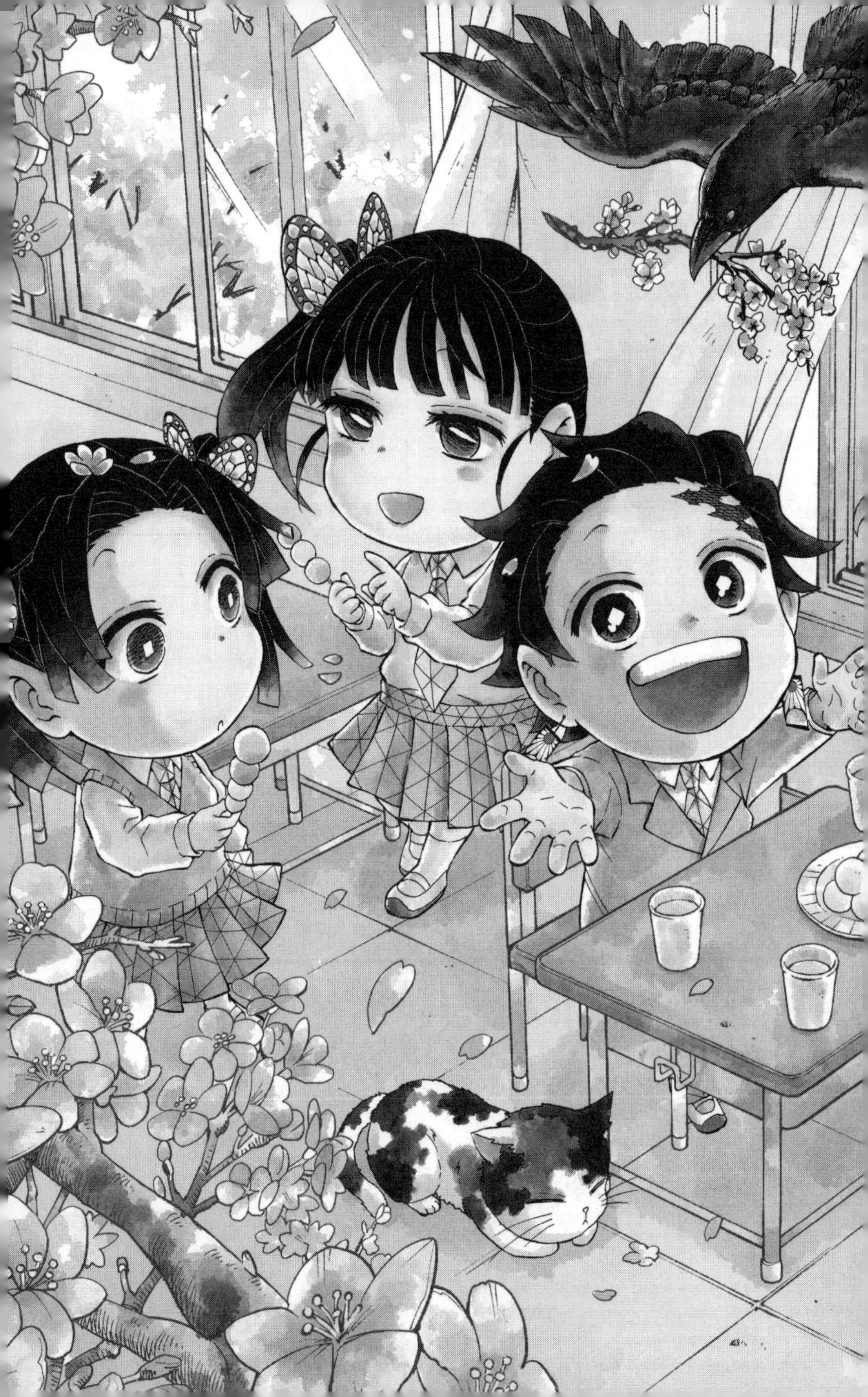

AFTERWORD

Welcome to volume 2! Thanks for reading! Just like with volume 1, this was only possible through the efforts of a lot of people, so thank you all very much. I'll be counting on you in the future too.

This volume goes on sale in July, and the story takes place from early summer to autumn, so I'm thrilled to see how the seasons have synced up. What a happy coincidence!

The serialized releases never match the actual season, so I drew the preceding two-page spread to match with the real world. Without any connection to the story, the sakura trees are in full bloom! I have to say, I like that illustration, but I was never satisfied with the color illustration of Makomo and the others for chapter 9, so I put them on the back cover of this volume.

I suspect volume 3 will take place from autumn to winter. Nothing is slated yet, though, so here's hoping it gets the green light!

STAFF

REGULARS
Nagashima
Kantaro Kumano
Keisuke Futta

HELPERS
Kojiro
Tachi Biwa

SPECIAL THANKS
Saikyo Jump editor: Toide-san
The *Demon Slayer: Kimetsu no Yaiba* original manga team
Graphic novel editor: Abe-san
Designers: Deguchi-san, Abe-san
Original creator: Koyoharu Gotouge
All the readers!

Natsuki Hokami

帆上夏希.

Good work! This is Gotouge! Volume 2 of *Kimetsu Academy* is on sale! Here's a big thanks to Hokami Sensei, the editors, assistants, and readers! The number of characters playing a role is ramping up, making these pages more boisterous than ever!

As the fun continues to take off, I hope you'll come along for the ride!!

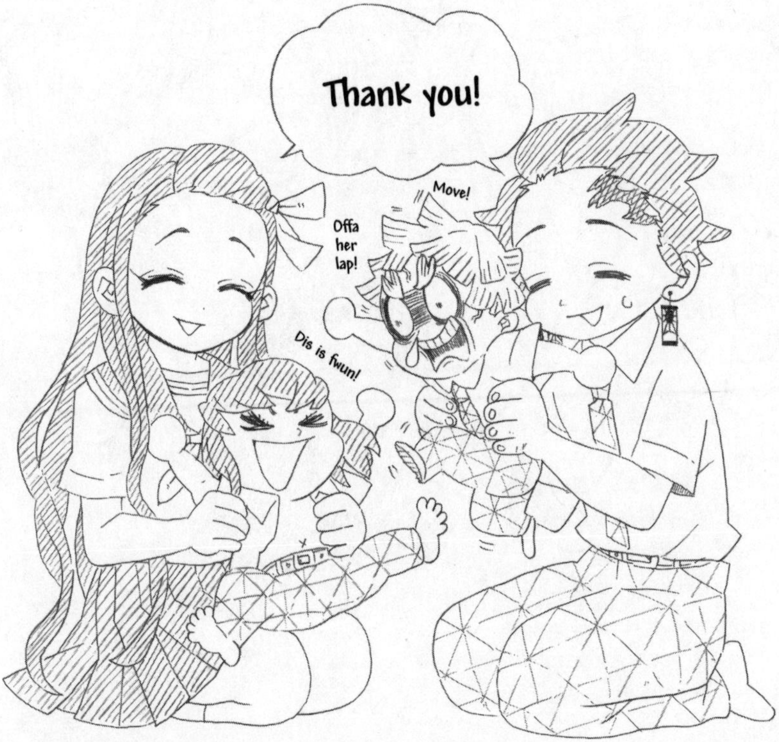
Thank you!
Move!
Offa her lap!
Dis is fwun!

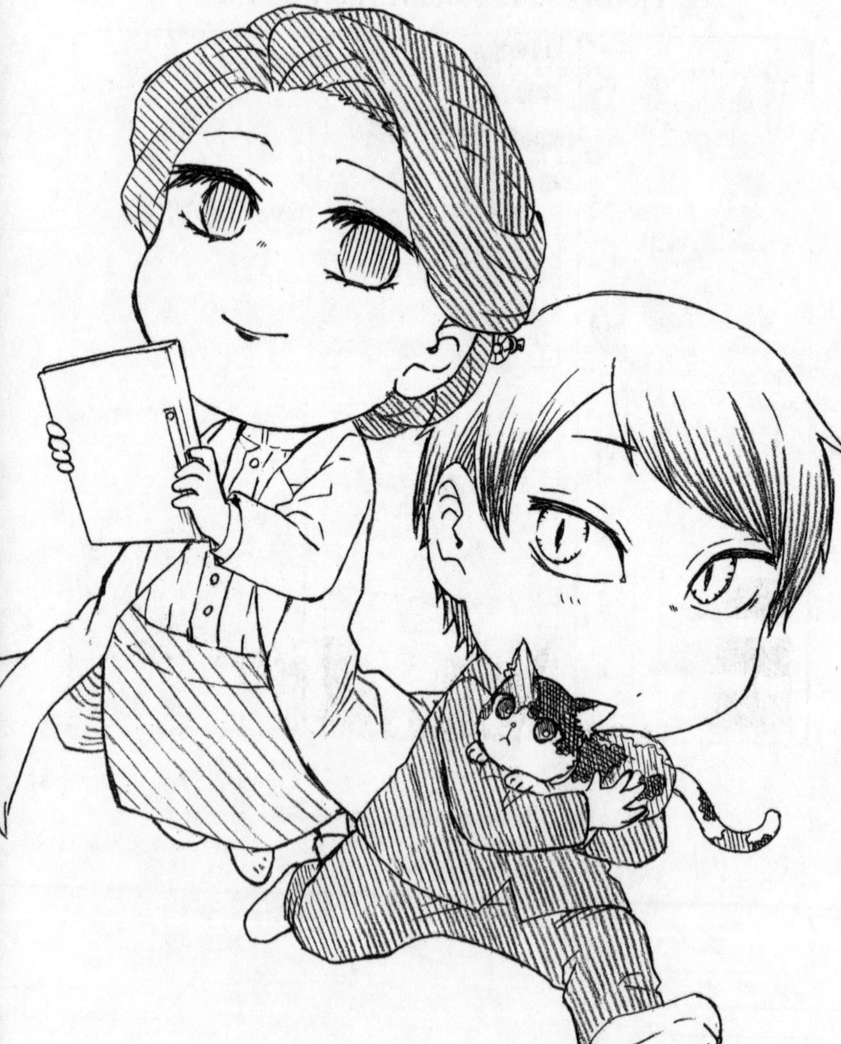

FIRST-YEAR TEXTBOOK DESIGNS FOR KIMETSU ACADEMY HIGH SCHOOL

CIVICS
CHEMISTRY
MATH A
BIOLOGY
HISTORY
ENGLISH
I

For a while, I only had a rough idea for these, but I asked my staff and they came up with proper designs. The other grades basically look the same.

You're reading the wrong way!

In keeping with the original Japanese comic format, *Demon Slayer: Kimetsu Academy* reads from right to left, meaning that action, sound effects, and word-balloon order are completely reversed from English order.

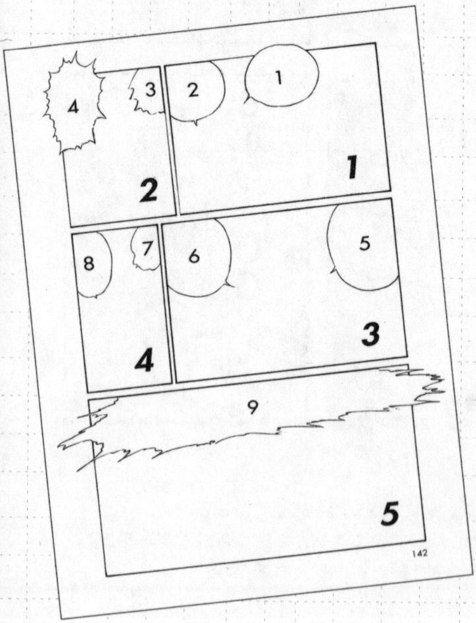
1
2
1
3
4
2
5
6
3
7
8
4
9
5
142

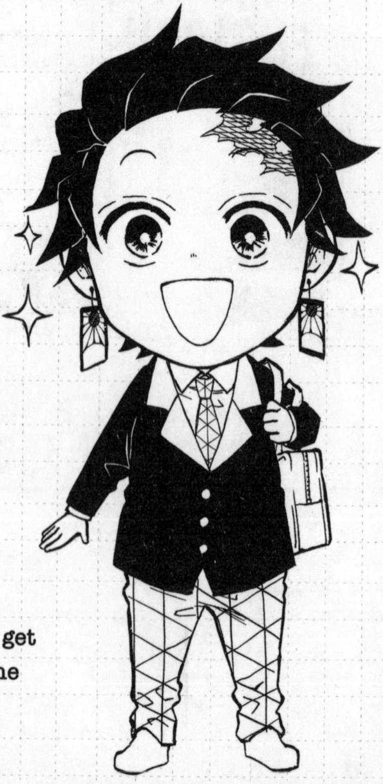

Check out the diagram shown here to get the hang of things, and then turn to the other side of the book to get started!